Room
AT THE
INN

TIM HAMPSON

BOOKS

Published by CAMRA, The Campaign for Real Ale
230 Hatfield Road, St Albans, Hertfordshire AL1 4LW
T 01727 867201
F 01727 867670
email: camra@camra.org.uk
www.camra.org.uk
Managing Editor: Mark Webb

First published 1996
Third edition 2003

Printed in the United Kingdom at
the University Press, Cambridge

Design/typography: Dale Tomlinson
Fonts: The Antiqua &Taz (lucasfonts.com)
Maps: John Macklin
Cover design: Rob Howells

ISBN 1 85249 184 1

*Every effort has gone into researching the contents of
this book, but no responsibility can be taken for errors.*

Contents

What is CAMRA?

CAMRA is an independent, voluntary, consumer organisation. Membership is open to all individuals, but corporate entities such as breweries and pubs are not members. CAMRA is governed by a voluntary, unpaid, national executive, elected by the membership. There is a small professional staff of eighteen responsible for central campaigning, research, administration of membership, sales and so forth.

How is CAMRA financed?

CAMRA is financed through membership subscriptions, sales of products such as books and sweatshirts, and from the proceeds of beer festivals. It receives no funding from the brewing industry other than a limited amount of advertising in the monthly newspaper What's Brewing.

CAMRA's objectives

CAMRA's mission is to act as champion of the consumer in relation to the UK and European beer and drinks industry. It aims to:

- Maintain consumer rights
- Promote quality, choice and value for money
- Support the public house as a focus of community life
- Campaign for greater appreciation of traditional beers, ciders and perries as part of national heritage and culture
- Seek improvements in all licensed premises and throughout the brewing industry
- CAMRA also seeks to promote real cider and perry through a sub-organisation called APPLE. Like ale, these are traditional British drinks and like ale, the traditional product is very different from the 'dead' version.

Campaigning

While CAMRA is a single industry group, it has a very wide area of campaigning interests. At present campaigns being actively pursued include the following:

- Improved competition and choice in the brewing industry
- Preserving the British pub and defending licensees from eviction by pub owners
- Seeking a fairer tax system for smaller brewers
- Seeking fuller information about the beer we drink, such as ingredients labelling
- A fundamental reform of licensing law
- Fighting take-overs and mergers
- Encouraging higher standards of pub design
- Encouraging brewers to produce a wide range of beer styles such as porter, mild and stout, in addition to their bitters.

Introduction

The pubs, inns and hotels listed in this guide cover a wide range of styles and tastes, to suit all budgets and age groups. From village and town locals to glorious country retreats and city centre alternatives to large anonymous hotels they should all offer a decent bed for the night, good beer and good cheer.

At their very best the establishments listed should be like staying in a rich friend's house – comfortable, friendly and with a hint of luxury and perhaps even just a touch eccentricity.

For many years the number of pubs offering accommodation was in decline and much of what was offered was poor.

But over the last few years there has been a silent revolution in the British pub, and a quantum change in quality has taken place.

Millions of pounds have been spent on improving facilities, many rooms now have a bathroom and toilet en suite – something unimaginable 20 years ago. Many offer a television and tea and coffee making facilities as the norm. And the quality of food is usually better than in many restaurants.

For the pub to survive and to compete with all the other alternatives in an increasingly competitive market for the leisure pound, the pub has had to change.

We live in an era of the short break and the weekend away and many of the establishments are ideal for a few days away from home to unwind and relax.

Increasing numbers of travelling business people clamour not for the bland anonymity of a branded hotel, but for a pub to stay in, where real people sit and drink real beer – where it is not unknown for a stranger to walk into a bar alone and find new friends – such places can be found in this book.

In this book there are Michelin star pubs and luxury hotels with the service and amenities to match the prices. There are comfortable little pubs off the beaten track, with maybe just two or three rooms without the most modern facilities. These should not be dismissed lightly, they offer peace and quiet, and evenings without the sound of a blaring television. And with the peace and tranquillity will often come good, homely cooking using locally farmed ingredients.

There are pubs which can accommodate families and those that can even provide a shelter for pets.

There are many inns where hospitality has been offered for centuries, each provides a unique snapshot of the history and heritage of England, Scotland and Wales, and there are modern rooms which have been open only for a few months.

There are pubs close to airports, and there are pubs close to city centres and there are rural retreats, ideal for a romantic weekend which, once found, can be very hard to leave.

There are many which offer that little bit extra, such as activity or themed breaks for golfers, anglers, walkers, cyclists and other sports enthusiasts. Whatever you require in the way of a bed for the night, you should find something here to fit the bill. Of course, at the end of your search you will be rewarded with a good pint of real ale.

How to use this guide

The entries in this guide are presented in a fairly straightforward way. The listings are by regions as defined by the British Tourist Authority.

This makes it easier for anyone who wants to know more about an area they plan to visit as information can be found via the www.visitbritain.com website.

Within each region, pubs are listed alphabetically by their location – be it rural area, village, town or city.

Where pubs are difficult to find, directions have been included in the descriptions.

In addition, if a pub has a website and email address it is listed. The web is an excellent tool for travellers who can see the pub and its facilities before they try and book.

Rooms are listed as single, double, twin-bedded or family rooms. In many cases pubs do not have single rooms and most charge a supplement for single occupancy of a double room. It is always advisable to check room rates at the time of booking, as even information which was correct at the time of going to press can change.

Increasingly many pubs now offer family rooms, and it is again advisable to check with the establishment when booking to ascertain what facilities are available – some pubs can offer a cot for a baby, but always check in advance.

Special needs

Very few older pubs have rooms adapted for wheelchair users. Such facilities are very difficult to provide in the very oldest buildings, This is mainly because of the inaccessibility of first-floor bedrooms, where it is impractical to install a lift. Many more cannot offer access because it is just impossible to widen a narrow ancient Grade I listed doorway.

However, more pubs, especially those which have recently undergone refurbishment are offering better access to both bars and bedrooms.

Where facilities for the disabled have been provided by the establishment details have been included in the listing, but where no information has been supplied it does not mean it does not exist – the advice has to be: ask what facilities are available before booking.

Breakfast and other meals

Most of the pubs listed include breakfast in the room price. This is usually a cholesterol-charged cooked breakfast, complete with egg, bacon, sausages and fried bread, but something simpler will often be available.

Good locally produced food is a vital component of many of the listings. One of the joys of travelling around the country is to discover the foods of hidden Britain. From real Cornish pasties to locally caught Cromer crabs, can be found in the British pub. But a journey around the pubs in this country is also a journey around the world: fine cooked foods using recipes from all over the globe are being cooked on a daily basis. This is exemplified by an increasing number of award winning pubs featured in this guide. A good pub these days is often much more than good beer. For many it is essential that it offers good food for all tastes and occasions.

Prices

Pubs often charge per room, rather than per person, but for the purposes of this book we have given price bands which refer to charges per person, per night for bed and breakfast (usually a cooked meal) as follows. The bands are only a guide and again it is advisable to check at the price at the time of booking.

£ = under £25 per person
££ = £25–35 per person
£££ = £35–45 per person
££££ = over £45 per person

Children are generally charged at half price or less. In some cases no charge is made at all for young children. Some pubs accept pet dogs and may charge for their accommodation, but always check in advance.

So what is real ale?

Real ale is a living fresh beer that undergoes a natural secondary fermentation in the cask. Like any natural product the beer will age and go off and therefore must be drunk within a strict timescale. It requires care in handling on its way to the pub, and care within the pub to bring it to perfection.

The usual practice is for the casks to be placed in a cool deep cellar. Some pubs keep their beer in a special cool room on the ground floor, a few keep their beer behind the bar – preferably nowadays with some modest external cooling system. Real ale is served at cellar temperature, which is somewhat cooler than room temperature. If real ale is too warm it is not appetising, it loses its natural conditioning (the liveliness of the beer due to the dissolved carbon dioxide). On the other hand, if the beer is too cold it will kill off the subtle flavour.

Real ale is not warm, cloudy, or flat – served properly it should be entirely clear (though there can be exceptions to this), refreshing, appetising, good to look at, good to smell and taste wonderful right down to the last drop in the glass.

Opening hours

All day opening (11am–11pm; noon–10.30pm on Sunday) is now well established, but many pubs do still close at least for a while during the afternoons. Opening hours may be seasonal, too; those in tourist areas may be open for the maximum permitted time during the holiday period, but revert to the old afternoon closure in winter.

Pubs with residential licences can serve food and drink at any time (provided they have the staff available). Children can stay in pubs with guest rooms, but under 18s cannot be served in bars, and children under 16 cannot be served alcohol in pub dining rooms. Children can be admitted to designated areas in the pub if it holds a children's certificate, but these certificates often impose a time limit on entry to those areas, for example, no children after 8pm. Children's certificates are more common in Scotland, where the scheme was started earlier than in the rest of the UK. Some pubs do not have a certificate but may have a separate family room.

The facilities offered by the pubs listed here were checked as late as possible in the production process, but unfortunately, information changes. The publisher appreciates any feedback from readers about the pubs in this guide, and any recommendations made for future editions will be well received. A form for this purpose is printed on the inside back cover of the book.

TIM HAMPSON

A taste of Britain

Tim Hampson swirls, smells and sups and goes on a sensory
tour of Britain as he visits some of his favourite inns

It is easy to take beer for granted. It is Britain's most popular
alcoholic drink, yet few people pause to think of the science,
art and craft that go into making the finest beers. And fewer
still pause and stop and reflect on the finer points of the beer
that they are drinking.

Some might argue, why should they? Because beer can be
enjoyed just as a thirst quenching, health giving drink. Yet,
there is much more to beer than this. In Britain there are more
than 1,200 different real ales brewed. And each is unique.

At its simplest, beer is an alcoholic drink made from a
malted cereal, but this hides the complexity of colour, aroma
and taste that can be found in Britain's beers.

And wherever one might be in Britain, it is possible to go
on a sensual journey of discovery, just by visiting a pub.

Geography of beer

In Britain beer, pubs and brewers are inextricably linked.
Without one there would not be the other.

Beer and pubs and inns have helped shape our culture,
villages, towns and cities.

There was a time when thousands of brewers worked
tirelessly to produce pints of flowing ale. That has changed
but around Britain there are still hundreds of brewers
producing local ales for local drinkers.

And the joy of a journey around England, Wales and
Scotland is that it can still be a voyage of discovery – finding
beers not drunk before, while at the same time like some
new-age archaeologist experiencing the living history that
breweries and pubs and the people who worked in them and
used them have bequeathed to us.

Walk around most towns and there is likely to be evidence
of a brewing heritage – perhaps it is in a street name: The
Maltings, or Tun Lane.

For a historian pubs are a living, breathing example of a primary source of information – the names the Red Lion, the Kings Arms, even the Rat and Parrot, each in its way reflects a moment in time, and each change charts something of the social, economic, fashion or political history that makes this country what it is.

South East England

My journey begins in the South East of England. In an area of pubs with long histories and an area where there are so many wonderful rural retreats it might seem a trifle odd to choose a pub that is barely a year old.

But the **Ship & Trades**, Chatham, Kent, close to Chatham's historic dockyard, has something special about it. Without its conversion into a pub with bedrooms, it faced a bleak future – it could have been raised to the ground or just left derelict.

But now it thrives as a focus for visitors to the area. The building has been thoughtfully converted and still retains glimpses of its maritime heritage.

Ship & Trades,
Chatham, Kent,

With wonderful views over water, it is an ideal place to begin my sensual journey with a glass of Shepherd Neame beer.

The Faversham brewer only uses the finest malted barley, Kent hops and pure water from the brewery's own artesian well, in the production of Spitfire, a multi-award winning ale.

See it and it is golden red to the eye. Ripe and fruity to taste, it is balanced by a deep fresh hop aroma, but then what else would you expect from one of the country's oldest breweries situated in one of the major hop growing areas of the country.

London

London is one of the most expensive cities in the world, it is also one of the most vibrant and exciting.

Few pubs offer accommodation, but the **Mad Hatter**, on the South Bank, London SE1 does. It is expensive, but it is much better value for money than most of the over-priced bland hotels in Central London with the added bonus of serving real ale. And what a place it is to drink beer.

Swirl a glass of Fuller's ESB and, as renowned Good Beer Guide editor Roger Protz says of this London brewer's beer, there is an explosion of malt, hops and marmalade fruit on the nose, a big malt and fruit palate balanced by spicy hops and a long finish with great Goldings floral hop character and hints of orange, lemon and gooseberry fruit.

The Mad Hatter is a good base from which to explore some of London's hidden gems, pubs down hidden alleyways, pubs where every brick and stone tells a story about its area and heritage.

And if one ever tires of Fuller's brews, then seek out a Young's pub, and marvel at how so much taste can be found in a glass of its Bitter. Malted barley, hops and water – that is all it takes – yet the results are sublime.

South of England

The Trooper Inn, Froxfield, in Hampshire is a remote pub, but the journey is worth it.

Situated at the highest point in Hampshire, in the heart of the countryside, the Trooper is one of Hampshire's finest pubs and its history goes back more than 400 years.

There was time when the rooms were full of the sound of hunting parties, stage coach passengers and even recruiting

The Trooper Inn,
Froxfield, Hampshire

sergeants calling young men to bear the King's arms and to march to the drums of war.

Today, a small hotel has been added to the pub and it is the place to try a glass of Ringwood beer.

The Ringwood Brewery is set in the heart of Hampshire. My personal favourite is its Best Bitter – simple perfection. But if it is available try the seasonal porter. Its XXXX Porter, 4.7 per cent, is almost as dark as the darkest night but there is the hint of a ruby red moon somewhere in the sky. An aroma of chocolate roasted malt leads to a rich chocolate taste with a hint of fresh ground coffee and a touch of orange and lemon fruit flavours. And it has an aftertaste that lingers long on the palate of healthy luscious malt and a silky moreish bitterness.

South West England

Rules are meant to be broken, and the South West stretching as it does through some of the most beautiful parts of England deserves more than one pub to be singled out.

If there was room I would choose them all – each has a reason for special acclaim.

But two have something special about them. **The Marquis of Lorne** in Nettlecombe, near Bridport, Dorset And the **Nobody Inn**, Doddiscombsleigh, just outside Exeter in Devon are exemplars of rural England at its finest.

Beer at the Marquis of Lorne is often served straight from the wood, and it is the place to try a beer from Britain's only thatched brewery Palmers of Bridport.

The Bridport Bitter is an excellent example of the brewer's art and craft. Light to taste, not too strong but a testament to a brewer's skill in producing taste where so many others just make blandness.

The Marquis of Lorne, Nettlecombe, near Bridport, Dorset

The Nobody Inn is a long way from anywhere but a warm welcome awaits anyone who wants to make the journey, and it is a perfect example of what being a local means – local beers, wines, ciders and cheeses are all sold.

The House Beer is brewed by one of the country's new wave of micro-brewers Branscombe Vale.

Nobody Inn,
Doddiscombsleigh,
near Exeter

The brewery is only just 10 years old, but from its former cowshed owned by the National Trust it has acquired a formidable reputation for brewing well-balanced beers.

Heart of England

Even in busy, crowded, car-reliant England it is still possible to find peace and calm close to a main road. **The Talbot Inn,**

The Talbot Inn,
Knightwick,
Worcestershire

Knightwick in Worcestershire is a perfect example of somewhere that is close by but seems far away.

Wiz Clift, who runs the restaurant, is one of a growing band of imaginative pub chefs, who not only buy locally produced ingredients but also see organic food as being very important.

The inn is also home to the Teme Valley brewery – famed for its This, That and T'Other brews, using hops from the nearby Lusley Court Estate, which until recently was owned by the Clift family.

Each year the pub brews a range of seasonal brews, single-hop varietal beers using fresh unkilned hops. These Hops Nouvelle beers have rightly acquired a reputation not just for their taste and quality but for showing what a big contribution hops in all their varieties can make to the taste and aroma of a beer.

Another favourite has to be the **Hare & Hounds**, Fulbeck, Lincolnshire, far to the East in this region. Not only does this lovely old 16th century pub sell one of my favourite beers Bateman XB, but it overlooks the green of one of Lincolnshire's prettiest villages.

East of England

Some pubs stand out not just because of the quality of the accommodation, but because the licensees are working hard not just to ensure that their pub survives but also that it is firmly at the heart of its community.

The White Hart Blythburgh in Suffolk is one such pub. Following the closure of the village shop and post office, the enterprising licensees decided to convert an out-building to a new use. In too many parts of Britain schools are closing, post offices shutting and pubs make way for a housing development.

As each of these important institutions goes, so part of the fabric that binds a community together goes too.

Converting part of the pub or one of its out-buildings into a shop-cum-post office really does create a community focus as has been recognised by Prince Charles whose Pub is the Hub initiative encourages pubs to diversify.

Now the White Hart is not just the place to drink Adnams beers, it is also the place to post a letter, buy a paper and do the grocery shopping.

The pub itself is also an example of how, with sensitivity, accommodation can be added onto a building.

Northumbria

Good food and good beer are an essential element of any pub. Add to it good accommodation and it could be a candidate for this book. The **Shipwrights Hotel**, North Hylton, Sunderland has all three.

The Shipwright is a 350 year-old coaching inn on the banks of the River Wear in the shadow of the Hylton Bridge. In its time it has been a post office, a ships chandlers and the place where men were press-ganged in to the Navy.

What makes it stand out is the quality of its service. Nothing seems too much for the staff, who make visitors to the area welcome and are always willing to help.

Any visitor to this region should take the opportunity to visit the **Star Inn**, Netherton in Northumberland.

This unspoilt gem, unchanged for the last 80 years, is one of only 17 to have appeared in all 30 editions of the Good Beer Guide. It was originally built as a hotel for a new railway line, which was never completed. Step into it and it is like stepping back in time. The Castle Eden Ale is served direct from the cellar at a hatch in the panelled entrance hall.

Yorkshire

Yorkshire offers the beer lover so much. Yorkshire's oldest brewery is Samuel Smith in the brewing town of Tadcaster, which in its prime rivalled Burton on Trent as a centre for brewing pale ales. Sam's, a fiercely independent and idiosyncratic company, stands next door to the John Smith brewery now owned by Scottish and Newcastle. And while the Berlin Wall may have fallen in Europe ending the Cold War, it is said locally that the wall that divides the two sites will stay forever. Sam Smith's continues to distribute its Old Brewery Bitter to pubs locally in wooden casks. It is a rich malty beer, with a bold burst of hops and fruit in the taste.

One of my favourite places to stay is the **Kings Head** in Masham. It is a fine Georgian building dating back to the 18th

Kings Head, Masham

century, situated in the Market Square of this picturesque town. The 10 stylish bedrooms are all individually designed and named, with some using a brewing theme. Masham is a remarkable town. It has a splendid church, a beautiful square and two breweries, Theakston and Black Sheep, both of which have visitor centres.

Cumbria

Jennings was once one of the Lake District's best kept secrets. Today its well-balanced ales can be found throughout the North-west and Lancashire. And Santon Bridge, Wasdale is a wonderful place to enjoy a glass of malty Jennings Bitter, or even the fruity Cumberland Ale or the stronger and complex Sneck Lifter.

The Bridge Inn, once a modest mail coaches' halt, is now a fine, well-situated, comfortable country inn providing good food and accommodation surrounded by the western lakes and fells of the English Lake District.

Close by is breathtaking lake and mountain scenery, Scafell Pike – England's highest mountain, Wastwater – the deepest lake and St Olaf's – the smallest church.

Not faraway from Santon Bridge you can take one of the most beautiful train journeys imaginable on the La'al Ratty.

The independently minded Cumbrians, are fond of their real ale and the area is home to many small, independent breweries. Business is tough for many of them, as they find it harder and harder to find free houses to sell their brews as any pub that comes on to the market is likely to be bought by one of the big pubcos that doesn't support local producers.

These craft brewers rely on visitors during the summer months to survive, and they should be sought out and enjoyed.

The Bridge Inn,
Cumbria

North West England

Until recently there were many family-brewers who could trace their history back to Victorian Britain and some are even older than that, but time, incompetence and greed have taken their toll and few remain.

However, the North West is home to several of them, and the beers of Holts, Hydes, Lees and Robinson's still thrive – drunk by people who are proud of their local brews.

Alongside the wonderful old can be found the new. Manchester is also the home of the Marble Brewery, founded in 1997, whose beers are made with organic ingredients and are suitable for vegetarians and vegans.

A favourite bed and breakfast has to be the **Little Mill Inn**, Rowarth, Derbyshire. The pub itself lies in the foothills of the Derbyshire Peak District, just outside Greater Manchester.

The overnight accommodation at this pretty little pub is situated in a converted railway dining car, the Derbyshire Belle, from the old Brighton Belle. A long way from its first home, the London Brighton rail line, the carriage now contains three tastefully converted rooms.

The building that accommodated the mill wheel was swept away by a great flood in 1930 but the wheel, believed to be the biggest in north west England, has since been restored to full working order and may be seen working every day.

Scotland

Anyone who thinks Scotland has no real ale should think again. Many of its beers are now award winners, and Deuchars IPA brewed at the Caledonian Brewery in Edinburgh is at the time of writing this book the Champion Beer of Britain. It is a superb example of a session beer, not too strong, but full of taste and once you have had one, you want to have another.

Scotland has many outstanding pubs too.

The Oak Tree Inn, Balmaha in Stirlingshire is close to Loch Lomond and the West Highland Way.

The pub stands in the shade of a magnificent 500 year old oak tree, a focal point in the village and the perfect setting in which to relax. Every detail of design and construction has been meticulous in order to create a truly unique environment for visitors and guests. Of special note is the bar area, constructed from a 300 year old oak tree. In a remarkable salvage operation, timbers and panelling were dismantled from a neighbouring country house dating from 1864, a local slate quarry was reopened for this one building and all the slates were reclaimed from the roof of Buchanan Castle. All this ensures its uniqueness in the area.

Wales

Wales is home to many beers. There can be few places better than the **Clytha Arms**, Clytha, Abergavenny, Monmouthshire to enjoy real ale.

This superb multi-award winning pub, offers a fine restaurant and excellent accommodation.

The landlord and his wife are both life members of CAMRA and the regular beers are complemented by a range of guests, usually from independent brewers, and always in first class condition.

Wales is also home to a marvellous example of a mild ale, a style of beer which CAMRA is committed to preserving.

Mild was once the drink of working Britain, a source of fluid and nutrients for people who had sweated long hours in farms or factories.

But it has become a fashion victim and is wrongly seen as a weak, watery, down market brew.

Brains Dark is brewed in Cardiff, South Wales. A skilful blend of pale and chocolate malts gives this rich dark mild a fine flavour.

The beer has a delicate hop and chocolate aroma. While the palate starts malty with a slight nuttiness, it gives way to a light dry moreish finish. A good traditional mild ale that deserves to be sought out and savoured, not as a museum curiosity but as a vibrant example of this beer style.

Do not be deterred from enjoying a beer if you experience something different from any of my descriptions. Beauty is in the eye of the beholder. As each of us is different, so each of us will experience subtle differences and use different words to describe the complexity of the beers we drink. However, one thing should unite us, the ability to drink a glass of real beer and enjoy it. I am sure we would all say cheers to that.

Cumbria/Lake District

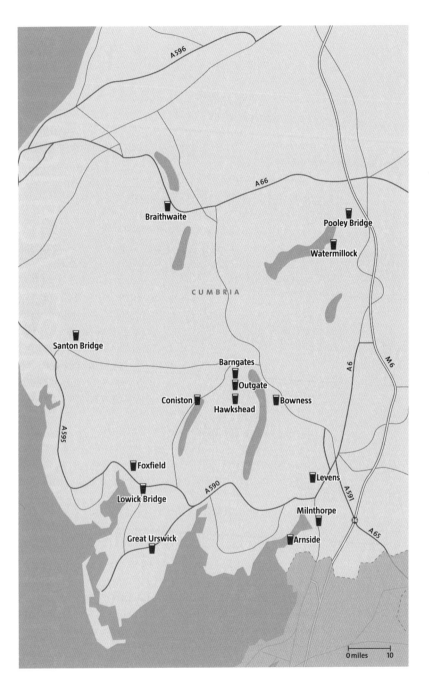

Braithwaite

Pooley Bridge

Watermillock

A 596

A 66

CUMBRIA

Santon Bridge

Barngates

Outgate

Coniston

Hawkshead

Bowness

A 6

M 6

A 595

Foxfield

Lowick Bridge

A 590

Levens

A 591

Milnthorpe

Great Urswick

Arnside

A 65

0 miles 10

CUMBRIA, which includes the Lake District National Park and the Hadrian's Wall World Heritage Site has been awarded a prestigious world first for managing its environment in a sustainable way.

Green Globe 21, the independent accreditation body, originally established by the World Travel and Tourism Council following the Rio Earth Summit, has developed a rigorous assessment programme to help tourism destinations manage the economy and communities in an environmentally sustainable manner. Cumbria is the first destination in the world to demonstrate its ability to balance these needs and be awarded the Green Globe Destination status.

In UK terms Cumbria is a relatively remote area, mainly composed of sparsely populated areas but with concentrations of populations along the 100 miles of varied coastline.

The world famous gem is of course The Lake District, an established tourist destination that offers something for everyone, young and old, from the wonderful rural experience to the plethora of cultural events, museums and galleries. This activity points to a healthy and prosperous community. There has also been a rebirth in the desire for locally produced beer and foods. Some of the best culinary offerings can be recognised by the Culinary Cumbria kitemark.

Unlike many parts of the UK, Cumbria is dominated by small owner-managed businesses. This scale of business contributes enormously to a sustainable tourism destination. Wealth created by small businesses, in the main, is retained in the local economy and thus helps support other industries.

Brewers play their part in this – in the quaint market town of Cockermouth can be found the Jennings Castle Brewery. Its brewing history can be traced back to 1783 with the birth of its founder John Jennings. Visitors can enjoy a guided tour of the brewery and also sample some of its superb Lakeland ales.

Not to be forgotten is the Coniston Brewery, home to the Champion Beer of Britain in 1998, Bluebird Bitter. The Hesket Newmarket Brewery is run by a co-operative of villagers and the Hawkshead Brewery is run by BBC radio presenter Alex Brodie.

Also worth seeking out are beers from the Barngates, Dent, Derwent, Foxfield, Great Gable, Tirril and Yates breweries.

Cumbria's turbulent history is steeped in legend and myth and for King Arthur fans, claims more Arthurian sites than any other area of the UK. Religion also contributes to the unique heritage of Cumbria, the birthplace of the Quaker movement, the impressive Cistercian Furness Abbey, prehistoric stone circles and numerous spectacularly sited churches are all key contributors to a fabulous place to visit.

ARNSIDE

Ye Olde Fighting Cocks

The Promenade, Arnside,
via Carnforth, Cumbria LA5 0HD
T 01524 761203   F 01254 761822
E neil@yeoldefightingcocks.co.uk
www.yeoldefightingcocks.co.uk
Licensees: Neil and Sue Taplin
Directions: On B5282 – five miles from M6 J36

A traditional pub, overlooking the Kent Estuary, with restaurant built over the original cock pit. The pub is an ideal base for visiting Lake Windermere, Levens Hall and the nearby Knot landmark. Children welcome and pets can be accommodated. All of its nine bedrooms are en suite.

🛏 Six double, one twin, one honeymoon, one family
£ ££
🍺 Thwaites Bitter, Thwaites Lancaster Bomber
🍴 Lunch, evening and snack menus
💳 Credit cards accepted

BARNGATES Ambleside

Drunken Duck Inn

Barngates, Ambleside, Cumbria LA22 0NG
T 015394 36347   F 015394 36781
E info@drunkenduckinn.co.uk
www.drunkenduckinn.co.uk
Directions: Take the Hawkshead turn off the B5285, after a mile turn right up Duck Hill

Despite its isolated position, this famous old inn is perennially popular, and brews its own beer. One could be inclined to stay a long time here enjoying the mountain views, open fires and imaginative meals. An added bonus is the lack of juke box, TV and other electronic intrusions that so often spoil the atmosphere of our rural pubs. The pub is in fact set in 60 acres of privately owned woodland and fell, yet is close to many popular tourist attractions such as Ambleside, Coniston and Langdale. Children are welcome and dogs can be accommodated.

🛏 Eight double and one twin-bedded room
£ £££
🍺 Barngates Cracker Ale, Chesters Strong & Ugly, Jennings Bitter, Theakston Old Peculier
🍴 Lunch, evening and snack menus
💳 Credit cards accepted

BOWNESS

The Albert Hotel

Queen Square, Bowness-on-Windermere, Cumbria LA23 3BY
T/F 015394 43241
Licensee: David Reid
Directions: on A592

A family run six-bedroom hotel set in the heart of Bowness. All rooms are en suite. The restaurant has an extensive menu with seafood and vegetarian dishes a specialty; bar snacks are available. It is an ideal location for all outdoor pursuits. Families and pets welcome.

🛏 Six double/twin
£ ££
🍺 Robinson's Best plus seasonals
🍴 Lunch, evening and snack menus
💳 Credit cards accepted

The Black Bull, Coniston

Royal Oak

Braithwaite, Nr Keswick, Cumbria CA12 5SY
T/F 017687 78533
E tpfranks@hotmail.com
www.royaloak-braithwaite.co.uk
Licensee: Terry Franks
Directions: Just off A66, between Cockermouth and Keswick

Braithwaite is a friendly place, offering a wide variety of amenities for visitors. The Royal Oak is a traditional country inn with 10 en suite bedrooms offering a Cumbrian bed and breakfast. The Royal Oak Hotel offers a Cumbrian bed and breakfast at its best. It caters for all from family holidays to walking weekends and is ideally located in the heart of the Lake District with Grisedale Pike and the dramatic Whinnlater Pass and visitor park easily accessible. The food features local specialities including hotpot and Cumberland sausages.

🛏 One single, one family, two four-poster, two twin, four double
£ ££ £££ single
🍺 Full range of Jennings beers
🍴 Lunch, evening and snack menus
💳 Credit cards accepted

Black Bull

Yewdale Road, Coniston, Cumbria LA21 8DU
T 01539 441335   **F** 01539 441168
Licensee: Ron Bradley
Directions: On A593 in village centre

The Black Bull is an historic 16th century coaching inn which brews its own beer including the 1998 Champion Beer of Britain, Bluebird Bitter. It is a cosy, warm and inviting base from which to explore the area. Many famous people have passed through the doors of the inn including John Ruskin, Turner – the landscape painter, Coleridge and de Quincey. The speed ace Donald Campbell used the pub before attempting his water speed records and the pub can be seen in the film *Across the Lake*, which depicted the last 60 days of his life. Coniston is a perfect Lake District village, in the shadow of the Old Man mountain. Children welcome.

🛏 All rooms
£ £££
🍺 **Coniston Bluebird Bitter, Bluebird XB, Old Man Ale**
🍴 Lunch, evening and snack menus
💳 Credit cards accepted

The Crown Hotel

Tiberthwaite Avenue, Coniston, Cumbria LA21 8EA
T 015394 41243   **F** 015394 41804
E info@crown-hotel-consiton.com
www.crown-hotel-coniston.com
Licensees: Enn and Adrienne Tiidus

The Crown Hotel has been completely refurbished to a very high standard and is an ideal base from which to enjoy Coniston and the Lake District. Close by is the Coniston Old Man, which rises to 2,633 feet and can be walked in various ways to suit all abilities, and Dow Crag provides some of the best rock climbing in Great Britain, while lake-shore walks to Torver are very popular. Children welcome.

🛏 Four double, four twin, two family
£ £££
🍺 **Robinson's Best Bitter, Hartleys Cumbria Way** plus seasonals
🍴 Lunch, evening and snack menus
💳 Credit cards accepted

FOXFIELD

Prince of Wales

Foxfield, Broughton-in-Furness, Cumbria LA20 6BX
T 01229 716238
E info@princeofwalesfoxfield.co.uk
www.princeofwalesfoxfield.co.uk
Directions: On A595 opposite Foxfield Railway Station

A beer drinkers' pub, the Prince of Wales is home to the Foxfield brewery. It offers basic,

comfortable accommodation in its two en suite double rooms. The pub is an ideal base for anyone wishing to walk in the area. It is listed in the Good Beer Guide, and was Furness CAMRA Branch Pub of the Year 2000/2001. Regular beer festivals are held, including a *wild mild* weekend and a *rare breweries in Cumbria* weekend. Its normal range of beers include an ever-changing range of guests but there is always a mild and usually a beer from Tigertops or Foxfield Brewery as well as draught continental wheat beer. The pub has no lunch or evening menus but offers excellent homemade snacks to accompany the beer on Friday, Saturday and Sunday. There is a discount on accommodation for CAMRA members. The pub is closed on Monday and Tuesday. Open 5pm Wednesday and Thursday, Noon Friday-Sunday. Good access by bus and rail.

🛏 Two double
£ £ Discount to CAMRA members
🍺 **Foxfield** and **Tigertops** beers plus guests
🍴 No lunch or evening menus, snacks only Friday-Sunday
💳 Credit cards not accepted

GREAT URSWICK

The Derby Arms

Great Urswick, Ulverston, Cumbria LA12 0SP
T 01229 586348   **F** 01229 585223
E thederbyarms@yahoo.co.uk
www.geocities.com/thederbyarms
Licensee: Gwyneth Dickinson

The Derby Arms (Stables), Urswick

A small well maintained pub with en suite accommodation in a converted stable block. The bar of the Derby Arms is well known for its fine ales, friendly atmosphere and open log fires. Dalton Wild Animal Park, Barrow Dock Museum and the Lake District National Park are all close by. Children are welcome but. The pub does not serve food at lunch or in the evenings.

🛏 Two double, two twin
£ £££
🍺 Hartleys XB
🍴 No lunch, evening or snack menus
💳 Credit cards not accepted

The Queens Head Hotel

Main Street, Hawkshead,
Ambleside, Cumbria LA22 0NS
T 015394 36271   **F** 015394 36722
E enquiries@queensheadhotel.co.uk
www.queensheadhotel.co.uk
Licensee: Anthony Merrick

Quaint village centre 16th century inn, with a flagged floor and oak beams. The Lake District is the pub's larder – offering locally reared wild pheasant, organic trout, lamb, ham and cheeses. All bedrooms are en suite and several have four-poster beds.

Close by are Coniston Old Man, Weatherlam and Latterbarrow, all with breathtaking views. Close too is Grizedale Forest, a woodland wonderland, 9,000 acres of walks, cycle paths and a sculpture trail. Hawkshead is a delightful village with winding streets, where no cars are allowed. Wordsworth went to school in the village. The hotel also has several self-catering properties.

🛏 14 double, one twin
£ £££
🍺 Robinson's Best Bitter, Hartleys XB
🍴 Lunch, evening and snack menus
💳 Credit cards accepted

The Queens Head Hotel, Hawkshead

LEVENS

Gilpin Bridge Inn

Bridge End, Levens, Nr Kendal Cumbria LA8 8EP
T 015395 52206   **F** 015395 52444
www.frederic-robinson.com
Licensee: Philip Rea

Sir Richard de Gilpin, a Crusader knight, gave his name to the nearby river and to The Gilpin Bridge Inn which is owned by Stockport brewer Frederic Robinson's. It is a friendly, family run pub with 10 en suite letting rooms. Situated in the south of the beautiful unspoilt Lyth Valley, it is close to the South Lakes. Children welcome.

- Seven double, three twin
- £ £££
- Frederic Robinson's Best Bitter
- Lunch, evening and lunch menus
- Credit cards accepted

LOWICK BRIDGE

Red Lion Inn

Lowick Bridge, Nr Ulverston, Cumbria LA12 8EF
T/F 01229 885366
E redlion@lowick.fslife.co.uk
www.redlionlowick.co.uk
Licensee: Tony Gray

From the beer garden there are beautiful views of the Old Man of Coniston. The Red Lion is a traditional Lakeland Inn with cosy log fires, beamed ceilings and a selection of real ales. The pub has close connections with Swallows and Amazons author Arthur Ransome and one of the bedrooms is

dedicated to his memory. Windermere is 20 minutes away and it is close to Haverthwaite Steam Railway. Children are welcome and the two letting bedrooms have recently been modernised – both en suite.

- One double, one twin
- £ ££
- Hartleys XB, Robinson's Mild plus seasonal beers
- Lunch, evening and snack menus
- Credit cards accepted

MILNTHORPE

The Cross Keys Hotel

1 Park Road, Milnthorpe, Cumbria LA7 7AD
T 015395 62115   **F** 015395 62446
E info@thecrosskeyshotel.co.uk
www.thecrosskeyshotel.co.uk
Licensee: Ian Mills

The Cross Keys is a family run hotel and has undergone a major refurbishment and modernisation programme. Milnthorpe has surroundings of great tranquillity. The river Bela winds lazily through parkland to the Kent Estuary at Sandside, where the dramatic expanse of Morecambe Bay has a backdrop of brooding Lakeland Fells. The hotel has won several awards for the quality of its beer cellar. All rooms are en suite. A self-catering cottage sleeps six. Children welcome.

- Seven double, one twin
- £ ££
- Robinson's Best Bitter, Hartleys XB plus seasonals
- Lunch, evening and snack menus
- Credit cards accepted

OUTGATE

Outgate Inn

Outgate, Nr Hawkshead, Ambleside,
Cumbria LA22 0NQ
T 01539 436413
E info@theoutgateinn.co.uk
www.theoutgateinn.co.uk
Licensees: Roy and Maureen White

Dating back to the late 18th century anglers
will enjoy using the pub's two permits for
game and coarse fishing in some of
England's most attractive waters. There are
three en suite bedrooms, which
unfortunately are not suitable for children.
A pleasant and comfortable pub popular
with locals, an added attraction is the live
jazz music each Friday evening. Hawkshead
village – in the heart of the National Park –
is close by.

🛏 Two double, one twin
£ ££
🍺 **Hartleys Cumbria Way**
🍴 Lunch, evening and snack menus
💳 Credit cards accepted

POOLEY BRIDGE

The Sun Inn

Pooley Bridge, Ullswater, Cumbria CA10 2NN
T 017684 86205   **F** 017684 86913

Situated on the north shore of Ullswater is
the pretty Lakeland Village of Pooley Bridge
where you will find this perfect traditional
Lake District inn. Ideally positioned for
touring the Lakes or as a walking holiday
base. Despite being in one of the most
beautiful corners of England, the Sun Inn is
only 10 minutes from the M6. All rooms are
en suite. There is ample parking on site and
dogs are most welcome.

🛏 Nine twin/double
£ £
🍺 **Jennings Bitter** and **Cumberland Ale**
🍴 Lunch, evening and snack menus
💳 Credit cards accepted

Outgate Inn, Outgate

SANTON BRIDGE

The Bridge Inn

Santon Bridge, Wasdale, Cumbria CA19 1UX
T 019467 26221   **F** 019467 26026
E info@santonbridgeinn.com
www.santonbridgeinn.com
Licensees: Lesley Rhodes and John Morrow

The Bridge Inn offers an experience which softer, prettier places cannot pretend to match. The Western Lakes and Fells are spectacular and here in this quiet valley there is still the peace and tranquillity that should be Lakeland. There are still more sheep than people in this area. Each year, in November, a contest is held in the pub, to award the title of The Biggest Liar in the World to the person who is worthy of following in the footsteps of "Auld Will". The contest attracts world wide attention, and in recent years the audience has learned facts like how the Lake District was formed – not by ice or volcanic action, but by large moles and eels! The food and Jennings beers are all excellent.

- 18 double/twin
- **£** ££
- **Jennings** range
- Lunch, evening and snack menus
- Credit cards accepted

WATERMILLOCK Ullswater

Brackenrigg Inn

Watermillock-on-Ullswater, Penrith, Cumbria CA11 0LP
T 017684 86206   **F** 017684 86945
E enquiries@brackenrigginn.co.uk
www.brackenrigginn.co.uk
Licensees: John Welch and Garry Smith
Directions: on A592

The Brackenrigg is a 17th century coaching inn overlooking Ullswater in the north lakes. It has a bar, lounge and dining room and an outside terrace which has stunning views down Ullswater to Helvelyn. All food is freshly prepared and where possible uses local ingredients. Children welcome.

- Three suites, three single, five twin/family and six double
- **£** £££
- **Black Sheep Bitter, Jennings Cross Buttock, Theakston Best Bitter, Coniston Bluebird,** regular guests
- Lunch, evening and snack menus
- Credit cards accepted

The Bridge Inn, Santon Bridge

East of England

Bedfordshire
Cambridgeshire
Essex
Hertfordshire
Norfolk
Suffolk

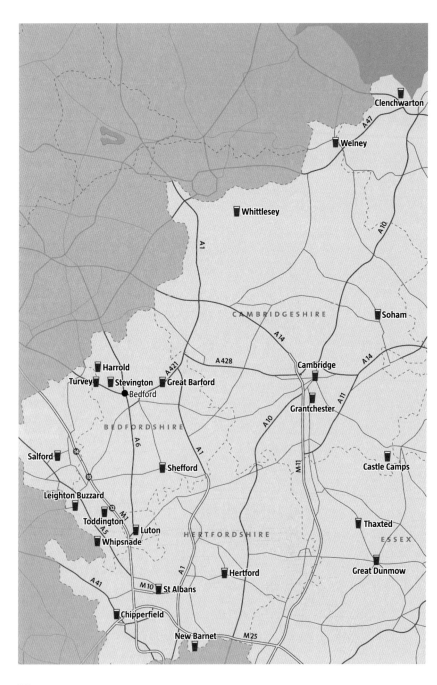

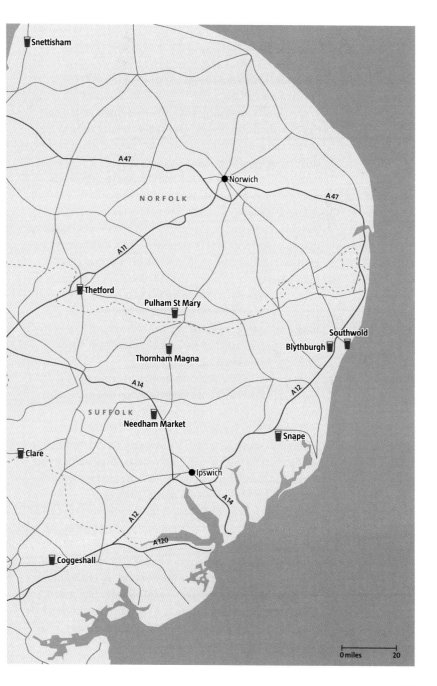

Snettisham

A 47

Norwich

NORFOLK

A 47

A 11

Thetford

Pulham St Mary

Southwold

Blythburgh

Thornham Magna

A 14

SUFFOLK

A 12

Needham Market

Snape

Clare

Ipswich

A 14

A 12

A 120

Coggeshall

0 miles   20

Step into the EAST OF ENGLAND, and you step into a subtly different world. This is England as you always thought it should be.

Gentle landscapes straight from an 18th century Constable painting.

Living, working villages of heart-stoppingly lovely, half-timbered cottages. Magnificent stately homes and awesome Gothic cathedrals. Traditional seaside resorts where children can play on sandy beaches. Oceans of Fenland shimmering beneath huge open skies. Lakes and rivers teeming with wildlife. Cities brimming with history and culture. The East of England has all this and more. And yet much of it has a delightful unspoilt, unassuming air. A corner of the country that's somehow missed the relentless march of time. And all with that unique East Anglian additive – a very quirky individuality.

This quirkiness is reflected in the area's beers, from Charles Wells in Bedford to Adnams in Southwold on the haunting Suffolk coast, the region's brewers produce beers of idiosyncratic distinction with a well earned reputation which goes far beyond their heartland.

Visitors to Cambridgeshire should take time to visit Elgood's Brewery and Gardens in Wisbech. There are tours and tastings to be had in the Georgian brewery.

A trip to Bury St Edmunds in Suffolk would be wasted unless the Greene King Brewery Museum was on the itinerary.

The museum includes displays of coopering and the vats where Old 5X matures for two years before being blended with a younger beer to make Strong Suffolk Ale.

If you are in search of culinary adventure, then the East of England is full of mouth-watering surprises which can be sampled with some of the many local ales.

In Bedfordshire you can try a clanger, a local delicacy of baked suet crust with savoury meat at one end, and something sweet at the other – a complete meal in one handy parcel.

Cambridgeshire is home to The Fens, an area of rich fertile soil ideal for growing cereals, flowers, fruit and vegetables and the local delicacy of eel.

Essex is a great place for trying seafood. Start in Colchester, whose famous oysters have been farmed since Roman times.

Hertfordshire is noted for its mills – at the 18th-century Mill Green Museum in Hatfield you can buy freshly milled flour, whilst at Kingsbury Watermill in St Albans, delicious waffles are the speciality.

During the 18th century droves of Norfolk turkeys were made to walk to the London markets, their feet coated with tar for protection.

Suffolk is noted for its delicious meats, such as hams sweet-cured with black treacle, sugar and beer, or dry-cured and oak smoked bacons.

BLYTHBURGH

White Hart

London Road, Blythburgh, Suffolk IP19 9LQ
T/F 01502 478217
Licensee: Michael Davis
Directions: Main A12 road

Southwold the home of Adnams beer – one of God's many gifts to beer drinkers – is only four miles away from this recently refurbished traditional English country inn. Open fires roar on winter nights. Overlooking the Blyth Estuary, it offers inland and coastal walks, lots of Royal Society for the Protection of Birds (RSPB) sites nearby; much of the countryside and coast is completely unspoilt. It has a large selection of daily specials and of course beer from Adnams. The recently built accommodation offers four large rooms that can be single, double or twin. Children welcome.

- Four rooms
- **£** ££
- **Adnams** full range
- Lunch, evening and snack menus
- Credit cards accepted

CAMBRIDGE

Clarendon Arms

35 Clarendon Street, Cambridge CB1 1JX
T 01223 313937
Licensee: Barry Fagg

Cosy welcoming two bar local, very popular for its good value food. The right hand bar has half-timbered walls and is mainly devoted to eating. The main bar is on two levels, the higher of which is the more pubby. Out the back is a sun trap of a patio/garden. Live music on Monday and Thursday is quiz night. Children welcome, no food Sunday evening.

- One double, one twin, one single
- **£** ££
- **Greene King IPA, Abbot** plus guest
- Lunch, evening and snack menus
- Credit cards not accepted

CASTLE CAMPS

Cock Inn

High Street, Castle Camps, Cambridgeshire CB1 6SN
T 01799 584207
Licensees: Mr and Mrs Feull

Tucked away in a remote corner of the Essex/Suffolk borders, the Cock is a very friendly local with a small public bar, large L-shaped lounge and separate restaurant. Food is available for residents on all days but limited for others. Folk music on the second Monday of each month. A large patio/garden is set beyond the accommodation extension. Children welcome.

- Three twin
- **£** ££
- **Greene King IPA, Adnams Bitter,** plus weekly guest
- Lunch, evening and snack menus
- Credit cards not accepted

CHIPPERFIELD

The Two Brewers

The Common, Chipperfield, Kings Langley,
Hertfordshire WD4 9BS
T 01923 265266 **F** 01923 261884
E info@twobrewers.com
www.twobrewers.com
Licensees: Alan Rodonsky, Nigel Clark and
Matthew Lancaster
Directions: On A4251

Chipperfield village centres on the Common – 60 acres of pleasant woodland fronted by the village cricket field. Nothing is more English on a fine summer's day to spend a little time watching the local XI take on a visiting side.

The Two Brewers, a 16th-century inn with much of its original features but providing modern amenities, overlooks the Common. Regarded as one of the finest buildings in the village it was once a training headquarters for bare-knuckle prize fighters. Close by is a 160-year-old church with a fine east window, and the old Queen Anne-fronted Manor House. The bar is traditional complete with log fires and there are 20 en suite bedrooms including a bridal suite.

🛏 20
£ £££££
🍺 **Courage Best, Directors**
🍴 Lunch, evening and snack menus
💳 Credit cards accepted

CLARE

The Bell Hotel

Market Hill, Clare, Sudbury, Suffolk CO10 8NN
T 01787 277741 **F** 01787 278474
www.oldenglishinns.co.uk
Directions: On A1092

This half-timbered coaching inn dates from the 16th century and is situated in the heart of Constable country. Close to the town centre is Nethergate Street where filming for TV's Lovejoy series took place. The town is home to the Nethergate Brewery which since its formation in 1986 has been in the forefront of innovative brewing, while maintaining strictly traditional methods.

Its Umbel beer claims to be the first beer brewed in England to use coriander for more than 150 years.

There are 16 beautifully furnished en suite rooms each with its own character. Clare boasts a ruined Norman castle and a country park with splendid walks. Nearby is Newmarket racecourse, Lavenham and Long Melford.

🛏 16 rooms
£ ££££
🍺 **Greene King** range plus **Nethergate** range
🍴 Lunch, evening and snack menus
💳 Credit cards accepted

CLENCHWARTON

The Victory Inn

Main Road, Clenchwarton,
Kings Lynn, Norfolk PE34 4AQ
T 01553 660682
E trevorswift8@btopenworld.com
Directions: on A17 just outside Kings Lynn

The Victory Inn is situated on the main road in Clenchwarton, a small, friendly village within easy access of the major tourist attractions in the Norfolk area. The pub has two traditional bars, both with log fires, and provides wholesome food throughout the day. The pub serves an excellent pint of Elgood's Cambridge or Black Dog Mild plus four guests. Beer garden plus a barbecue in the summer months.

The Bell Hotel, Clare

Two twin
£ ££
Elgood's Cambridge, mild and seasonal ales plus four guests
Lunch, evening and snack menus
Credit cards not accepted

COGGESHALL

White Hart Hotel

Market End, Coggeshall, Essex CO6 1NH
T 01376 561654 F 01376 561789
Directions: A12, follow signs to Kelvedon – B1024 to Coggershall

A Roman road, heading to Colchester once passed through the heart of this Essex town. Today it is famous for its superbly preserved 16th century Tudor half-timbered house Paycocke's. Once the home of a wealthy merchant it still contains many of its original features. The White Hart dates back to the 15th century and its wealth of original features, including timbered rooms, provide a warm and welcoming atmosphere. Situated in the heart of the town it is close to many antique shops.

18 rooms
£ ££££
Greene King IPA
Lunch, evening and snack menus
Credit cards accepted

GRANTCHESTER

Blue Ball Inn

57 Broadway, Grantchester, Cambridgeshire CB3 9NQ
T 01223 840679
Licensee: John Roos

Delightfully compact Victorian pub, though there has been a Blue Ball in Grantchester for much longer, comprising two small rooms with only five tables. It was the CAMRA Pub of the Year in 2002. Photographs of the pub and village decorate the walls along with a complete list of landlords since 1767.

The Blue Ball was a hot air balloon flown from Trinity Hall Farm to Wickhambrook, Suffolk in 1785. Ring the Bull is played. Food is served excepted Sunday evening and Monday. Within easy reach of Cambridge. The Old Vicarage, Grantchester is home to Jeffery Archer. Neither bedroom is en suite.

One double, one twin
£ ££
Adnams Bitter, Adnams Broadside
Lunch, evening and snack menus
Credit cards not accepted

GREAT BARFORD

Anchor

High Street, Great Barford, Bedford MK44 3LF
T 01234 870364
E attheanchorinn@aol.com
Directions: Opposite river bridge, about one mile south of A421

Busy pub overlooking the bridge and picturesque water meadows next to the River Great Ouse. Food served in bar and restaurant. Two guest beers usually available. Extensive wine list. The pub is set in an attractive part of the Great Ouse valley, three miles from 16th century National Trust dovecotes at Willington.

Two double, one single
£ £ ££ single
Charles Wells Eagle, Bombardier usually two guest beers
Lunch, evening and snack menus
Credit cards accepted

GREAT DUNMOW

Kicking Dickey

4 Ongar Road, Great Dunmow, Essex CM6 1ES
T 01371 872071
www.pickapub.co.uk/thekickingdickey.htm
Licensees: Lawrence and Diane Daniels
Directions: South side of town near junction with
        B184 – Ongar Road

Formerly known as The Railway Tavern, the Kicking Dickey's new licensees Lawrence and Diane Daniels take a genuine hands-on interest in seeing that their customers really enjoy themselves, in this old town pub. It's a very civilised dining pub, which makes a good place to come for a special occasion. The letting rooms are of a high standard situated in an out-building conversion at the rear and separate to the pub. There is a large menu with daily specials. Twenty miles from Stanstead Airport. Children welcome.

🛏 One double, one twin, one family
£ ££ single £££
🍺 **Ridleys IPA**, **Ridleys Prospect**
🍴 Lunch, evening and snack menus
💳 Credit cards accepted

HARROLD

The Oakley Arms

98 High Street, Harrold, Bedfordshire MR43 7BH
T 01234 720478
www.theoakleyarms.co.uk
Licensee: Anne Wildman
Directions: In village centre, four miles north of A428

Located in the delightful rural setting of North Bedfordshire. This Grade II listed pub was built in two parts, the first in the 16th century and the second part in the 17th century. The older part of the building is now used for the new bed and breakfast. Some pubs claim Kings and Queens have stayed, the Oakley claims the king of rock and roll Paul McCartney first played Hey Jude in public in the lounge in 1969.

The bed and breakfast is an ideal base for those wishing to explore all of the delights of rural north Bedfordshire, with its country park and wildlife centre literally at the end of the road. Also nearby is the Santa Pod raceway, and Silverstone Race Track is only a 45 minute drive away. Harrold is also ideal if you want to visit places further afield such as London, Oxford, Cambridge and the home of Shakespeare, Stratford-upon-Avon, these all being within one hour travelling time. Children welcome.

🛏 Two double, one twin, one suite
£ £££
🍺 **Charles Wells Eagle**, **IPA** plus guests
🍴 Lunch and evening menus
💳 Credit cards accepted

HERTFORD

Salisbury Arms

Fore Street, Hertford, Hertfordshire SG14 1BZ
T 01992 583091 F 01992 552510
E reception@salisbury-arms-hotel.co.uk
www.salisbury-arms-hotel.co.uk
Licensees: Mike and Sharon Howell

The Salisbury Arms Hotel, Hertford's oldest hostelry, has been in the ownership of the Hertfordshire family brewers McMullen since 1891. There are 31 bedrooms including two that are specially adapted for the needs of disabled guests. All bedrooms have en suite bath or shower rooms, hair dryer, hospitality tray, colour television with satellite channels, trouser press, personal safe, direct dial telephone and computer modem connection. In addition there are two family rooms and two executive rooms, one with a spa bath. There are many local places of interest including the great houses of Knebworth, Hatfield and Luton Hoo.

🛏 31 all
£ £££
🍺 **McMullen** range
🍴 Lunch, evening and snack menus
💳 Credit cards accepted

LEIGHTON BUZZARD

The Hunt Hotel

Church Road, Linslade, Leighton Buzzard,
Bedfordshire, LU7 2LR
T 01525 374692 Fax: 01525 382782
E bobpatrick@thehunthotel.freeserve.co.uk
Licensees: Bob and Sandra Patrick
Directions: Near Railway station

This small family-run hotel has a pleasant
outlook and is situated only 150 metres from
Leighton Buzzard main line railway station.
All 13 bedrooms are en suite, there is a small
bar, lounge, restaurant and car parking for 25.
Leighton Buzzard is an old market town,
surrounded by open countryside with the
National Trust's Ascott House and
Waddesdon Manor both within easy reach.
It is 16 miles from Luton Airport.

🛏 Three single, six double, three twin rooms, and
   one family
£ £££
🍺 **Fuller's London Pride**, **Tetley Bitter**
🍴 Lunch evening and snack menus
💳 Credit cards accepted

LUTON

Leaside Hotel

72 New Bedford Road, Luton, Bedfordshire LU3 1BT
T 01582 417643   **F** 01582 734961
E leasidehotel@aol.com
www.leasidehotel.com
Directions: Access to car park via Old Bedford Road

Located a few minutes' walk from Luton town
centre, this family owned hotel is an impressive Victorian villa. Set in its own gardens, it
retains many original features in the public
areas. These include a choice of bars and games
lounges and an elegant restaurant where
imaginative dishes are offered. Bedrooms
are well equipped for both the business and
leisure guest. All rooms are en suite, with
TV and telephone. Guide dogs welcome.

🛏 13 rooms
£ £££
🍺 Range of real ales
🍴 Lunch, evening and snack menus
💳 Credit cards accepted

NEEDHAM MARKET

The Limes Hotel

99 High Street, Needham Market,
Ipswich, Suffolk IP6 8DQ
T 01449 720305   **F** 01449 722233
E limes.hotel@elizabethhotels.co.uk
www.elizabethhotels.co.uk
Directions: On High Street

A historic 15th century town centre pub
with an imposing frontage. With two
distinct bars – Bugs Bar has flagstone floors,
exposed beams and an unusual walk-round
inglenook fireplace. His Lordship's Bar is
comfortable with oak panelled walls and
well upholstered seating. Children are
welcome in the lounge area.

There are regular live music sessions
including jazz on Sundays. It offers special
deals on food and accommodation.
Constable country is a 20 minute drive
away and Sudbury and Ipswich are nearby.
Needham Market is a graceful town with
Georgian houses in the High Street and
excellent examples of Tudor Architecture

🛏 11 double/twin all
£ £££
🍺 **Adnams Bitter**, **Greene King IPA** and **Abbot**
🍴 Lunch, evening and snack menus
💳 Credit cards accepted

The Hadley Hotel

113 Hadley Road, New Barnet,
Hertfordshire EN5 5QN
T 020 8449 0161   F 020 8441 0329
Directions: 10 minutes walk New Barnet BR station,
15 minutes walk High Barnet tube station

Owned by the Turley family for many years
this comfortable Victorian hotel is hidden
away in leafy suburbia but is on the
outskirts of London. One bar serves three
drinking areas, one of which is decorated
with a mural depicting the civil war Battle of
Barnet which took place on nearby Hadley
Common, another has an exhibition of
paintings by a local artist, which are for sale.

- 🛏 One single, two twin, two double, one triple
- £ ££ and £££ single
- 🍺 **Fuller's London Pride, Greene King IPA** plus guests
- 🍴 Lunch and evening menus most days
- 💳 Credit cards accepted

Kings Head

The Street, Pulham St Mary, near Diss,
Norfolk IP21 4RD
E graham.scott@barbox.net
www.kingsheadpulham.com
T 01379 676318

The Kings Head is a late 17th century
timbered frame pub. The cosy main bar is
warmed on cool evening, by the embrace of
a large woodburner. The attractive village is
famous for the first dual crossing of the
Atlantic by an airship in 1919. The dirigible
was one of many built at a nearby airfield

which were known as Pulham Pigs. A
wooden propeller is displayed above the
fireplace. The freehouse has a large garden
with a play area for children, and the barn
has been converted into a play area for adults.
It has its own bowling green. Bressingham
Steam Museum is 12 miles away. The pub
which supports local brewers is very popular
with locals and supports a cricket team,
football team and the bowls club.

- 🛏 One double, one family, one double plus sofa bed
- £ ££
- 🍺 **Adnams Bitter, Buffy's Bitter House Beer** plus guest ales
- 🍴 Lunch, evening and snack menus
- 💳 Credit cards accepted

The Red Lion

Wavendon Road, Salford, Nr Milton Keynes,
Buckinghamshire MK17 8AZ
T 01908 583117
E redlionhotelmk@hotmail.com
Licensee: Bob Sapsford
Directions: Off A421, two miles from M1 Js 13 and 14

Salford is one of the attractive villages that
lie on the outskirts of Milton Keynes, just
six miles from the centre, but far enough
away to maintain its own character. The
restaurant draws business people as well as
families, with its extensive menu, and
children are welcome to stay at the pub
(although there is no designated family room).
Woburn Abbey, with its famous collection of
Canalettos, Safari Park, Antiques Centre and
extensive grounds is just four miles away.

Three of the guest rooms, decorated in
cottage style, are in the main pub building,
the rest are in a more modern, chalet-style
building in the pub grounds. All but two of
the rooms have en suite amenities, and
some feature four-poster beds. TV,
telephones and tea/coffee making facilities
are available in all the rooms.

- 🛏 Six double, two twin-bedded rooms
- £ ££
- 🍺 **Charles Wells Bombardier, Eagle IPA**

🍴 Lunch, evening and snack menus
💳 Credit cards accepted

SHEFFORD

White Hart Hotel

North Bridge Street, Shefford, Bedfordshire SG17 5DH
T 01462 811144   **F** 01462 850970
Directions: In town centre, off A600 and A507
immediately beside the traffic lights

The White Hart is an original coaching inn;
its heyday was when Shefford was on the
0main Bedford to London coach route.
Although the present front is 18th century,
behind the brick and under the rendering is
a fine timber framed building. Inside you
will find many photographs of old Shefford.
The pub has four letting rooms. Bar snacks
and full menu served in bar or restaurant
and petanque is played in the garden.
Shefford is the home of the B&T brewery
and its Tap, the Brewery Tap, is just down
the road. The town's most famous former
resident is Robert Bloomfield, who wrote
the *Farmer's Boy* in 1800.

🛏 Four twins
£ ££
🍺 **Greene King IPA**, **Abbot** and occasional guest
beers
🍴 Lunch, evening and snack menus

SNETTISHAM

The Rose & Crown

The Rose & Crown, Old Church Road,
Snettisham, King's Lynn, Norfolk PE31 7LX
T 01485 541382   **F** 01485 543172
E info@roseandcrownsnettisham.co.uk
www.roseandcrownsnettisham.co.uk
Licensee: Anthony Goodrich
Directions: On A149 King's Lynn to Hunstanton road

A great place to escape to – The Rose & Crown
is a 14th century village inn in one of the
most stunning and least known parts of
Britain. Snettisham has a superbly decorated
church, St Marys and is close to Sandringham,
Houghton, Holkham and the amazing
North Coast Beaches. It is within easy reach
of Norfolk Lavender and RSPB Snettisham.
Inside, the core of The Rose & Crown is still
much as it has been over the last few
centuries, a proper local pub with three bars
with ancient timbered ceilings, twisting
corridors, large open fires and worn
pavement floors.

The pub has recently been awarded an
AA Rosette for the food. The eleven bedrooms
are decorated in great style with wrought
iron bedsteads and fresh white linen.
Each has its own well-equipped bathroom.
Larger groups and those with children
enjoy the Garden Room, with its huge
fireplace and old farmhouse tables, which
leads directly onto a lovely walled garden.

🛏 Three twin, eight double
£ ££££
🍺 **Fuller's London Pride**, **Adnams Broadside**,
Greene King IPA
🍴 Lunch, evening and snack menus
💳 Credit cards accepted

SNAPE

The Crown Inn

Bridge Road, Snape,
Nr Saxmundham, Suffolk IP17 1SL
T 01728 688324
Licensee: Diane Maylott
Directions: On B1069

A 15th century inn with a wealth of wooden
beams, large double settles around an
inglenook fire place. Intriguing old brick
floors. Adnams beers, fine wines, the dining
room is open seven days a week. Interesting

menu and the food is cooked on the premises. It is five minutes from the famous Snape Maltings Concert Hall. Three en suite bedrooms. Orford Medieval Castle and Minsmere Bird Research are nearby. Children over 14 welcome.

🛏 Two double – including one four-poster, one twin
£ ££
🍺 Adnams Bitter, Broadside, Regatta
🍴 Lunch, evening and snack menus
💳 Credit cards accepted

SOHAM

The Fountain

1 Churchgate Street, Soham,
Cambridgeshire CB7 5DS
T 01353 720374   F 01353 722103
E enquiries@thefountain.co.uk
www.thefountain.co.uk

The Fountain which was originally known as the White Lion is thought to date back to the 15th century. Unfortunately on Friday 4th May 1900 the original building was largely destroyed by fire. It was re-built in very much the same style, keeping the imposing three gabled structure. Thankfully one of the most interesting relics, an ancient steelyard weighing machine and part of what now forms the lounge survived the fire and still remain to this day.

The Fountain is situated under the shadow of St Andrews Church in the centre of the market town of Soham. It offers excellent value accessible accommodation within easy reach of Ely, with its famous Cathedral, Newmarket, the home of horse-racing and Cambridge, the seat of learning with its many elaborate and picturesque colleges. Major roads nearby include the A10, A14 and the M11. Home cooked bar lunches and evening meals are served in the newly constructed conservatory at the back of the pub.

🛏 Three twin all
£ £
🍺 Greene King IPA, Adnams Bitter
🍴 Lunch, evening and snack menus
💳 Credit cards accepted

SOUTHWOLD

The Kings Head

25 High Street, Southwold, Suffolk IP18 6AD
T 01502 724517
Licensee: Phil Tompkins
Directions: On High Street

A fine pub with large bars and a separate restaurant area and a family room in the summer months. There is a varied menu of home cooked food with locally caught fish featuring. All the accommodation is en suite. Children welcome.

The Kings Head, Southwold

🛏 Two twin, one double
£ ££
🍺 **Adnams** range
🍴 Lunch evening and snack menus
💳 Credit cards accepted

ST ALBANS

The Lower Red Lion

36 Fishpool Street, St Albans, Hertfordshire AL3 4RX
T 01727 855669   F 01727 838660
E info@thelowerredlion.co.uk
www.thelowerredlion.co.uk

St Albans' oldest freehouse, this charming 17th century two-bar pub is close to the Cathedral and Roman Verulamium. It has a range of at least five constantly changing real ales from micros as well as two permanent house beers – the award winning Oakham JHB and Fuller's London Pride. Regular beer festivals are held over the May Day and August bank holidays which can feature up to 50 unusual and highly drinkable beers.

All the letting rooms have TV and tea and coffee making facilities. No evening meals are served (but the home-cooked lunches are very good) and there is a good choice of restaurants within walking distance. The guest rooms are cosy and comfortable, just two of them have en suite facilities.

🛏 One double, one twin, two twin, one double, two single
£ £££
🍺 **Oakham JHB, Fuller's London Pride** plus regular guests
🍴 Lunchtime only
💳 Credit cards accepted

STEVINGTON

Red Lion

1 Park Road, Stevington, Bedford MK43 7QD
T 01234 824138
E pubredlion@aol.com
Licensees: Geoff and Karen Gallimore
Directions: At village centre, two miles north of A428

Prominent pub at village crossroads, with a friendly, informal atmosphere. The large garden includes an aviary and petanque pitch. Separate games room. Home cooked food (not Monday evening) and three-course Sunday lunch. Holds a key to the restored 18th century Stevington Windmill museum and is two miles from the restored water mill museum at Bromham. The village is on the Bunyan Trail circular walk linking local features that John Bunyan used in Pilgrim's Progress. Bunyan is said to have preached from the village cross outside the pub. The garden has a number of exotic birds in the aviary and a parrot next to the entrance of the garden which likes to wolf whistle and say goodbye to visitors (be careful, he bites!).

🛏 One double, two double, one single
£ ££
🍺 **Charles Wells Eagle** and **Bombardier** plus guest
🍴 Lunch, evening and snack menus
💳 Credit cards accepted

THAXTED

Rose & Crown

31 Mill End, Thaxted, Essex CM6 2LT
T 01371 831152
Licensees: George and Suzanne Carless
Directions: In town centre, off High Street

A friendly, traditional two bar pub with an open fire. The public bar has darts, pool and TV. In the saloon the restaurant is separate from the main bar. The menu is sourced extensively from quality local produce at value for money prices. The pub is the home of the Thaxted Morris. Thaxted has a 14th-century Guildhall, and a fine tower windmill housing a small museum.

The local church is famous, not least for its annual music festival, inspired by Gustav Holst, a one-time resident of Thaxted. The town claims to be the original home of Morris Dancing and between 150 and 300 dancers gather every year to put on a spectacular display. One of the bedrooms is en suite, the other has an adjoining bathroom. Children are welcome.

🛏 Two twin-bedded rooms
£ ££
🍺 **Ridleys IPA**, guest beers
🍴 Lunchtime, evening and snack menus
💳 Credit cards not accepted

Swan Hotel

The Bull Ring, Thaxted, Dunmow, Essex CM6 2PL
T 01371 830321 F 01371 831186
Directions: M11 to Stansted, A120 to Great
Dunmow, B184 to Thaxted

The 180 foot tower of the St John the Baptist
church dominates this small Essex town
and indicates the importance of Thaxted,
once as a centre for cutlery and later cloth
making. The Swan is a traditional coaching
inn, with a large roaring fire warming the
bar on cooler days. The Swan's 21 en suite
rooms are all well equipped. Nearby is a
well-preserved Tower windmill which
houses a museum of rural life.

🛏 21 rooms
£ ££££
🍺 **Greene King** range
🍴 Lunch, evening and snack menus
💳 Credit cards accepted

The Crown Hotel

Crown Road, Mundford, Thetford, Norfolk IP26 5HQ
T 01842 878233 F 01842 878982
Licensee: Barry Walker
Directions: Five miles from the Suffolk Border
where the A1065 crosses the A134 – 5 miles
Brandon, 10 miles form Swaffham and Thetford

The Crown Hotel dates back to 1652 and was a
renowned hunting inn – situated on the edge
of the Thetford forest. The beamed bars have
large open fireplaces, with a spiral staircase
leading to the eating area upstairs. Locally
brewed Iceni and Woodforde's beer are
usually on sale and the food is good. When
the couple who first recommended the
Crown stayed there in 1996 they parked their
Caterham 7 in the well protected courtyard,
and stayed in one of the attic rooms. Six years
later the Caterham was gone and replaced by
a three year old dog and they stayed in the
newly converted Smithy, which has been
converted into a self contained flat.
"My husband had a locally brewed Iceni beer
before the meal and I tried it, it was so lovely,
I had half a pint afterwards, and I don't
normally drink beer," said the nominator.

🛏 16 double, two family, 16 single
£ ££ £££ single
🍺 **Woodforde's Wherry Best Bitter,
Iceni Fine Soft Day**
🍴 Lunch, evening and snack menus
💳 Credit cards accepted

Four Horseshoes

Nr Eye, Suffolk IP23 8HD
T 01379 678777 F 01379 678134
E 6448@greeneking.com
Directions: One mile off the A140, the main
Ipswich to Norwich road

A charming thatched inn dating back to the
12th-century with a patio and rear garden.
Its rambling bars and restaurant provide
many fascinating features including
inglenook fireplaces and a genuine wishing
well – and the place to wish for all real ale
being served as well as it is here. There are
eight comfortable bedrooms all recently
refurbished and including CD players.
Nearby is the village of Thornham Magna
with its thatched Norman church complete
with a 13th-century painted ornamental
screen showing the crucifixion. Nearby is
the town of Bressingham which houses a
steam museum.

🛏 Eight rooms
£ ££££
🍺 **Greene King** range plus guests
🍴 Lunch, evening and snack menus
💳 Credit cards accepted

TODDINGTON

Sow & Pigs

19 Church Square, Toddington,
Dunstable, Bedfordshire LU5 6AA
T 01525 873089
www.sowandpigs.co.uk
Directions: M1 J12, behind Toddington Services

This is one of only 17 pubs in the country that has appeared in every edition of the Good Beer Guide, 30 in total, so the beer is guaranteed to be worth the journey. It is a 19th century commercial inn, with one long, dog friendly bar, heated by three real log fires. The pub displays assorted pig and golfing memorabilia. Residents are offered a choice of a hot meal in the evening or a cooked breakfast as part of the basic package. The accommodation offers comfortable rooms at reasonable prices. No rooms are en suite but there is a large spacious bathroom. Much friendlier than a Travelodge, and the beer is much better too.

🛏 Three twin, one single
£ £ £29 for evening meal and breakfast
🍺 **Greene King IPA, Abbot**, seasonal beers
🍴 Lunch – evening meal for residents only
💳 Credit cards accepted

TURVEY

Three Cranes

High Street, Turvey, Bedfordshire MK43 8EP
T 01234 881305 **F** 01234 881305
www.oldenglish.co.uk
Directions: on A428, midway between Bedford and Northampton

Some say that Turvey is the perfect old English village. An 11-arch bridge carrying the main road over the Great Ouse dates from the 15th century, but the picturesque olde-worlde village is mainly a 19th century development when it was rebuilt of local stone. The Three Cranes is a 17th-century former coaching inn which stands in the conservation area, next to the Anglo Saxon church. Of special interest in the church is the 12th century Anglo-Danish nave and tower and a 14th century painting of the crucifixion in the south aisle.

The restaurant offers a good choice of freshly prepared food. The traditional bar has open fireplaces and many corners for quiet conversations. There is a wide range of real ales, which can be sampled in the pretty garden. Good for rural pursuits such as walking in Harrold Country Park and fishing on the River Ouse, it is also convenient for Santa Pod Raceway, Silverstone and Woburn Abbey and Safari Park.

🛏 One single, one double, one twin
£ ££
🍺 **Greene King IPA, Abbot, Hook Norton Best Bitter** and guest beers
🍴 Lunch, evening and snack menus
💳 Credit cards accepted

WELNEY

Lamb & Flag

Main Street, Welney, Nr Wisbech,
Cambridgeshire PE14 9RB
T 01354 610242
Licensee: Georgina Webb

On the very edge of Norfolk, the Boston creeper covered Lamb & Flag is pleasantly situated in the small village of Welney, well known for its fishing and birdwatching. It is close to the Welney Wildfowl and Wetlands Trust. Families are welcome in the pub which has an open fire in its bar. Ely Cathedral is a short drive away. All rooms are en suite.

🛏 One double one twin, one family
£ £
🍺 **Elgood's** range plus guest ales
🍴 Lunch, evening and snack menus
💳 Credit cards accepted

WHIPSNADE

Old Hunters Lodge

The Cross Roads, Whipsnade, Bedfordshire LU6 2LN
T 01582 872228   **F** 01582 872518
T old-hunters@compuserve.com
www.old-hunters.com

An attractive 15th century thatched inn and restaurant, set on the edge of Whipsnade

Common. It is set in a fold of the Chiltern Hills very close to Dunstable Downs and a large area of National Trust land. Whipsnade Zoo is near by and is one of the most interesting modern wild animal breeding and conservation centres in the world. Children welcome, but no family room or cots – all rooms are en suite.

🛏 Three double, two twin, one single
£ £££
🍺 **Greene King Abbot** and guest from micros
🍴 Lunch, evening and snack menus
💳 Credit cards accepted

WHITTLESEY

The Boat Inn

2 Ramsey Road, Whittlesey, Peterborough PE7 1DR
T 01733 202488
Licensee: Philip Quinn
E quinnboatinn@aol.com
Directions: On B1040

Small, child friendly, family run pub with five letting rooms. Close to the diving training centre and several renowned fishing lakes.

🛏 Three twin, one triple, one single
£ £
🍺 **Elgood's Pageant, Cambridge** and **Black Dog**
🍴 Lunch menu, restrictions in evening
💳 Credit cards not accepted

Old Hunters Lodge, Whipsnade

Heart of England

Birmingham
Black Country
Cherwell & North
Coventry & Warwickshire
Derbyshire
East Gloucestershire
Herefordshire
Leicestershire
Lincolnshire
Northamptonshire
Nottinghamshire
Rutland
Shropshire
South Warwickshire
Staffordshire
West Oxfordshire
Worcestershire

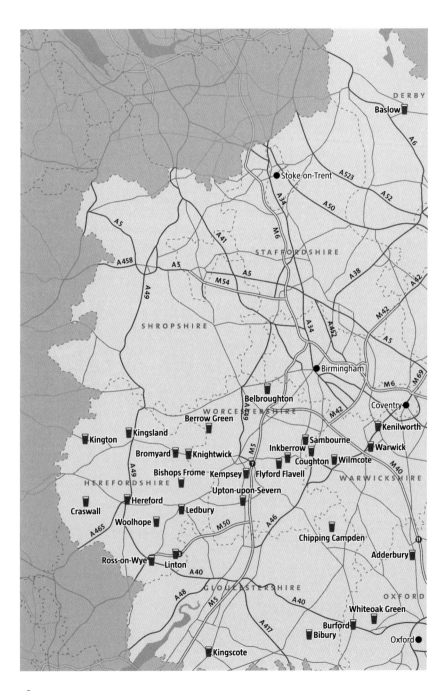

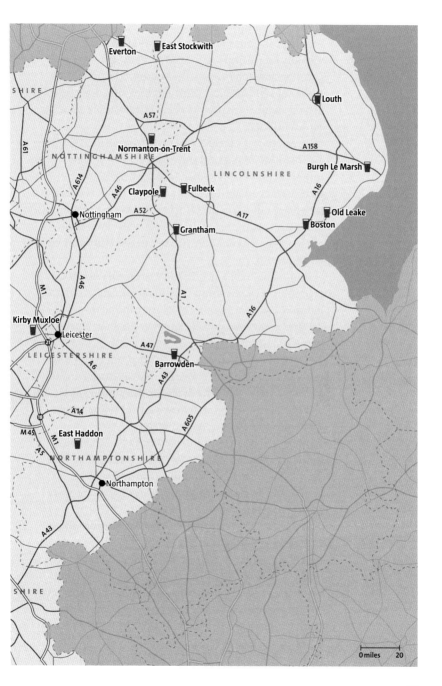

This massive British Tourist Authority area is the place to experience sights, sounds and sensations that will live in the memory forever: rosy red sunsets over the Cotswold hills and its yellowstone houses, the beauty of the Derbyshire Peaks, the sight of Lincoln's magnificent cathedral on the hill and the rugged brutality of England's industrial revolution can all be found.

The story of the HEART OF ENGLAND is written in a time-capsule of stone and steel and wrought iron – mighty castles, cathedrals and stately homes, working factories and picturesque cottages in countless sleepy hamlets where, at the village inn, the tradition of hospitality spans centuries. These sit cheek by jowl with bustling cities of intense economic activity and areas where farmers still farm and fields flourish.

Burton-on-Trent is not the most beautiful town in the region, but it is the spiritual heartland of England's brewing industry. Its Coors Museum of Brewing includes an Edwardian bar, vintage vehicles, gorgeous Shire horses, a harness room and shop.

Not to be forgotten are the town's two other breweries – the craft brewer Burton Bridge established in 1982 and the mighty Marston's – a cathedral of British brewing where the sublime Burton Union system works hard day and night fermenting pints of perfect Pedigree.

Travellers to Lincolnshire should visit the Batemans Brewery Experience and Visitor Centre at the Salem Bridge Brewery in Wainfleet, Lincolnshire and marvel at the determination of a family to stay in brewing and produce good honest British beer.

Worcestershire is the home of some of England's finest craft cask ale brewers, who use locally grown hops to flavour their brews including the renowned Teme Valley and Wyre Piddle breweries.

And every traveller to Oxfordshire should visit the Hook Norton Brewery Visitors' Centre. Hard to find, but worth the journey, it is a testament to the dedication of a family to pass on the brewery, generation to generation, still intact, still working and still producing beers of exquisite beauty.

People in search of cultural pursuits need look no further than Shakespeare's Stratford-upon-Avon, plus there are hundreds of music and arts festivals, theatres, concert halls, museums and art galleries that abound in the region.

Last but not least, experience those singularly English pleasures, cricket on the village green, real ale, the summer garden fete, and the Christmas pantomime.

All are there waiting to be found.

ADDERBURY

Red Lion

The Green, Adderbury, Nr Banbury,
Oxfordshire OX17 3NG
T 01295 810269   **F** 01295 811906
E redlion.adderbury@oldenglishinns.co.uk
Directions: From M40 J11 into Banbury, take A4260 towards Oxford through Bodicote

The Red Lion overlooks the village green of this hilly village. It is a former coaching inn with old oak decoration and stone chimneys. The bar has a list of the inn's landlords dating back to the Civil War when it was a Royalist-owned hostelry. The historic town of Banbury, known as the gateway to the Cotswolds, is just a couple of miles away. The 12 comfortable en suite bedrooms all have modern facilities.

🛏 12 rooms
£ £££
🍺 **Greene King IPA** plus guests
🍴 Lunch, evening and snack menus
💳 Credit cards accepted

BARROWDEN

Exeter Arms

Main Street, Barrowden-in-Rutland, LE15 8EQ
T 01572 747247
E info@exeterarms.com
www.exeterarms.com
Licensees: Peter and Elizabeth Blencowe
Directions: One mile off A47

A very friendly and welcoming 17th century country inn which brews its own beer. It is an idyllic setting overlooking the village green and duck pond with southerly views over the Welland Valley. The three bedrooms have recently been refurbished and all offer en suite facilities.

The Blencowe Brewery is situated in a barn at the end of the garden and even though extra capacity has been installed demand still outstrips supply. The owners are big supporters of live music and hold regular jazz and folk sessions. Fish and game dishes are regularly on the menu.

The CAMRA member who nominated the pub describes it as peaceful but never dull. Children welcome.

🛏 One double, two twin
£ ££
🍺 **Blencowe** range of **Boys** bitters
🍴 Lunch, evening and snack menus
💳 Credit cards accepted

BASLOW

The Robin Hood

Chesterfield Road, Baslow, Bakewell,
Derbyshire DE45 1PQ
T 01246 583186   **F** 01246 583032
Licensee: Peter Fairey
Directions: On A619 between Baslow and Chesterfield

The Robin Hood is an idyllic country pub on the edge of Chatsworth Estate, providing a warm and inviting environment for all. There is an immaculate golf club/course to the rear, outside drinking area and ample parking, making this pub a pedigree amongst similar style outlets.

The pub is an ideal staging post for ramblers/fell walkers with access to Peak National Park walks adjacent to the pub. The pub has a children's certificate and families are welcome to stay. The two bedrooms share a bathroom.

🛏 One twin, one single
£ ££
🍺 Marston's Pedigree, Mansfield, Banks's Bitters
🍴 Lunch, evening and snack menus
💳 Credit cards accepted

BELBROUGHTON

Olde Horseshoe

High Street, Belbroughton, Worcestershire DY9 9ST
T 01562 730233
Licensees: Alex and Sue Townhill-Key

This is a very popular and busy two roomed pub set in the heart of the village. It has an excellent menu and a relaxed friendly atmosphere. Once a private house, it has been licensed since 1830. It offers en suite accommodation with tea and coffee making facilities but does not provide breakfast unless a block booking is made for several people by prior arrangement. The Clent Hills are nearby. Children welcome.

🛏 Two doubles, one single
£ £
🍺 Boddingtons Bitter, Draught Bass, Marston's Pedigree, Greene King Old Speckled Hen, Theakston Old Peculier
🍴 Lunch, evening and snack menus
💳 Credit cards accepted

BERROW GREEN near Martley

The Admiral Rodney

Berrow Green, Martley, Worcestershire WR6 6PL
T 01886 821375   F 01886 822048
E rodney@admiral.fslife.co.uk
Licensees: Kenneth Green and Gillian Nelson
Directions: On B4197, two miles from A44 (follow brown signs from Knightwick), seven miles west of Worcester

The main bar area comprises two delightfully decorated rooms, both with real open fires.

One is a designated non-smoking bar with a children's licence. The back door of the locals bar leads out into the skittle alley, which also has a pool table and dart board. The pub is a big supporter of local micros and has a list of constantly changing guest ales. Bar food is served in both bars at both lunchtimes and evenings.

The beautiful restaurant is a feature in itself! A converted barn, complete with exposed beams and brickwork and dried hops, plus wonderful à la carte food at very reasonable prices. Sample dishes include haunch of venison on a bed of horseradish mash, boneless loin of lamb with rosemary and garlic and chicken roulades stuffed with thyme, coriander and mozzarella. Vegetarians or special diets also catered for. Fish is supplied direct from Cornwall to ensure top quality dishes such as spiced skate wings with lime mayonnaise and steamed swordfish with hoi sin and damson sauce.

There are two double rooms and one twin, which are priced by the room and include a full English breakfast. Breakfast time is negotiable, the later the better! The Worcestershire Way runs across the front of the pub. Sir Edward Elgar's birthplace and museum is approximately five miles from the pub with Worcester City just over seven miles away.

🛏 Two doubles, one twin
£ ££
🍺 Wye Valley Bitter, Greene King IPA and two guests, real cider
🍴 Lunch, evening and snack menus
💳 Credit cards accepted

BIBURY

The Catherine Wheel

Bibury, Gloucestershire GL7 5ND
T 01285 740250
E catherinewheel.bibury@eldridge-pope.co.uk
Directions: Bibury is located on the B4425 about five miles northeast of Cirencester

Bibury is a simply superb Cotswold village described by William Morris as the most beautiful in England. The houses like this pub are made of golden local stone and are a glorious site on a summer's evening. A tranquil place even though the village can seem very busy at times. Many of the houses are now owned by the National Trust and front onto the River Coln. Over the bridge, at the other end of the village, is one of the best trout farms in England and the fish is a regular feature on the pub's menu.

The four beautifully refurbished rooms are designed and named to reflect different parts of the village's fascinating history. A romantic, intimate pub with log fires and candles.

🛏 Four double/twin
£ ££££
🍺 Changing range of real ales
🍴 Lunch, evening and snack menus
💳 Credit cards accepted

BOSTON

Kings Arms

13 Horncastle Road, Boston, Lincolnshire PE21 9BU
T 01205 364296
Licensee: Terry Durdey

Within five minutes walk of the Boston Stump, which at 272.5 feet is said to be the second highest church tower in England, the Kings Arms is an honest, down to earth pub and the ideal base for anyone wanting to explore one of the country's most historic but forgotten towns. And after climbing the 365 steps up to the top of the Stump it is an ideal place to return to try a pint of Batemans.

🛏 Three double, one family
£ £
🍺 **Batemans XXXB, XB**, and seasonals
🍴 Lunch, evening and snack menus
💳 Credit cards not accepted

BISHOPS FROME

Chase Inn

Bishops Frome, Worcestershire WR6 5BP
T 01885 490234   F 01885 490547
E anthony.james@tesco.net
Licensees: Tony and Suzanne James

Directions: On B4214, turn off the A4103, midway between Hereford and Worcester, towards the direction of Bromyard for one mile. Within easy reach of mainline stations at Ledbury, Hereford, and Great Malvern

The Chase Inn is situated in the heart of Bishops Frome, an attractive village on the eastern border of Herefordshire. It was built in the 19th century specifically to cater for the influx of labour to the fertile Frome valley during the busy harvest and hop picking seasons. Bishops Frome is at the centre of Herefordshire and Worcestershire, with the Malvern Hills, Brecon Beacons and breathtaking countryside on the doorstep. The inn retains its original exterior which is complemented by the surrounding picturesque village scenery.

The spacious open plan bars and restaurant areas have retained the Inn's character and charm providing a warm and cheerful welcome to all. There are many events held at the Chase, including folk nights and quizzes, and there are active cribbage, pool and darts teams. There are racecourses with regular meetings close by at Cheltenham, Hereford, Worcester and Ludlow. Families are welcome and takeaways available.

🛏 Two double, one twin, two single
£ £
🍺 **Worthington Best, Valley Bitter**, occasional guest beers
🍴 Lunch, dinner and snack menus
💳 Credit cards accepted

BROMYARD

Falcon Hotel

4 Broad Street, Bromyard, Herefordshire HR7 4BT
T 01885 483034   F 01885 488818
Licensee: Jane Findler
Directions: Centre of town, it is situated on the A44 between Worcester and Leominster

A very interesting and unspoilt 600-year-old hotel with two bars, two restaurants and conference facilities. One bar is quiet while the other has a pool table and juke box. Meals include bar snacks, carvery and à la carte. Own car park. The town stands on a plateau over 120m above sea level and was once surrounded by orchards and hop fields. The Frome flows through this, the smallest of Hereford's market towns which has several outstanding traditional Herefordshire black and white houses.

- Three family, four double, one single
- £ ££
- **Wye Valley Butty Bach**, **Bitter** and **Boddingtons Bitter**
- Lunch, dinner and snack menus
- Credit cards accepted

BURFORD

The Golden Pheasant

High Street, Burford, Oxfordshire OX18 4QA
T 01993 823223   **F** 01993 822621
Directions: From A40 take A361 into the High Street

In one of the most beautiful of Cotswold towns, the Golden Pheasant is built with the mellow yellow stone for which the area is renowned. This small country inn in the centre of this ancient wool town enjoys a superb reputation with locals and visitors alike.

The twelve en suite bedrooms are individually furnished and a number have four-poster beds – there are two outside ground floor rooms.

Nearby are beautiful walks on the plateau between the Evenlode and Windrush valleys, where sheep safely grazed in medieval times, the source of the town's wealth. Burford is busy and bustling with many small stores and is an ideal base to visit Oxford, the Cotswolds and the Cotswold Wildlife Park.

- 12 rooms all
- £ ££££
- **Greene King** range
- Lunch, evening and snack menus
- Credit cards accepted

BURGH LE MARSH

Bell Hotel

High Street, Burgh Le Marsh, Skegness, Lincolnshire PE24 5JP
T 01754 810318
E info@bell-hotel-burgh.co.uk
www.bell-hotel-burgh.co.uk
Licensee: Craig Russell
Directions: On main A158

Situated in Burgh Le Marsh, some 3½ miles from the very popular family holiday resort of Skegness, Burgh provides a haven of tranquillity from the bustle of the coastal activities. The unspoiled village, once a small market town, is steeped in history, and boasts of several small restaurants pubs, and delightful surrounding countryside. A visit to the working mill several hundred yards away is a must.

For ramblers, the delightful Lincolnshire Wolds with miles of secluded pathways are only three miles away. The Bell is located on the High Street – that is the main A158 that passes through the heart of the village.

The hotel is traditional, informal and is an ideal location for a quiet weekend break, or as a venue for both a business and a family function. The Bell offers comfortable hotel accommodation. For those seeking independence, enquire about its self-catering cottages.

- 11 rooms including four deluxe with four-posters, three cottages
- £ £
- **Batemans XB**, **Dark Mild**, **XXXB**, guest ales
- Lunch, evening and snack menus
- Credit cards accepted

CHIPPING CAMPDEN

Volunteer Inn

Lower High Street, Chipping Camden, Gloucestershire GL55 6DY
T 01386 840688   **F** 01386 840543
E saravol@aol.com
Licensee: Hilary Sinclair
Directions: just off main High Street

This 17th-century, former coaching inn lies just off the High Street, once described as the most beautiful village street now left in the island. The same family have run this 300-year-old stone inn for more than 17 years and have transformed it into a thriving pub enjoyed by locals and visitors. The owners are big supporters of local brews and it is one of only a handful of pubs in the Cotswolds to sell Stanway beers. Named after a volunteer army of the 1840s, the lounge bar has a golden stone fireplace and cushioned seats in bay windows; old village photos and army artefacts hang in both bars.

The pub stands at the start of the Cotswold Way so is ideal for hikers and for anyone wishing to discover this delightful area, with Stratford-upon-Avon just 12 miles away and other attractions such as Hidcote Gardens and the Elizabethan Stanway House even closer. Children are welcome. Pets can be accommodated.

🛏 Three double, two twin-bedded rooms
£ ££
🍺 **Hook Norton Best Bitter**, **Stanway Stanney Bitter**, plus guests
🍴 Snacks and meals daily, lunchtime and evening
▭ Credit cards not accepted

COUGHTON

The Throckmorton Arms

Coughton, Warwickshire B49 5HX
T 01789 766366   F 01789 762654
Licensee: Jeremy Collins
Directions: On A435

A large, well positioned pub on the main road. The large open plan interior is divided into raised seating areas and cosy corners with settees and open fires. Good food is served along with four real ales, with one normally from a local micro. There is a car park and an outside seating area. The pub is opposite Coughton Court and is nine miles from Stratford-upon-Avon. Warwick and Worcester are within easy reach.

🛏 10 double/twin
£ ££
🍺 **Draught Bass**, **Fuller's London Pride**, **Timothy Taylor Landlord** and a guest ale
🍴 Lunch, evening and snack menus
▭ Credit cards accepted

CLAYPOLE

Five Bells

95 Main Street, Claypole, Nottinghamshire NG23 5BJ
T 01636 626561
Licensee: Martin Finney
Directions: About four minutes off A1 between Grantham and Newark

A friendly, village freehouse close to Newark, Grantham and Lincoln. The pub takes its name from the local parish church. A former coaching inn built in the 1800s, the stables have recently been converted into three letting rooms – one family room and two twin. Friendly, helpful and welcoming, the licensees keep the place bright and spotlessly clean. More than 100 different real ales a year are served, with two normally coming from local micros. The food menu is varied and reasonably priced.

🛏 Two twin, one double/family room
£ £ £££ single, discounts available for two or more nights
🍺 **Tetley** plus regular local guests
🍴 Lunch, evening and snack menus
▭ Credit cards accepted

CRASWALL

Bull's Head

Craswall, Hereford, Herefordshire HR2 0PN
T 01981 510616   F 01981 510383
E denise@thebullsheadcraswell.fsnet.co.uk
www.thebullsheadcraswell.com
Licensee: Denise Langford
Directions: On Longtown to Hay road – grid ref SO 278360

The recent transformation of this drover's inn high in the foothills of the Black Mountains has been remarkable. From selling cider to a few locals and walkers, it now offers real ale and an exciting range of food to a growing number of customers. This has been achieved without altering the central ancient bar with its serving hatches, sloping flagstone floor and peeling wallpaper.

Ideal for exploring Hay Bluff and Offa's Dyke Path, the village is set in wild, beautifully wooded country. Crasswall is home to the remains of an ancient Grandmontine priory, where a strict order of monks used to live. It is a unique site where the complete unconserved remains of a small medieval priory are now exposed to view. Booking at the Bull's Head is recommended for meals at weekends. Real cider and perry available. Closed Monday in winter and Sunday evenings

🛏 One double, one bunk room (double+ single), one small double
£ £
🍺 **Wye Valley Butty Bach**
🍴 Lunch, dinner and snack menus
💳 Credit cards accepted

EAST HADDON

The Red Lion Hotel

Main Street, East Haddon,
Northamptonshire NN6 8BU
T 01604 770223   F 01604 770767
www.redlionhoteleasthaddon.co.uk
Licensee: Ian Kennedy
Directions: Located just off the A428, seven miles from M1 J18

An imposing stone-built and thatched inn with oak settles, oak and mahogany tables, and low beams, The Red Lion provides the ideal setting for that quiet and peaceful weekend away.

It's a good base and watering hole for visitors to Coton Manor Gardens, which has a brilliant bluebell display in spring, as well as Althorp House, home of Earl Spencer. All bedrooms have en suite facilities with telephones, televisions and hospitality trays. Most comfortably decorated with a superb residents' lounge, all in keeping with the old world atmosphere to be seen throughout the hotel.

🛏 Five twin and double
£ £££
🍺 **Adnams Broadside, Charles Wells Eagle IPA, Charles Wells Bombardier**
🍴 Lunch, evening and snack menus
💳 Credit cards accepted

EAST STOCKWITH

The Ferry House

27 Front Street, East Stockwith,
Gainsborough, Lincolnshire DN21 3DJ
T 01427 615276   F 01427 612419
Licensees: Margaret Barratt, Lee and Clare Slingsby
Directions: On Trentside Road, four miles from Morton, Gainsborough

Large family run pub which attracts a wide range of clientele. Separate dining room and large function room. Large menu and all the food is home prepared and represents great value. Pub closes all day on Monday but rooms are un-effected. Gainsborough Old Hall is four miles away. Three of the rooms have Trent views – from where it is possible to watch the Agair (like the Severn Boar). Children welcome.

🛏 Three double, one twin
£ £
🍺 **John Smith's Bitter, Webster's Yorkshire Bitter** plus guests
🍴 Lunch, evening and snack menus
💳 Credit cards accepted

EVERTON

Blacksmith's Arms

Church Street, Everton, Nottinghamshire DN10 5BQ
T 01777 817281
Licensee: Deborah Anderson
Directions: Located in centre of the village, off A631

Everton is an ancient North Nottinghamshire village, which straddles the busy A631, once part of the main Roman route from Lincoln to York. The remains of a Roman fort are to be found at the western edge of the parish, where one can imagine Roman soldiers pausing before crossing the River Idle to Bawtry. The Blacksmith's is a genuine 18th century freehouse at the heart of a thriving village.

Everton is a popular area for ramblers and the pub offers a warm welcome in the locals' bar which still has the original tiled floor and settle. Duck under a low-beam and you enter the games room, formerly the smithy. The restaurant puts an emphasis on home-cooked food. The en suite accommodation is in the converted stables.

Nearby is Barrow Hills Sand Pit Site of Special Scientific Interest (a nationally important site for wildlife), Sherwood Forest, Doncaster Racecourse and the Earth Centre.

- 🛏 Four double
- £ £££
- 🍺 **Theakston Old Peculier**, **Barnsley Bitter**, **John Smith's Bitter**, **Marston's Pedigree**
- 🍴 Lunch and evening menus
- 💳 Credit cards accepted

FLYFORD FLAVELL

The Boot Inn

Radford Road, Flyford Flavell,
Worcestershire WR7 4BS
T 01386 462658
Licensees: Susan Hughes and Oliver Wortley
Directions: In village off A422

The front door of this pub opens on to a pleasant, largish bar with a small pool room to one side. A short passage leads to the main lounge with its open beams and supports showing the age of the pub, which is about 600 years. The décor is tasteful with wooden furniture and old plates giving a sophisticated farmhouse kitchen effect. To the side is a large conservatory. There is no piped music and there are two open fires. There are two garden areas and a car park.

The pub is close to Hanbury Hall, Coughton Court and Ragley Hall. Warwick, Worcester and Stratford-upon-Avon are within easy reach. Five en suite rooms classified AA red diamond and English Tourist Board four diamonds.

- 🛏 Four doubles and one twin
- £ ££
- 🍺 **Greene King Old Speckled Hen**, **Fuller's London Pride** plus three others including a local micro
- 🍴 Lunch, evening and snack menus
- 💳 Credit cards accepted

FULBECK

Hare & Hounds

The Green, Fulbeck, Grantham, Lincolnshire NG32 3JJ
T 01400 272090   **F** 01400 273663
Licensees: Mr and Mrs Nicholas
Directions: just off the A17, at junction with the A607 Grantham to Lincoln road

This lovely old 16th century pub overlooks the green of one of Lincolnshire's prettiest villages. The Inn is a grade II listed building and was built as a maltings and used as such until 1910. Set on a ridge, it offers splendid views of the surrounding countryside. There is a bar and separate restaurant serving high quality food. With its steep streets and old stone houses, Fulbeck is very popular with visitors who enjoy the Manor Stables Craft Workshops and Fulbeck Hall, home of the Fane family since 1632, which is open to the public for most of the summer.

The bedrooms are all en suite with bath or shower, colour TV and tea/coffee making facilities, some are on the ground floor and may suit guests with mobility problems – the bar and restaurant are both accessible to wheelchairs. Children are welcome; the pub has its own garden with a popular boules pitch.

- 🛏 Four double, two twin-bedded, two family rooms
- £ £ single ££
- 🍺 **Bateman XB**, **Fuller's London Pride**, **Marston's Pedigree**, **John Smith's Bitter**, guest beer
- 🍴 Snacks (lunchtime) and meals daily, lunchtime and evening
- 💳 Credit cards accepted

GRANTHAM

Angel & Royal Hotel

High Street, Grantham, Lincolnshire NG31 6PN
T 01476 565816   **F** 01476 567149
T enquiries@angelandroyal.co.uk
www.angelandroyal.com
Directions: off the A1, in the town centre

The Angel Inn at Grantham is reputedly Britain's oldest inn still in use and is an important historical site. It was Knight's Templar property in 1213, when it bore that name, derived from Salutation, or Angelus, as it originally represented the Angel appearing to the Virgin Mary. It is now known as the Angel & Royal Hotel. Two splendid bars are warmed in winter by open fires; there is also a no-smoking lounge and the beautiful restaurant with its stone walls.

The 29 en suite bedrooms are spacious and comfortable with modern amenities. Children are welcome to stay (high chairs, cots and even a baby listening service can all be provided). Popular local tourist destinations include Belvoir Castle and Belton House.

🛏 11 single, 10 double and eight twin-bedded rooms
£ £ (single ££££)
🍺 **Courage Directors**, **Marston's Pedigree**, **Theakston Best Bitter**, occasional guest beer
🍴 Lunchtime snacks; evening snacks and meals daily
💳 Credit cards accepted

HEREFORD

Salmon Inn

1 Hampton Park Road, Hereford HR1 1TQ
T 01432 272236 **F** 01432 271031
Licensees: Robert and Margaret Kite
Directions: On B4224 south west of city centre

Hereford is a gentle city and an ideal base from which to explore the county's famous black and white houses. Visitors can try the locally brewed Wye Valley beers in its tap Barrels in Owen Street. The cathedral church dedicated to the memory of Mary and Ethelbert contains the Mappa Mundi – a map of the flat world – drawn and painted in 1275. The city is also home to a cider museum. Converted in 1956 from a gentleman's residence to replace the historic Whalebone, the lower storey of which still remains nearby. The Salmon is now a popular, comfortably furnished pub with one large bar extending into a conservatory. Home cooked, traditional pub food is served. Garden and children's play area outside.

🛏 One double, three twin, one family
£ £
🍺 **Brains**, **Buckley's Bitter**, **Draught Bass**
🍴 Lunch, evening and snack menus
💳 Credit cards accepted

INKBERROW

The Bulls Head Inn

The Village Green, Inkberrow, Worcestershire WR7 4DY
T 01386 792233 **F** 01386 793090
Licensee: Lord Nigel Andrew Wilkes
Directions: On A422

The Bulls Head Inn is a centuries old coaching inn in the main street of Inkberrow, opposite the village green. There is a top bar adjacent to the restaurant area with steps leading down to a large bar decorated with a variety of sporting memorabilia. There are log fires, a real inglenook fireplace and a wealth of old oak beams above burnished flagstone floors. The pub has a car park and a small terrace outside the front door. Adjacent to the car park is a lawn with tables and a children's play area. The pub is close to Hanbury Hall, Coughton Court and Ragley Hall. Warwick, Worcester and Stratford-upon-Avon are within easy reach. Children welcome.

🛏 Four double one twin
£ ££
🍺 **Banks's Bitter**, **Timothy Taylor Landlord** and **Bulls Head Bitter** from **Church End Brewery**
🍴 Lunch, evening and snack menus – no meals Sunday evenings
💳 Credit cards accepted

KEMPSEY

Walter de Cantelupe

Main Road, Kempsey, Worcestershire WR5 3NA
T 01905 820572
E info@walterdecantelupeinn.com
www.walterdecantelupeinn.com
Licensee: Martin Lloyd-Morris
Directions: On A38, convenient for J7/M5

Situated three miles out of Worcester this tiny pub is named after a Bishop of Worcester, who helped Simon de Montfort and his army cross the River Severn, only for them to be captured and massacred by Edward II. A village pub with wooden beams and stone floors, it keeps a good selection of quality ales including the award winning Timothy Taylor Landlord bitter which is rarely found outside its native Yorkshire in such good condition.

The pub is run by a friendly, enthusiastic landlord and a friendly Labrador called Monti. Boldly decorated in red and gold, the interior comprises a friendly and relaxed bar area with an informal mix of furniture and a couple of steps up to a carpeted drinking area with old wind-up HMV gramophone and a good big fireplace.

The rest of the pub is devoted to the dining area which is pleasantly furnished with a mix of plush or yellow leather dining chairs, an old settle, a sonorous clock and candles and flowers on the tables. The large paella dish featured on the wall near the entrance is brought into use for the pub's annual paella party in July, and the pub organises other out-of-the-ordinary special events throughout the year. A pretty walled garden at the rear completes the picture when the weather allows. Children only allowed in garden.

🛏 Three double
£ ££
🍺 **Cannon Royal Kings Shilling**, **Timothy Taylor Landlord**, **Everards Beacon** and guests
🍴 Lunch, evening and snack menus
💳 Credit cards accepted

KINGSCOTE

Hunters Hall

Kingscote, near Tetbury, Gloucestershire GL8 8XZ
T 01453 860393   F 01453 860707
E huntershall.kingscote@oldenglishinns.co.uk
Directions: on the A4153

Situated close to Tetbury this rambling, ivy-covered inn which dates back to the 16th century has a wealth of charm with its fine high Tudor beamed ceilings, stone floors, ubiquitous bric-a-brac and no less than three open fires. Old settles and sofas add to the atmosphere of a bygone era. The guest rooms, however, are bang up-to-date, with modern facilities and en suite bathrooms. They are situated in a separate building which once served as the stables and blacksmith's shop.

Several of the rooms are on the ground floor and specially designed for guests with disabilities. An extensive range of bar meals is served in all three bars and there is also an informal restaurant with no-smoking area. There is a large garden and play area – perfect for summer lunches with the family.

🛏 Six double, five twin-bedded and one family room
£ ££££
🍺 **Greene King IPA** plus occasional guests
🍴 Snacks and meals daily, lunchtime and evening
💳 Credit cards accepted

KENILWORTH

Clarendon House Hotel

High Street, Kenilworth, Warwickshire CV8 1LZ
T 01926 857668   F 01926 850669
E info@clarendonhousehotel.com
www.clarendonhousehotel.com
Licensees: David and Karen Randolph

Historic plush hotel with modern facilities. The friendly and informal bar is well liked by locals as well as visitors. There are high standards throughout and much attention to detail. Nearby is Kenilworth Castle once described as the grandest fortress ruin in England. Norman, Plantagenet and Tudor monarchs all played a part in its development. Children welcome.

🛏 10 double, five twin
£ ££££
🍺 **Greene King IPA**, **Abbot**, **Hook Norton Best** plus two guests
🍴 Lunch evening and snack menus
💳 Credit cards accepted

KENILWORTH

The Old Bakery Hotel

12 High Street, Kenilworth, Warwickshire CV8 1LZ
T 01926 864111   **F** 01926 864127
E info@theoldbakeryhotel.co.uk
www.theoldbakeryhotel.co.uk
Licensee: Mike Bond
Directions: Just off the main Coventry road the A429

The original Old Bakery Hotel building has been part of Kenilworth's picturesque High Street for nearly 400 years. The hotel is operated as a family business by Gill and Mike Bond. In 2002 the local CAMRA branch – Coventry and North Warwickshire – presented the hotel with a special award for maintaining outstanding quality and increasing the popularity of real ale. Also the hotel has just won CAMRA Pub of the Year 2002 for the Warwickshire area.

There are 13 luxurious bedrooms, all with en suite facilities. Each room has a telephone, colour TV (inc. Sky), tea and coffee making facilities. A two room family suite, family room and a room for less able people are all available. All bedrooms are non smoking.

Close-by is Kenilworth Castle, which has been intimately linked with some of the most important names in English history. Today, with its Tudor gardens, its impressive Norman keep and John of Gaunt's Great Hall, it is the largest castle ruin in England

🛏 13 comprising single, double, twin, family and a room for the less-abled
£ £££ – ££££ single
🍺 **Hook Norton, Timothy Taylor Landlord, Black Sheep Best Bitter**
🍴 No food – breakfast provided with accommodation
💳 Credit cards accepted

KINGSLAND

Corners Inn

Kingsland, Leominster, Herefordshire HR6 9RY
T 01568 708385   **F** 01568 709033
www.cornersinn.co.uk
Licensees: Richard Dawes and Stewart Rees
Directions: On B4360, middle of village

Easy to spot with its whitewashed and timbered façade, the pub stands in the centre of Kingsland. Situated near the Welsh Border, the village of Kingsland lies in the quiet countryside of North Herefordshire, 12 miles north of Hereford, three miles west of the market town of Leominster and 10 miles south of the historic town of Ludlow.

This beautiful half-timbered inn dates back in part to the early 16th century and offers fine local ales and ciders, quality cuisine, beautifully appointed en suite bedrooms, large restaurant and function room with ample parking. It consists of a single, large lounge bar whilst a later extension houses a restaurant. A full range of food from bar snacks to restaurant meals is available including vegetarian and booking is recommended, especially for the Sunday carvery. The pub is on the black-and-white village trail.

🛏 Three double
£ £
🍺 **Hobson's Best Bitter, Wye Valley Butty Bach**
🍴 Lunch, dinner and snack menus
💳 Credit cards accepted

KINGTON

Swan Hotel

Church Street, Kington, Herefordshire HR5 3AZ
T 01544 230510   **F** 01544 230670
E enquiries@theswanhotelkington.co.uk
www.theswanhotelkington.co.uk
Licensee: Kevin Graham
Directions: West end of town centre

Home to the Dunn Plowman Brewery whose brewhouse is located to the rear of the pub. Close to Offa's Dyke Path and Hergest Ridge, this 17th century hotel, recently refurbished, has a one room bar divided into areas by a chimney breast. One area has chairs for bar meals and the other has settees. There is also a separate restaurant area with an à la carte menu. Previously known as the Upper Swan to distinguish it from another (Lower) Swan in the High Street.

🛏 Two family, two double, one twin, one single, one suite
£ £££

🍺 **Dunn Plowman Brewhouse Bitter**,
  Worthington Bitter and occasional guests
🍴 Lunch, dinner and snack menus
💳 Credit cards accepted

The Talbot Inn

Knightwick, Worcester WR6 5PH
T 01886 821235   **F** 01886 821060
E info@the-talbot.co.uk
www.temevalley.co.uk
Licensees: Annie and Wiz Clift
Direictions: On B4197 at junction with A44

This family run hotel is in an idyllic setting
close to the old coach bridge over the River
Teme, an area favoured by many naturalists
– otters have recently been introduced into
the river. The hotel is the home of the Teme
Valley brewery, which is also owned by the
Clift family. Imaginative, good food, made
wherever possible with local organically
grown ingredients, can be enjoyed in either
the bar or restaurant. On the Worcestershire
Way, it is close to many hop fields and farms.
Monthly farmer's market is held outside the
pub. A Green hop beer festival is held in
October.

🛏 Three single, five double, two twin
£ £££
🍺 **Teme Valley T'Other**, **This**, **That**, **Hobson's Best
  Bitter** plus seasonals
🍴 Lunch, evening and snack menus
💳 Credit cards accepted

KIRBY MUXLOE

The Castle

Main Street, Kirby Muxloe, Leicestershire LE9 2AP
T 0116 239 5337   **F** 0116 238 7868
E info@castlehotelkirby.com
www.castlehotelkirby.com
Licensees: Steve and Michelle Leonard
Directions: M1 J21/21a

Traditional inn with log fires and a large
garden. It also has a licence that enables
people to be married in the building. The
accommodation is of a very high standard.
Nearby is Kirby Muxloe Castle, a fortified
moated home built by Lord Hastings in 1480.
It wasn't able to save him, as he was
executed in 1483. Close by are Bosworth
Fields, Mallory Park and De Montfort Hall.

🛏 22
£ ££££
🍺 **Marston's Pedigree**, **Theakston Bitter**,
  Courage Bitter
🍴 Lunch, evening and snack menus
💳 Credit cards accepted

The Talbot Inn, Knightwick

LEDBURY

Olde Talbot Hotel

14 New Street, Ledbury, Herefordshire HR8 2DT
T 01531 632963   **F** 01531 633796
E talbot.ledbury@wadworth.co.uk
www.visitledbury.co.uk/talbot
Licensee: Andy Ward
Directions: Just off town centre

An ideal place to stay for anyone visiting this historic market town or the Malvern Hills, it is a superb black and white hotel dating back to 1596 and steeped in history. The plush bar boasts an impressive fireplace with an extra drinking area to the rear, whilst the beautiful oak-panelled dining room with its fine carved overmantle was once the scene of fighting between Cavaliers and Roundheads. Although a Wadworth tied house, it stocks a local beer and interesting guest beers. Traditional English food features on the menu. Well-behaved children welcomed.

🛏 Four double, two twin, one single
£ £££
🍺 **Wadworth Henry's IPA, 6X, Wye Valley Butty Bach** and guest beers
🍴 lunch, dinner and snack menus
💳 Credit cards accepted

LINTON

Alma Inn

Linton, Ross-on-Wye, Herefordshire HR9 7RY
T 01989 720355   **F** 01989 720355
www.almainnlinton.co.uk
Licensees: Graham and Linda Webb
Directions: Off B4221, west of M50 Junction 3 Grid ref SO 659255

CAMRA's runner up Pub of the Year for 2001, a freehouse, the Alma usually serves four beers, all from independents. Dating from the early 19th century, it was named after the Crimean Battle of the 1854 campaign. The interior has a Victorian feel although the main structure of the building is much older This pub is ample demonstration that rural pubs can survive by providing a friendly and comfortable place to drink good ale and do not need to be turned into restaurants. The main room is the large lounge at the front with a games area at the rear. A second, no-smoking bar is used for Sunday lunches. Snacks are available for guests if required. The extensive gardens look out on to attractive hilly countryside. A stair lift is available for guests. The pub is close to the Birds of Prey Centre, May Hill and the historic Forest of Dean.

🛏 Two double/family
£ £
🍺 **Butcombe Bitter, RCH Pitchfork, Smiles Best Bitter, Malvern Hills Red Earl** or **Dunn Plowman Brewhouse Bitter**
🍴 Normally no food, snacks can be ordered, but several pub/restaurants nearby
💳 Credit cards not accepted

LOUTH

Masons Arms Hotel

Cornmarket, Louth, Lincolnshire LN11 9PY
T 01507 609525   **F** 08707 066450
E info@themasons.co.uk
www.themasons.co.uk
Licensees: Roger and Justin Goldsmith
Directions: In the centre of Louth, off A157

In the heart of the fine Georgian town of Louth, on the Cornmarket, stands the Masons Arms, a former Posting Inn dating back to 1725. It has a vibrant bar for beer lovers, and the six cask ales are worth seeking out. Beer writer Roger Protz has described the dark mild as being kept in 'succulent' condition. The pub has 10 guest rooms, five en suite and an excellent restaurant open only on Friday and Saturday nights and Sunday lunch.

Louth is a friendly, bustling town packed with examples of good townscape. St James's Church a gothic masterpiece, with a 30-foot spire – the tallest on a parish church in England – dominates the town. Louth is in the heart of the Wolds and there are plenty of excellent walking and cycling opportunities nearby.

in June 2001 and now includes an attractive new annex comprising three double-bedrooms of the highest standard. One room is designed with disabled access and facilities. Cosy and friendly, it boasts a large wood-burning stove in the central fireplace, and encourages intimacy with several snug areas and alcove.

The restaurant, called the Gun Room, is decorated with game shooting memorabilia and stuffed birds, and (not surprisingly) specialises in game dishes. Vegetarians may prefer to eat in the bar where they are also well catered for. Less than ten miles from the centre of Newark, the pub is in a beautiful rural setting and has a well-equipped children's play area and beer garden. Adults can not only enjoy beers from the nearby Maypole but also play pin skittles.

- Three rooms – double or twin
- £ £ £££ single
- **Maypole** beers plus two guest ales
- Lunch, evening and snack menus
- Credit cards accepted

- Three single, five double, two twin
- £ £
- **Draught Bass, Bateman Dark Mild, XB, XXXB, Marston's Pedigree, Highwood Best Bitter** plus guests
- Snacks and meals lunchtime and evening - except Sunday
- Credit cards accepted

NORMANTON-ON-TRENT

Square & Compass

Eastgate, Normanton-on-Trent,
Newark, Nottinghamshire NG23 6RN
T 01636 821439   **F** 01636 822794
E info@squareandcompass.co.uk
www.squareandcompass.co.uk
Licensee: Kenneth and Fran Munro
Directions: Three miles from the A1, signed off the B1164, south of Tuxford

The Square and Compass at Normanton-on-Trent is reputed to be the oldest country pub in Nottinghamshire. More than 500 years old, this popular pub has been well converted from three cottages, with care taken to preserve its low timbered ceilings and traditional character. It was refurbished

OLD LEAKE

The Bricklayers Arms

Wainfleet Road, Old Leake, Boston
Lincolnshire PE22 9HT
T 01205 870657
Licensee: Mrs M George
Directions: on A52 between Boston and Skegness

An ideal base for exploring the lights of Skeggie or the delights of Boston. This family run local offers an open fire on cooler days, traditional home-cooked food and a glass of God's gift to Lincolnshire – Batemans beer. The pub has a nice garden where children can play and facilities for caravans to stay as well. There is a separate restaurant and a room with pool tables.

- One family, one twin, one single
- £ £
- **Batemans** range of beers plus occasional guests
- Lunch, evening and snack menus
- Credit cards not accepted

ROSS-ON-WYE

The Royal

Palace Pound, Ross-on-Wye, Herefordshire HR9 5HZ
T 01989 565105   F 01989 768058
Directions: Take B4260 into town, turn right up hill to hotel

Set in a red sandstone cliff, Ross throngs with visitors in the summer months. The Royal, where Queen Victoria stayed when she was young, stands high on a rocky cliff above the sweeping River Wye and with magnificent views of the countryside. The Wye Bar features an open fire and offers a varied menu and real ales. The 42 recently refurbished bedrooms offer comfort and style and range from large four-poster to single rooms in the old stable block. And for anyone tiring of this historic town, Hay-on-Wye, the second-hand book capital of the world, is a short drive away.

- 🛏 42 rooms – ranging from large four-poster to single
- £ ££££
- 🍺 **Greene King** range plus guests
- 🍴 Lunch, evening and snack menus
- 💳 Credit cards accepted

SAMBOURNE

The Green Dragon

The Village Green, Sambourne,
Warwickshire B96 6NU
T 01527 892465   F 01527 893255
Licensees: Peter and Ann Hardy
Directions: Village green

This 17th century inn overlooks the attractive village green. Oak beams, brasses, pewter mugs and an open fire add to the character of the two bars and restaurant. It enjoys a reputation for good food and boasts connections with the comedian, Tony Hancock. It has two car parks and two garden areas. The pub is near Coughton Court and is 10 miles from Stratford upon Avon. Warwick and Worcester are within easy reach. Well behaved children are welcome, particularly if eating, but because of its age the bars are not really suitable for general use by children. The garden areas are fine.

- 🛏 Six double rooms
- £ ££ ££££ single
- 🍺 **Draught Bass, Hobson's Best Bitter** and **M&B Brew XI**
- 🍴 Lunch, evening and snack menus – no food Sunday
- 💳 Credit cards accepted

UPTON-UPON-SEVERN

White Lion Hotel

21 High Street, Upton-upon-Severn,
Worcestershire WR8 0HJ
T 01684 592551   F 01684 593333
E info@whitelionhotel.biz
www.whitelionhotel.biz
Licensees: Jon and Chris Lear
Directions: Centre of Upton-upon-Severn on B4101

Sixteenth century ex-coaching inn with connections to Henry Fielding and the English Civil War. Comfortable lounge with comfy sofas and bar with bench seating; three real ales are served, with at least one from a local micro.

Its Pepperpot Brasserie has won many awards. Spear dispense from the cask ensures that the beers can survive regular flooding of the cellar. Close by are the Malvern Hills, the River Severn, The Cotswolds, Worcester with its cathedral and porcelain works, regency Cheltenham and Stratford-upon-Avon.

- 🛏 One four-poster, six doubles, three twins, one single
- £ ££££
- 🍺 **Greene King Abbot Ale** plus three guest ales
- 🍴 Lunch, evening and snack menus
- 💳 Credit cards accepted

WARWICK

Globe Hotel

8–10 Theatre Street, Warwick CV34 4DP
T 01926 492044   F 01926 407170
E theglobehotel@warwicktownfreeserve.co.uk
www.infotel.co.uk/47072
Directions: Just off the market square

Two elephants guard the entrance to this Grade II listed building. The hotel's restaurant is now the Warwick Thai Elephant serving excellent Thai cuisine. The plush lounge serves a choice of three quality ales, sometimes including a guest from a local independent brewery. Two first floor function rooms are available for hire and there are 11 bedrooms. Ideally situated for Warwick Castle and the town's other tourist attractions.

🛏 11 rooms
£ £££
🍺 M&B Brew XI plus guest
🍴 Lunch, evening and snack menus
💳 Credit cards accepted

Old Fourpenny Shop Hotel

27–29 Crompton Street, Warwick CV34 6HJ
T 01926 491360   F 01926 411892
E fourpennyshop@aol.com
www.a1tourism.com/uk/oldfourpenny.html
Licensees: Jan and Jane Siddle
Directions: Just off A429

The Old Fourpenny Shop Hotel is located within minutes of Warwick Castle, the racecourse and golf course. Easily accessible are Kenilworth, Stratford-upon-Avon and the Cotswolds, whilst the M40 motorway provides quick and easy access to the National Exhibition Centre, National Agricultural Centre, and the business centres of Birmingham and the rest of the Midlands. It has a wonderfully relaxed atmosphere and a wide range of guest beers and is a regular in the Good Beer Guide. Voted Warwickshire CAMRA Pub of the Year in 2000, its top quality food is said to match any in Warwick's other eating establishments. Children welcome.

🛏 Five double, three twin, one family, two single
£ ££
🍺 RCH Brewery plus four guests
🍴 Lunch, evening and snack menus
💳 Credit cards accepted

WHITEOAK GREEN

The Bird in Hand

Whiteoak Green, Hailey, Witney,
Oxfordshire OX29 9XP
T 01993 868321   F 01993 868702
Directions: On B4022

The Bird in Hand is one of Oxfordshire's best kept secrets. This 16 cottage bedroomed, Cotswold stone inn, which has won many accolades, is worth a visit as it is within easy driving not just of the Cotswolds but also of Oxford and Blenheim Palace. There is a huge feature fireplace in a very cosy restaurant, where the food is cooked and prepared by Lester Curnow who has a justified reputation for the range and variety of his menus. Children welcome.

🛏 Four twin, 10 double, two family
£ ££
🍺 Adnams Bitter, Fuller's London Pride
🍴 Lunch, evening and snack menus

WILMCOTE

Mary Arden Inn

Wilmcote, Stratford-upon-Avon,
Warwickshire CV37 9XJ
T 01789 267030   F 01789 204875
www.oldenglish.co.uk
Directions: Approaching Stratford-upon-Avon from any direction, follow brown tourism signs to Mary Arden's house. Hotel is opposite

Formerly a splendid private house, the Mary Arden Inn dates back to the 1700s. Standing opposite Mary Arden's house it is ideally located for exploring Stratford. The 11 en suite bedrooms have been refurbished in 2002 and include two four-poster rooms and a honeymoon suite called the Romeo and Juliet suite, which has a four-poster bedroom, small lounge area and a Jacuzzi bath. The village of Wilmcote is the birthplace of Shakespeare's mother, Mary Arden and the inn overlooks the farmstead which was her home. Anne Hathaway's House and Stratford-upon-Avon are just three miles down the road.

- 11 rooms including two four-posters and a honeymoon suite
- £ £££ ££££ single
- 🍺 **Greene King IPA** and **Abbot**
- 🍴 Lunch, evening and snack menus
- 💳 Credit cards accepted

Mary Arden Inn, Wilmcote

Butchers Arms

Woolhope, Hereford, Herefordshire HR1 4RF
T 01432 860281 **F** 01432 860821
E peter@thebutchersarms.org.uk
www.thebutchersarms.org.uk
Licensee: Peter Dunscombe
Directions: East end of village which is on high ground between Fownhope and Ledbury grid ref OS618358

An impressive black and white pub, formed in Victorian times by combining a butcher's shop and a beer house. Original beams are much in evidence including a very solid one at head height in the lounge (beware!) and the style of the furnishing is rustic. A good mix of customers use the pub for drinking and, mainly, for eating with home prepared food being served in both bars as well as the separate dining room. A stream runs along the side of the pub and garden.

Woolhope village is associated with Lady Godiva and her sister Wulvia who gave the manor to Hereford Cathedral in the 11th century. Silurian limestone can be seen protruding through the red limestone hills.

- Two double
- £ £
- 🍺 **Hook Norton Best Bitter**, **Old Hooky**, **Wye Valley Bitter**
- 🍴 Lunch, dinner and snack menus
- 💳 Credit cards accepted

London

Greater London

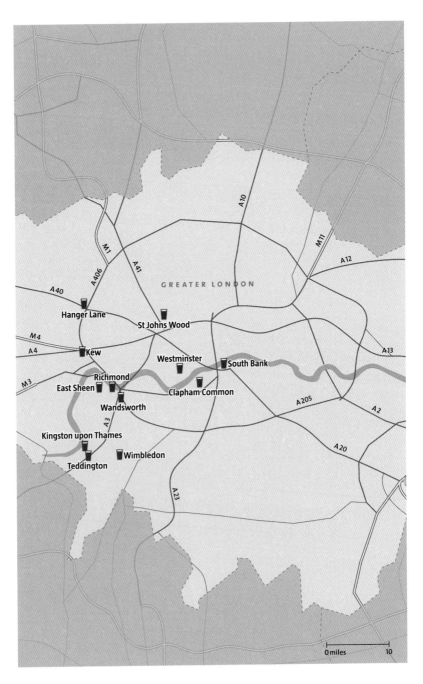

GREATER LONDON

A10

M11

A12

M1

A41

A406

A40

Hanger Lane

St Johns Wood

M4

A4

A13

Kew

Westminster

South Bank

M3

Richmond

East Sheen

Clapham Common

A205

A2

Wandsworth

A3

Kingston upon Thames

A20

Teddington

Wimbledon

A23

0 miles 10

LONDON is a vibrant, multi-cultural city, which embraces the diverse cultures of its population.

Whether it's reflected in its pubs, the food, colourful street markets, the music or at one of the city's many festivals, in London visitors can mix with the world.

It is as much a collection of villages as a city, with many local pubs reflecting the character of the area where they are found.

In recent years there has been a quiet revolution as more pubs in the capital have started to offer high class accommodation – and where better to stay than in a pub, with a welcoming, friendly bar, often filled with local people enjoying real ale, as opposed to the bland, stereotyped anonymity of a massive hotel?

London too has many historic pubs: a small number survive from the 16th and 17th century, there are some pubs that first opened there doors in the 18th century and there are many fine examples of Georgian and Victorian pubs which have survived the ravages of developers and world war.

London too is a brewing city, admittedly it no longer has the numbers of 100 or even 20 years ago, but the craft still thrives, with both cask ale producers Fuller's and Young's producing some of England's finest beers. And these two traditional brewers are ably supported by a growing band of micros.

Tours of Young's Brewery and Brewery Tap in Wandsworth can be arranged as can a tour of the stables where some of the most magnificent Shire horses in the country, which are still used to deliver beer to local pubs, can be seen along with the brewery's handsome ram.

Tours can be booked at Fuller's brewery too. Brewing has taken place on its West London site for more than 350 years. The brewery has a proud tradition of brewing real ale. In the 24 years that CAMRA has held the Champion Beer of Britain competition, Fuller's has won the Beer of the Year award five times. The beers have been Best in Class no less than nine times and Fuller's ESB, its strong pale brown ale of great character, has been voted Best Strong Ale an unprecedented seven times.

The capital also boasts a fashionable brew restaurant Mash in Great Portland Street. The in-house brewery produces international beer styles on a rotational basis including a blackcurrant porter, an India Pale Ale and an extra stout.

CLAPHAM COMMON

Windmill on the Common

South Side, Clapham Common, London SW4 9DE
T 020 8673 4578   **F** 020 8675 1486
E windmillhotel@youngs.co.uk
www.youngs.co.uk
Licensee: Jennifer Hale
Directions: on the A24, midway between Clapham
Common and Clapham South underground stations

The first of Young's hotels and once the home
of the brewery's founder, this old coaching
inn stands right on the common. Advertised
by Young's as a country hotel in London, the
recently refurbished large single bar with its
conservatory-cum-family room, does have
a comfortable feeling. It can get very busy,
especially in summer when the crowd spills
out over the common. Food is available in
the bar and the no-smoking room which
used to be the restaurant.

For hotel residents there is a separate
lounge for out of hours use, without a bar,
but with night porter service and cask ale
available until 11.30pm. Whilst the majority
of weekday guests are on business, there
remains a good business/leisure mix with
many overseas visitors using the hotel for
holidays.

🛏 19 double, 10 twin-bedded rooms
£ £££££
🍺 **Young's Bitter, Special**
🍴 Snacks and meals daily, lunchtime and evening
💳 Credit cards accepted

EAST SHEEN

Plough

42 Christchurch Road, East Sheen SW14 7AF
T 020 8876 7833   **F** 020 8392 8801
Licensee: Brian O'Donovan
Directions: Just off the South Circular road

The Plough originated as a row of farmer's
cottages over 200 years ago, when this was
still the countryside, a fair way out of the
city. Now London is within easy reach by
modern public transport (Waterloo in 15
minutes). The station is a few minutes'
walk. The long since redundant cottages
have become a comfortable inn, which
aims, in its decor and atmosphere, to
preserve a reminder of its rural beginnings.

The seven subtly decorated rooms have
been refurbished with up-to-date facilities;
all are en suite. Pets are accepted. Food at
the Plough comes highly recommended,
including the substantial breakfasts. The
pub is just a couple of minutes' walk from
Richmond Park and the Thames, with Kew
Gardens just a mile away.

🛏 Three double, three twin and one family room
£ £££ (single occupancy ££££)
🍺 **Courage Best Bitter, Directors**; occasional
guest beer
🍴 Lunch, evening and snack menus
💳 Credit cards accepted

The Victoria

10 West Temple Sheen, East Sheen, London SW14 7RT
T 020 8876 4238   **F** 020 8878 3464
E mark@thevictoria.net
www.thevictoria.net
Licensee: Mark Chester

The Victoria is a gastropub with rooms and
serves the style of food you would expect
from someone who worked for Terence
Conran for many years. There is a large
garden and play area and children are very
welcome at all times. It has seven simply
but stylishly furnished double bedrooms,
all of which are en suite and a priority has
been to ensure that guests can enjoy a
comfortable night's sleep and a really great
shower. In two rooms there is additional

space for a travel cot or a camp bed. Richmond Park is on the doorstep and an ideal place to walk off the effects of a good meal. Easy access to central London.

🛏 Seven double
£ ££££
🍺 Guest ales plus **Hoegaarden** beer on tap
🍴 Lunch, evening and snack menus
💳 Credit cards accepted

Roebuck

72 Hampton Road, Hampton Hill, Middlesex TW12 1JN
T 020 8255 8133   **F** 020 8255 9004
Licensee: Terry Himpfen
Directions: On A313, almost in Hampton Hill

Hampton Court Palace is less than three miles away from this comfortable pub which is close to Hampton Hill's main street. The owners have created a welcoming pub decorated with ships, trains, traffic lights, bank notes and other bric-a-brac. Three single rooms and one twin are available for bed and breakfast. The guest beer changes monthly. Not suitable for children, food served weekdays only. No evening meals.

🛏 Three singles, one twin
£ £££
🍺 **Badger Best Bitter**, **IPA**, **Tanglefoot** plus guest
🍴 Lunch and snack menus Monday-Friday
💳 Credit cards accepted

Fox & Goose Hotel

Hanger Lane, Ealing, London W5 1DP
T 020 8998 5864   **F** 020 8997 5378
E foxandgoose@fullers.co.uk
www.fullers.co.uk
Licensee: Mike and Michelle Menhennett
Directions: Off Hanger Lane roundabout – take A4005 towards Alperton and Sudbury, down the hill on the lefthand side. Two minutes from Hanger Lane underground

A large hotel on the edge of central London with easy access to the West End. Wembley Arena and Conference Centre are two miles away, and Heathrow Airport 10 miles. It has

73 bedrooms, Sky TV and disabled facilities. Special rates for children and at the weekend.

🛏 30 twins, 36 double, three family, three disabled double, one disabled twin
£ £££££ special rates at weekend
🍺 **Fuller's London Pride**, **ESB**, **Chiswick** and seasonal ale
🍴 Lunch and snack menus
💳 Credit cards accepted

Coach & Horses

8 Kew Green, Kew, Richmond, Surrey TW9 3BH
T 020 8940 1208   **F** 020 8948 8787
E coachandhorses@youngs.co.uk
www.youngs.co.uk
Licensee: John Bamford
Directions: On A4205, South Circular Road

This 17th century coaching inn has recently been refurbished. It boasts 31 en suite air-conditioned bedrooms and a traditional bar. It is licensed to hold civil weddings. Excellently located opposite Kew's Botanical Gardens the hotel is only a few minutes walk away from the Public Records Office and tube and rail stations. Kew Bridge Steam Museum is half a mile away. It has a justifiable reputation for home-cooked food. Easily accessible to M4 and Heathrow Airport.

🛏 31 rooms
£ ££££
🍺 **Young's Bitter**, **Special** plus seasonal ales
🍴 Lunch, evening and snack menus
💳 Credit cards accepted

KINGSTON UPON THAMES

Owl & Pussycat

144 Richmond Road, Kingston upon Thames KT2 5HA
T 020 8546 9162
Directions: On junction of Windsor Road and
Richmond Road (A307) north of town centre.
Less than ½ mile from Kingston railway station

A freehouse with a modern pastel decor,
with some soft sofas, serving Adnams Bitter
and Young's Bitter. A third handpump is
sometimes used. Good food menu lunchtimes and evenings, popular traditional
Sunday lunches. Has a small number of
letting rooms but breakfast not served.

- Small number of letting rooms
- **£** £££
- **Adnams, Young's** plus occasional guests
- Snack and full menu – no breakfast
- Credit cards accepted

The White Hart Hotel

1 High Street, Hampton Wick,
Kingston upon Thames KT1 4DA
T 0208 977 1786   **F** 0208 977 7612
E whitehart.hotel@fullers.co.uk
www.fullers.co.uk
Licensee: Redmond Walsh
Directions: On Kingston Bridge

The White Hart Hotel is newly refurbished
and offers 37 well appointed air conditioned
bedrooms, all en suite with remote
controlled television, satellite and radio,
direct telephone, tea and coffee making
facilities. Kingston town centre is five
minutes' walk away and Hampton Court
Palace is a mere five minutes drive. Also
nearby are Chessington World of
Adventures, Kempton and Sandown Park
Racecourses, Wimbledon Lawn Tennis
Museum and Twickenham Museum of
Rugby. A roaring fire makes it a comfortable
place to be on a winter's evening.

- 21 double, six twin, six family, four superior
  suites
- **£** ££££ special rates at weekend
- **Fuller's London Pride, ESB** and seasonal beers
- Lunch, evening and snack menus
- Credit cards accepted

RICHMOND

Red Cow

59 Sheen Road, Richmond, Surrey TW19 1YJ
T 020 8940 2511   **F** 020 8940 2581
E tom@redcowpub.com
www.pub-explorer.com/olpg/red-cow/richmond
Licensee: Tom Dillon
Directions: On A305

The Red Cow dates back to the early 19th
century. It has recently been refurbished,
but has retained many of its original
features, including some wonderful
Victorian glasswork. A popular local, it is
only a few minute's walk away from
Richmond's shops and station. There are
three distinct drinking areas, where rugs on
bare floorboards and period furniture
create a traditional atmosphere. The first
floor has been converted to provide four en
suite bedrooms. Tuesday is quiz night and
music is played on Friday, Saturday and
Sunday evenings.

- Four double/twin, two family
- **£** £££
- **Young's Bitter, Special** plus seasonal ales
- Lunch, evening snack menus – no food
  Saturday/Sunday evenings
- Credit cards accepted

Dukes Head

42 The Vineyard, Richmond Upon Thames,
Surrey, TW10 6AN
T/F 020 8948 4557
E info@dukeshead.com
www.dukeshead.com
Licensees: Pat and Moraid Dalton
Directions: Off Richmond Hill

Irish hospitality in a traditional English
two-bar pub in an affluent residential area
of Richmond upon Thames, one of
London's finest villages. For the last 15 years
Pat and Moraid Dalton have managed the
Duke's Head, a small, friendly, pub whose
history dates back to Victorian times. With
a small patio to rear, the pub has frequently
won awards for its blaze of floral colour.
Good English menu available throughout

the day and evening, together with excellent range of traditional ales. Within easy reach of Richmond town centre, Richmond Theatre, District Line tube station (connecting to central London, Knightsbridge etc), and Richmond Park.

Since 1997 the Duke's Head has operated as a traditional English inn, offering bed and breakfast accommodation. Resident guests are served a hearty English breakfast every morning – although Moraid does sometimes give it a bit of an Irish flavour. All bedrooms have en suite shower and WC, remote control colour TV and central heating. Ironing facilities are available – children welcome.

- 🛏 11 bedrooms – range of double, twin and a triple
- £ £££ single ££££
- 🍺 **John Smith's** plus guests
- 🍴 Lunch, evening and snack menus
- 💳 Credit cards accepted

ST JOHNS WOOD

The New Inn

2 Allitsen Road, St Johns Wood, London NW8 6LA
T 020 7722 0726   F 020 7722 0653
E thenewinnlondon@aol.com
www.newinnlondon.co.uk
Licensee: Janet Rooney

Sat on the corner with Townshend Road, and originally built in 1810, this one-bar pub with a small raised area set aside for dining, is less than 10 minutes walk from St Johns Wood tube (Jubilee line). It sits in a quiet, tree-lined residential area with Regent's Park, London Zoo, Primrose Hill and Lords cricket ground all within a short walking distance. In better weather tables are placed on the pavement outside and on Saturday night/Sunday afternoon a live band might be found playing easy listening and light blues. The pub has five basic B&B rooms, three double and two twin, all with en suite showers, TV and tea/coffee making facilities. Children allowed in dining area. For the area, the accommodation represents very good value for money.

- 🛏 Three double, two twin
- £ £££
- 🍺 **Greene King IPA** and **Abbot**
- 🍴 Lunch, evening and snack menus
- 💳 Credit cards accepted

SOUTH BANK

Mad Hatter

3–7 Stamford Street, South Bank, London SE1 9NY
T 020 7401 9222   F 020 7401 7111
E mad.hatter@fullers.co.uk
www.fullers.co.uk
Licensee: Dave McLelland
Directions: Close to south side of Blackfriars Bridge

A typical 19th century façade hides a Fuller's Ale & Pie pub with a welcoming atmosphere and some great home cooked food. It is expensive but offers much better value for money than the over-priced bland hotels in central London, with the added bonus of serving real ale. In the dining area there are great scenes of Alice in Wonderland on the ceiling which are worth the visit alone. The pub is close to the Tate Modern, Shakespeare's Globe Theatre, the National Theatre, The Old Vic and the London Eye.

- 🛏 12 double, 18 twin
- £ ££££
- 🍺 **Fuller's London Pride**, **Chiswick**, **ESB** and seasonal ales
- 🍴 Lunch, evening and snack menus
- 💳 Credit cards accepted

WANDSWORTH

Brewers Inn

147 East Hill, Wandsworth SW18 2QB
T 020 8874 4128   F 020 8877 1953
E brewersinn@youngs.co.uk
www.youngs.co.uk
Licensee: Scott Parker
Directions: On A3 – by car approach down East Hill and turn into St Annes Hill

Superbly located for access to central, south and west London it is only a few minutes walk from Wandsworth Station. Parking is available but the complexities of Wandworth's one-way system can deter

Brewers Inn, Wandsworth

even the most determined of London's car drivers. The pub is split into three main areas – a bar with bare floorboards and wooden tables, a more comfortable carpeted area and an oak panelled candle lit restaurant. There is a bistro menu with daily specials for more informal dining.

The 16 bedrooms all have their own shower or bath, trouser press and telephone. London is an expensive city to stay in but look out for special prices at weekends when it can be considerably cheaper. Children are welcome and special rates apply.

- Four singles, seven doubles, three twin and two family rooms
- £ £££ (££ weekend), single ££££
- **Young's Bitter** and **Special** plus seasonals
- Lunch, evening and snack menus
- Credit cards accepted

WESTMINSTER

The Sanctuary House

33 Tothill Street, London SW1H 9LA
T 020 7799 4044   F 020 7799 3657
E sanctuary@fullers.co.uk
www.fullers.co.uk
Licensee: Liz McLelland
Directions: by St James's Park underground station

A traditional style of pub, including bars, food, family room, with many notable features. The main bar has airy spaces and large windows decorated with feature chandeliers. The hotel is immaculately furnished to a very high standard and all rooms are en suite. Close-by is Westminster Abbey, Big Ben, the Houses of Parliament and Buckingham Palace.

- 24 double, 10 twin
- £ £££££
- **Fuller's London Pride**, **ESB** and seasonal ales
- Lunch, evening and snack menus
- Credit cards accepted

WIMBLEDON

Rose & Crown

55 High Street, Wimbledon Village, London SW19 5BA
T 020 8947 4713   F 020 8947 4994
E roseandcrown@youngs.co.uk
www.youngs.co.uk
Licensees: Karen and Jeff Messitt

This is Wimbledon's oldest inn still standing in its original form. Built in 1651 this traditional pub was recently refurbished by adding a courtyard and a conservatory. Serves traditional 'best of British' food including a full English breakfast and a snack menu. There is an emphasis on real beers from the Young's brewery in Wandsworth.

This former coaching inn was the first stage from London, and until the 19th century passengers had to take Dutch courage before facing the hazards of highwaymen like Dick Turpin. Within walking distance of the All England Lawn Tennis Club.

- 13 new air-conditioned rooms suitable for single, double, twin or family – disabled welcome.
- £ £££££ – special offers at weekend
- **Young's Bitter**, **Special** and seasonal plus **Smiles Bitter**
- Lunch, evening and snack menus
- Credit cards accepted

North West England

Cheshire
Greater Manchester
Lancashire
Merseyside
High Peaks of Derbyshire

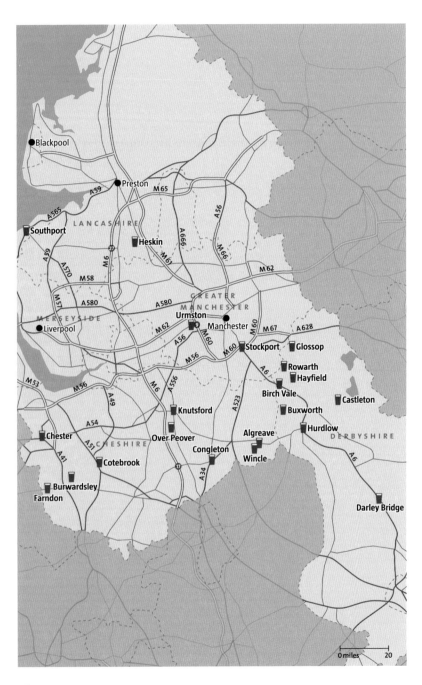

THE NORTH WEST OF ENGLAND is an area of dynamic cities, exciting countryside and vibrant coastal towns.

It is an area rich in history – pre-historic Britain, Roman Britain, the industrial revolution and even today's e-revolution can all be found cheek by jowl.

Explore the picturesque half-timbered villages of Cheshire in the heart of lush farmland. Discover Lancashire's rolling moorland hills and outstanding scenery – from the dramatic Pennine Moors to the spectacular Forest of Bowland or the peaceful Lune Valley.

The North West contains some of Britain's most unspoilt countryside and a warm welcome and a friendly chat await those who venture on the highways and byways.

From the stunning Derbyshire Dales, to Chester – in many eyes, Britain's finest historic city, to the majestic towns of Liverpool and Manchester it is an area of glorious pubs, fabulous beers and some wonderful brewers.

The rivers Ribble, Hodder and Calder wind freely through the Lancashire Valley's rich pastures, where contented woolly sheep graze alongside riverbanks where Romans once trod.

Cheshire is a special place. Its location, on the border with Wales and at the meeting point of the Midlands and England's rugged North Country, has led to a rich and eventful history set within a melting pot of landscapes. Here outdoor enthusiasts are rewarded with intimate glimpses of peaceful English countryside, ranging from magical wooded hillsides and gentle pastoral lowlands, to the panoramic heights of purple moorland and wild hills.

Cheshire, with its lush green pastures and sandstone outcrops – all within an area of just 2,000 sq. km, is where the visitor can discover much of what is best about traditional England. Not just some fine walking country, but also flourishing local crafts, world famous historic towns and beautiful villages.

Explore some of Cheshire's finest countryside using way marked trails and circular routes. The Sandstone and Gritstone Trails are two spectacular, contrasting routes with fine views over the surrounding countryside.

And visit Chester – its Walls are the most complete in

Britain and the unique two-tiered shopping galleries, the Rows are not found anywhere else in the world.

The resorts here offer ideal locations for day trips. There is such a choice – from Morecambe in the north to the Wirral in the south, along with Blackpool, Fleetwood and Lytham St Annes, each offering its own distinctive style of entertainment.

ALGREAVE, Macclesfield

Rose & Crown

Algreave, Macclesfield, Cheshire SK11 0BJ
T/F 01260 227232
E info@theroseandcrown.net
www.theroseandcrown.net
Licensee: Mrs J A Fagan
Directions: on A54

This friendly hillside pub is a long, narrow building that inside is a bit mixed up but full of character. The far end of the function room used to house a smithy; next is the comfortable lounge with open fire. Then beyond the narrow bar with a wooden pew, rocking chairs and fish tank is the new-looking dining room with views over the valley below. Families and dogs welcome. All rooms are en suite. The garden is set into the hillside to the rear. It is an ideal base to visit Alton Towers and Buxton Spa.

🛏 Two double, one twin
£ ££
🍺 Robinson's Best Bitter plus seasonal ales
🍴 Lunch, evening and snack menus
💳 Credit cards accepted

BIRCH VALE

Waltzing Weasel

New Mills Road, Birch Vale, High Peak, Derbyshire SK22 1BT
T/F 01663 743402
E w-weasel@zen.co.uk
www.w-weasel.co.uk
Licensees: Mike and Linda Atkinson
Directions: on the A6015, between Hayfield and New Mills

The Derbyshire Dining Club of the Year in 2002, the Weasel successfully combines the quality (and prices) of an upmarket hotel with the pleasurable atmosphere of a local pub set within the heart of the Peak District hills. The warmth of the welcome is as high as Kinder Scout which it stands by. It has a quiet, traditional bar, replete with old settles, grandfather clock, prints and a log fire. It offers an alternative to the anonymous urban hotel and yet is only forty minutes away from Manchester and its international airport, Sheffield and Stockport. The entrenched forces of conservatism guarantee the absence of music, machines and mobiles. Chef Tracy Young provides fine, honest food, served in a widely acclaimed restaurant, which, through its mullioned windows, offers some dramatic views.

🛏 Five double, two twin-bedded rooms
£ £££ – ££££
🍺 Marston's Bitter and Pedigree, guest beers (occasionally)
🍴 Lunch, evening and snack menus
💳 Credit cards accepted

BUXWORTH

Navigation Inn

Bugsworth Basin, Buxworth, High Peak, Derbyshire SK23 7NE
T 01663 732072
E linda@navigationinn.co.uk
www.navigationinn.co.uk
Licensee: Alan and Lynda Hall
Directions: One and a half miles off A6, between Whaley Bridge and New Mills, towards Chinley – not easy to find as it is not on every map

The Navigation Inn is situated at the historic Bugsworth Basin in the village of Buxworth in the heart of the scenic High Peak, part of Derbyshire's Peak District. Once owned by the late Pat Phoenix, Coronation Street's Elsie Tanner, the Navigation became an inn over two hundred years ago, and still retains its original character and atmosphere. There are five double rooms of which four are en suite and a large family room. Food is served in the bar, restaurant or outside on the large patio. There is an extensive and varied menu to choose from as well as the daily specials' board. In the bar you will find a wide selection of beers and ales. The guest ales are changed regularly so there's always something new to take your fancy. The Navigation is a listed building situated right by the Buxworth Basin, itself a listed ancient monument, and the only remaining canal/tramway interchange in the UK; now defunct it is currently the subject of a restoration programme. Special rates for children.

🛏 One singles, two doubles – one with a four-poster, one twin, one family
£ £ ££ single
🍺 **Marston's Pedigree, Timothy Taylor Landlord, Webster's Yorkshire Bitter** and guest beers
🍴 Lunch, evening and snack menus
💳 Credit cards accepted

Pheasant Inn

Higher Burwardsley, Tattenhall, Cheshire CH3 9PF
T 01829 770434   **F** 01829 771097
E reception@thepheasant-burwardsley.com
www.thepheasant-burwardsley.com
Directions: Eight miles from Chester, via the A41

The Pheasant Inn is a three-hundred year old inn of half timbered and sandstone construction, on the top of the Peckforton Hills with magnificent views over the Cheshire Plain to Wales. The pleasant Lounge Bar is full of old world charm and boasts what must be the biggest log fire in Cheshire, open both sides to toast you on cool evenings. The Bistro Restaurant was the original farmhouse kitchen and is a mixture of old oak sandstone and with a traditional farmhouse cooking range.

The ten en suite guest rooms are in a converted barn and equipped to a very high standard with hospitality tray, colour TV and direct dial telephone. Most of the rooms have panoramic views and, being away from the main public area, they offer a peaceful night's rest. Weekend guests who are able to stay over from Friday to Monday, are not charged for accommodation on the

Sunday night. Children are charged at £10 per night bed and breakfast. Pets can be accommodated by arrangement.

🛏 Six double, two twin-bedded and two family rooms
£ ££ (££££ single occupancy)
🍺 **Draught Bass**, guest beer
🍴 Lunch, evening and snack menus
💳 Credit cards accepted

Bulls Head

Cross Street, Castleton, Hope Valley, Derbyshire S33 8WH
T 01433 620256   **F** 01433 623839
E info@bullsheadcastleton.co.uk
www.bullsheadcastleton.co.uk
Licensee: Philip Hobson

A traditional pub offering comfort and service in the heart of the beautiful Peak National Park. Located in the heart of the village many of the finest walks in the Peak District start right on the doorstep and in nearby Edale can be found the start of the Pennine Way. It is close to Castleton's famous Caverns and Blue John mine.

Two large log fires often roar in the dining room and beamed lounge. Children welcome. Five bedrooms, all en suite.

🛏 Four double, one family
£ ££
🍺 **Robinson's Best Bitter**
🍴 Lunch, evening and snack menus
💳 Credit cards accepted

CHESTER

George & Dragon

Liverpool Road, Chester CH2 1AA
T 01244 380714   **F** 01244 380782
Directions: Just outside the city wall, off St Oswald's Way, which lies parallel to the canal

Chester has some of the most visually stunning town centre architecture in Britain and is the most complete walled city in Britain. It is famed for its fine Roman remains, and medieval Rows linking quaint, delightfully decorated shops full of old-world charm and character. Close to the city centre the George & Dragon Hotel sports Cheshire's famous black-and-white magpie design, and itself is a Grade II Listed building, built on a Roman site and reputed to have its own resident ghost.

The recently refurbished guest rooms all offer en suite facilities and the usual amenities. A full English breakfast is included in the room rate. Meals can be taken in either the restaurant or the bar, which has one of the widest selection of real ales in Chester. It doesn't accommodate children.

🛏 Seven double and seven twin-bedded rooms
£ ££
🍺 **Boddingtons Bitter, Flowers IPA, Fuller's London Pride** plus guest beers
🍴 Lunch, evening and snack menus
💳 Credit cards accepted

Mill Hotel

Milton Street, Chester CH1 3NF
T 01244 350035   **F** 01244 345635
www.millhotel.com
Licensees: Gordon and Gary Vickers
Directions: Between the ring road and station

A jewel in the centre of the Roman City of Chester. The original, Griffith's Corn Mill, was built circa 1830. The latest extension was completed in 2001. The spacious Club Rooms, with 14 satellite channels, enable guests to relax in style. Four bars compliment the Mill Hotel's relaxed atmosphere. The public bar has 16 hand pulled beers and has been featured in the Good Beer Guide for the last 10 years. The bar serves over 1,000 different

Mill Hotel, Chester

traditional beers per year and was awarded the Millennium Pub of the Year by the Chester and South Clwyd Branch of CAMRA.

In the Canaletto Restaurant diners can experience superb food overlooking its waterside location, or try the 60 seat Restaurant Boat where the same excellent food can be sampled whilst cruising on Chester's waterway. The health club's sauna, steam room, swimming pool and beauty spa are the places to relax, at the end of the day. For those that require a little more from their stay the latest Technogym equipment, used three times a week for six weeks, will increase your personnel fitness level 38 per cent guaranteed!

🛏 One single, 55 double, 21 twin-bedded and four family rooms
£ ££ (££££ single)
🍺 **Boddingtons Bitter, Mill Premium, Weetwood Best Bitter,** many guest beers
🍴 Lunch, evening and snack menus
💳 Credit cards accepted

CONGLETON

Bulls Head

4 Mill Street, Congleton, Cheshire CW12 1AB
T 01260 273388   **F** 01260 273435
E bullshead@hydes40.fsnet.co.uk
Licensees: Tony and Gill Massey

A town centre pub which has been run by the same family for the past 40 years. Close to the Peak District, Alton Towers and Jodrell Bank.

🛏 Three single, four double, six twin
£ £££
🍺 **Hydes**
🍴 Lunch, evening and snack menus
💳 Credit cards accepted

COTEBROOK

Alvanley Arms

Cotebrook, Tarporley, Cheshire CW6 9DS
T 01829 760200   **F** 01829 760696
www.thealvanleyarms.co.uk
Licensee: Janet King

Comfortable, friendly local, with a large dining area and large car park. It is next to the Cotebrook Shire Stud and Native Wild Breeds Park. Oulton Park is eight miles away. Children welcome.

🛏 Three double, three twin, one single
£ ££

🍺 **Robinson's Best Bitter** plus guest
🍴 Lunch, evening and snack menus
💳 Credit cards accepted

DARLEY BRIDGE

Square & Compass

Station Road, Darley Bridge, Matlock, Derbyshire DE4 2EQ
T 01629 733255   **F** 01629 732400
Licensee: David Lees
Directions: on B507

Good beer is a priority at this traditional 18th century pub in Darley Dale. The former bar and farm cottage have been converted to provide excellent bed and breakfast. Overnight visitors can enjoy their full English breakfast in the conservatory with its views across the Derwent Valley. Fishing enthusiasts can obtain day tickets for the pub's private fishing stretch of the River Derwent. For historians, Derbyshire offers the finest stately homes, including Chatsworth House and Riber Castle, and families can visit the Gulliver's Kingdom which is an easy drive away. All rooms are en suite, children welcome.

🛏 Five double, two family, five single
£ ££
🍺 **Robinson's Best Bitter**
🍴 Lunch, evening and snack menus
💳 Credit cards accepted

Square & Compass, Darley Bridge

FARNDON

Farndon Arms

High Street, Farndon, Cheshire CH3 7PU
T 01829 270570 **F** 01829 271428
E beerseller.farndonarms@virgin.net
www.farndonarms.com
Licensee: Martin Bouchier

The most noticeable aspect of the Farndon Arms is the striking black and white façade. This 16th century coaching inn was formerly known as the Raven – a fact apparent by the attractive etched windows. There are up to four real ales on tap and usually two are from local micros. The accommodation has recently been refurbished and includes full en suite facilities. The pub is approximately 15 minutes drive from the centre of Chester and is handy for the nearby Carden Park golf complex. The Victorian style first floor restaurant offers some of the very best cuisine in the area using all fresh market produce.

🛏 Three double, two single, one twin, one family
£ £££
🍺 Range varies – normally two from local micros
🍴 Lunch, evening and snack menus
💳 Credit cards accepted

Greyhound Hotel

High Street, Farndon, Nr Chester, Cheshire CH3 6PU
T/F 01829 270244
E greyhound-farndon@line1.net
Licensees: Marco and Sarah Paoloni
Directions: B5130, off A534 – M6 J17

Situated in the pleasant border village of Farndon close to the River Dee, the Greyhound makes an excellent base for exploring West Cheshire and North Wales. The pub is divided into three distinct areas with one acting as the dining room – where there is a real log fire. The menu has an emphasis on Italian food, due to the landlord's origins. There are usually two guest beers on tap as well as Greenalls Bitter and Tetley Mild. There are 10 golf courses within a 30 minute drive of the pub. Fishing for pike, salmon and other freshwater fish is very popular. Four bedrooms – all en suite – and a self-catering cottage are available. Children are welcome.

🛏 One double, one twin, one single, one family, and a holiday cottage with three double
£ ££
🍺 **Greenalls Bitter**, **Tetley Mild** plus two guests
🍴 Lunch, evening and snack menus
💳 Credit cards accepted

GLOSSOP

George Hotel

Norfolk Street, Glossop, Derbyshire SK13 7QU
T 01457 857033 **F** 01457 855449
E enquiries@georgehotelglossop.co.uk
www.georgehotelglossop.co.uk
Licensees: Jean and George Wharmby
Directions: in the town centre, opposite the station

The George is very conveniently situated, both for the centre of the market town of Glossop itself, and also for Manchester (accessible by train) and its airport. As

Glossop is surrounded on three sides by the Peak District National Park, this friendly, family-run establishment is also a popular choice as a base for touring. The George has a warm and welcoming bar offering hand-pulled Theakston and guest ales.

Six of the nine guest rooms have a private bathroom, and they all have tea/coffee making facilities, TV and telephone. A solid stone building, occupying an extensive corner site, the hotel also has two lounge bars open to the public, sometimes frequented by coach parties, and a dining room. It has a good reputation for its hearty meals produced using ingredients from local suppliers.

🛏 Four singles, three doubles, one twin-bedded and one family room
£ £
🍺 **Theakston Best Bitter** and guest beers
🍴 Snacks and meals daily, lunchtime and evening
💳 Credit cards accepted

HURDLOW

Bull I'Th' Thorn

Ashbourne Road, Hurdlow, Buxton, Derbyshire SK17 9QQ
T/F 01298 83348
Licensee: Annette Maltby-Baker

Low beams and antiques are a feature of the main bar. There is a large function room which is used for medieval banquets. The spa town of Buxton is nearby and access to the Peak District National Park. Children welcome.

🛏 Three double
£ £££
🍺 **Robinson's Best Bitter**
🍴 Lunch, evening and snack menus
💳 Credit cards accepted

HAYFIELD

Royal Hotel

Market Street, Hayfield, Derbyshire SK22 2EP
T 01663 742721   F 01663 742997
E royalhotel.hayfield@virgin.net
Directions: In the village centre, just off the A624

Overlooked by Kinder Scout, Hayfield is an old village which was once a staging post on the pack-horse route across the Pennines from Cheshire to Yorkshire. The main importance of Hayfield for the visitor is that it is the gateway to the west side of Kinder, and the narrow road which leads off the side of the Royal Hotel takes you in that direction. The Royal has at various times in its history served as both a pub and a parsonage. Originally built as a home for the vicar of St Matthew's Church, the Rev. Bradley, a particular friend of John Wesley who stayed and preached in Hayfield several times.

The Royal offers a relaxed atmosphere in its bars and bistro restaurant. All the guest rooms (where a no smoking rule applies) are en suite and have TV and tea and coffee making facilities. The Honeymoon suite boasts a Jacuzzi and four-poster bed. Short break packages are available and there are many opportunities locally for rural pursuits in this area of outstanding natural beauty. Noted for its selection of real ales, the pub hosts a beer festival in October.

🛏 Three doubles, one twin-bedded and one family room
£ £££
🍺 **Marston's Pedigree**, **John Smith's Bitter**, **Theakston Best Bitter**, two ever-changing guest beers
🍴 Lunch, evening and snack menus
💳 Credit cards accepted

HESKIN

Farmers Arms

Wood Lane, Heskin, Chorley, Lancashire PR7 5NP
T 01257 451276   F 01257 453958
E info@farmersarms.co.uk
www.farmersarms.co.uk
Licensee: Malcolm Rothwell
Directions: On B5250, M6 J27

A family run 18th-century inn with a reputation locally for good food and the quality of its beer. The pub is about one mile from the Park Hall Conference Centre and Camelot Amusement Park. There are five en suite guest rooms, one of which has a four-poster bed.

🛏 Five double/twin
£ ££
🍺 **Castle Eden Ale, Timothy Taylor's Landlord, Flowers IPA, Boddingtons Bitter**
🍴 Lunch, evening and snack menus
💳 Credit cards accepted

KNUTSFORD

The Cross Keys

King Street, Knutsford, Cheshire WA16 6DT
T 01565 750404   **F** 01565 750510
Licensees: Andrew and Rachel Burke

Set on a picturesque and thriving street in quirky Italianate Knutsford, the Cross Keys is a former coaching inn. Knutsford is a lovely small market town, the Cranford of Elizabeth Gaskell. There is easy access to Manchester and its international airport, and Tatton Park, the home of the RHS North Flower Show. It is only two miles from the motorway network. There is private parking off the street and many restaurants within an easy stroll. All the rooms are en suite and were converted from the old coaching house and stables.

The cellar restaurant is reached by a barrel-vaulted passageway. The public rooms comprise a games room with wide-screen TV for sport, and a lounge, separated by a rare timber and glass screen. Traditional cider is often available, and the bar boasts a bank of gleaming hand-pumps, offering typically three guest beers in what is the only real free house in the town. Children welcome.

🛏 10 double, three single
£ ££££
🍺 **Boddingtons Bitter, Tetley Bitter, Timothy Taylor Landlord** plus three guest beers
🍴 No evening meals Sunday or Monday
💳 Credit cards accepted

OVER PEOVER

Dog Inn

Well Bank Lane, Over Peover, Nr Knutsford, Cheshire WA16 8UP
T 01625 861421   **F** 01625 864800

E Thedog-inn@paddockinns.fsnet.co.uk
Licensee: Steve Wrigley
Directions: Take the A50 in direction of Holmes Chapel from Knutsford, turn left on to Stocks Lane. Dog Inn is on left after two miles

The Dog is a large, comfortable, rambling building, part of a long row of 18th century cottages. Converted to the New Inn early last century as can be seen from the photograph in the front room, later renamed the Gay Dog and finally simply The Dog as a result of the modern slant on the former nomenclature! There are three main sections: the tap-room with pool table and darts board popular with younger clientele, the friendly lounge bar and an extensive eating area. In fact the demand for food has necessitated two evening sittings at weekends, so booking is advisable.

Two locally brewed Weetwood ales are now served, replacing ales which were once supplied by nationals. The food is also made from locally grown produce. Since 2002, there has been a summer beer festival in a marquee in the car park. Convenient for Manchester International Airport, Tatton Park (venue of the RHS North Flower Show) and Jodrell Bank Radio Telescope.

🛏 Four double, three twin-bedded rooms
£ £££ single ££££
🍺 **Weetwood Best Cask, Weetwood Old Dog, Moorhouses Black Cat, Hydes B**
🍴 Lunch, evening and snack menus
💳 Credit cards accepted

ROWARTH, Marple Bridge

Little Mill Inn

Rowarth, via Marple Bridge, Derbyshire SK22 1EB
T 01663 743178
E chrisbarnes@littlemillrowarth.fsnet.co.uk
www.littlemillrowarth.fsnet.co.uk
Licensee: Chris Barnes
Directions: Signed off Siloh Road, off Mellor Road

This waterside inn was built in 1781 as a candlewick mill. The lower floor consisted of a public house and shop supplying the workers from here and surrounding mills with food and refreshment. A real must for rail buffs: the overnight accommodation at this pretty little pub is situated in a converted dining car, the Derbyshire Belle, from the old Brighton Belle. A long way from its first home, the London to Brighton rail line the carriage now contains three tastefully converted rooms, all en suite. In addition there are some cottages which can sleep up to five.

The pub itself lies in the foothills of the Derbyshire Peak District, just outside Greater Manchester. A trout stream runs through the grounds, which also contain a small adventure playground. The building that accommodated the mill wheel was swept away by a great flood in 1930 but the wheel, believed to be the biggest in north west England, has since been restored to full working order and may be seen working every day.

🛏 Three double rooms and a holiday cottage which sleeps five
£ ££ £££ single occupancy
🍺 Banks's Mild and Bitter, Camerons Strongarm, Marston's Pedigree, Robinson's and guest beers
🍴 Lunch, evening and snack menus
💳 Credit cards accepted

SOUTHPORT

The Berkeley Arms Hotel

19 Queens Road, Southport, Merseyside PR9 9HN
T 01704 500811   F 01704 548787

Whilst catering for the individual, the Berkeley Arms is well suited to parties including hen and stag nights, golfers and conference delegates. Its 11 family, twin, double and single bedrooms offer en suite facilities with colour TV and hospitality trays. The Berkeley Arms is also home to a lively real ale pub. Popular with locals, the CAMRA award-winning bars serve no less than nine cask ales at any time. A lively hotel, well known for its home-made pizza.

🛏 11 twin, double and single room
£ ££
🍺 Adnams, Black Cat Mild plus many guests
💳 Credit cards accepted

STOCKPORT

Blue Bell

King Street West, Shaw Heath, Stockport, Greater Manchester SK3 9DY
T 0161 480 5055
Licensee: Nicola Ball
Directions: Behind Stockport Rail Station

Impressive late Victorian/Edwardian pub, recently refurbished and rebranded as a Holts Free House. A good drinking pub, it has two lounge bars and a pool room and large garden at the rear. Accommodation is simple, no food at lunch times and only occasionally in the evenings

🛏 10 double, three family
£ £
🍺 Joseph Holts Bitter
🍴 Some evenings only
💳 Credit cards accepted

URMSTON

Manor Hey Hotel

130 Stretford Road, Urmston, Greater Manchester M41 9LT
T 0161 748 3896   F 0161 746 7183
E joanne@manorhey.com
www.manorhey.com
Licensee: Peter Matthews
Directions: B5213 (Flixton to Stretford road) – about one kilometre from Urmston railway station and from junction 9 of the M60

Convenient for Old Trafford football and cricket grounds, Trafford Park, the Trafford Centre and the new Imperial War Museum (North), all of which are about three miles away. Small suburban hotel rather than a pub, with a bar-cum-bistro that is open to non-residents and always features two cask conditioned ales. The beers change frequently and tend to come from independent family brewers such as Robinsons. Recent beers were Gales Summer Haze and Coach House Summer Sizzler. The bar/bistro also offers interesting meals, very different from standard pub fare. Children welcome.

- 12 double or twin bedded, two single
- £ £££
- Always two cask ales served by handpump, from a variety of regional brewers
- Snacks and meals
- Credit cards accepted

WINCLE

Wild Boar

Wincle, Macclesfield, Cheshire SK11 0QL
T/F 01260 227219
E info@thewildboar.co.uk
www.thewildboar.co.uk
Licensee: Andrew and Carry Brown
Directions: On A54

Built in the 16th century the Wild Boar was situated on the edge of the King's hunting grounds where wild boar roamed. The only wild boar to be seen now however are on the menu, along with a range of traditional, freshly prepared meals and bar snacks. The boar and some of the other meats on the menu are reared by the tenants who also farm locally. Nestling in the Peak District, it is a traditional pub with coal fires and offers a warm welcome to tourists and locals alike. En suite rooms and the re-opening of the caravan and campsite make it an ideal touring base. Children welcomed.

- Two double
- £ ££
- **Robinson's Best Bitter** plus guest
- Lunch, evening and snack menus
- Credit cards accepted

Durham
Northumberland
Tees Valley (Darlington Borough,
Hartlepool Borough, Redcar
and Cleveland, Middlesbrough,
Stockton-on-Tees Borough)
Tyne and Wear

Northumbria

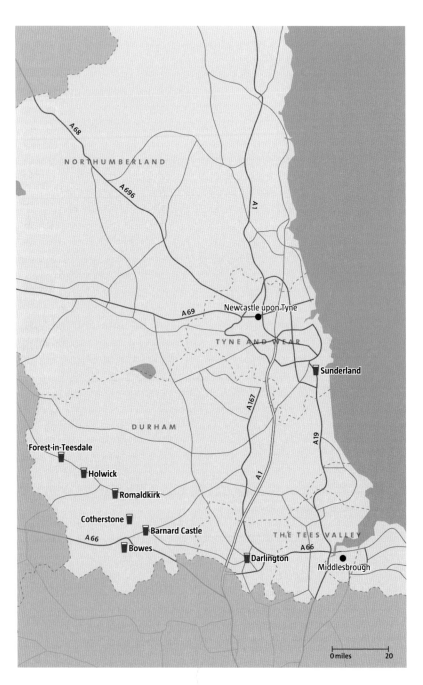

It is said that NORTHUMBRIA is an idyllic region, and its magic has certainly caught the attention of filmmakers as parts of the Harry Potter films have been shot in the area.

The Hogwarts School with its beautiful emerald green landscapes and turret-style classrooms is none other than the awesome grandeur of Alnwick Castle.

The pub's always been at the heart of the community and in Northumbria many of them have been in the thick of local history.

Take the Shipwright's Hotel in Sunderland – 350 years old and a former chandlery, it was also a prime spot for Navy press-ganging and only one of two pubs in the area that has been listed in every edition of CAMRA's Good Beer Guide. Or mind your head on the beams of a genuine Tudor warehouse – the Cooperage on Newcastle's Quayside. Stay in the Old Well Inn at Barnard Castle, the town where Dickens researched Nicholas Nickleby. Or as you travel around stop for a pint in any of the dozens of old coaching inns – the London to Edinburgh Great North Road cut a swathe right through Northumbria.

If you like your pub to include something to see, there's none better than Newcastle's Crown Posada, which unfortunately doesn't have bed and breakfast, with its stunning Victorian stained glass windows – this pub is possibly architecturally the finest in Newcastle.

In Stockton, Fitzgerald's was once a gentlemen's club, with imposing granite pillars and historic bar fittings salvaged from long-gone inns and at Blanchland, the Lord Crewe Arms is a converted monastery.

Visitors to Sunderland should seek out beers from the Darwin Brewery. It specialises in historical recreations of past beers such as Flag Porter, a beer produced with the yeast rescued from a shipwreck in the English Channel.

Look out too for beers from the Mordue Brewery, Shiremoor in Tyne and Wear. Launched by a former home brewer Garry Fawson and his younger brother Matthew in 1995, their first beer Wookie Ticket went on to become Champion Beer of Britain at the Great British Beer Festival in 1997.

And the food! If you want Craster kipper pate, kangaroo steaks, fresh-caught fish and great big chips; or some of the classiest modern British cookery – Northumbria's got it on the menu. But best of all, the pub's always at the heart of town and village life. You'll always be warmly welcomed, there'll be somebody who's delighted to chat.

BARNARD CASTLE

Old Well Inn

21 The Bank, Barnard Castle,
County Durham DL12 8PH
T 01833 690130   **F** 01833 690140
E reservations@oldwellinn.co.uk
www.oldwellinn.co.uk
Licensees: The Mackay family

Solid old three-storey stone 18th-century inn in the centre of Barney, one of the most attractive and historic towns in the country and the gateway to Upper Teesdale. The picture window which gives views over the sloping, antique-shop filled main street from the small front bar is not an original feature in an otherwise perfectly proportioned frontage. The larger – but still nicely snug – lounge bar at the rear tends to be the busier. It links into the main dining areas – a restaurant and a new conservatory. Rabana's restaurant (non-smoking) next door is in the same ownership.

🛏 Eight double/twin, two family
£ ££ and £££
🍺 **Courage Directors**, **John Smith's Cask Bitter**, **Theakston Best Bitter**, **Ruddles Best Bitter**
🍴 Lunch, evening and snack menus
💳 Credit cards accepted

BOWES

Ancient Unicorn

On the Pennine-Way, Bowes, Teesdale,
County Durham DL12 9HL
T 01833 628321
E Management@Ancient-Unicorn.co.uk
www.ancient-unicorn.co.uk
Licensees: Tony Leete and Linda Birkett

This old coaching inn used to be an essential overnight stop for travellers on the often bleak, high cross-Pennine route. Now, thanks to the A66 bypass, the village is blissfully tranquil and stays are a matter of choice rather than necessity. The small village has, over the years, seen Roman, Norse and Norman invaders come and go, and their legacy remains in features such as the wonderfully-named Lavatris Roman fort and the ruined 12th century Bowes Castle, which still towers over the village. Charles Dickens stayed and drank at the Unicorn while researching Nicholas Nickleby. Some present day invaders arrive more peaceably on the Pennine Way which passes through the village. The one-time stables around the spacious courtyard have been adapted for use as guest bedrooms. Inside the pub part of the inn consists of a large main room with an imposing stone fireplace and smaller rooms off. Children welcome.

🛏 Four bedrooms in cottages around courtyard
£ ££/£££
🍺 **Theakston Best Bitter**, two guests
🍴 Lunch, evening and snack menus
💳 Credit cards accepted

COTHERSTONE

Fox & Hounds

Cotherstone, Barnard Castle,
County Durham DL12 9PF
T 01833 650241   **F** 01833 650518
Licensees: Nichola and Ian Swinburn

A cosy, relaxed country pub whose modest appearance belies its role as a coaching inn almost 200 years ago. It stands back from the road at the north end of the village, atop a sloping village green and close to where the River Balder enters the Tees. Until the re-drawing of local government boundaries in 1974 this was Yorkshire's most northerly dale, now it is Durham's most southerly and most beautiful. The village is known for its soft cheese, but it's not always easy to find. The public areas comprise a soft-furnished beamed, lounge bar – with a log fire taking pride of place – a small split-level dining room with home cooked food and a pool room. Two of the bedrooms feature original cast iron fireplaces and boast pleasant country views.

A separate stone built two-bedroom cottage at the rear of the pub is also available for hire.

🛏 Two double, one twin
£ ££ and £££
🍺 **Black Sheep Best Bitter**, plus two guests
🍴 Lunch, evening and snack menus

DARLINGTON

Devonport Hotel

16–18 The Front, Middleton-One-Row, Darlington, County Durham DL2 1AS
T 01325 332255
T thedevonport@aol.com
Licensees: Duncan and Joanna Millar

The Devonport is a traditional small country hotel and freehouse overlooking a scenic stretch of the Tees and a quiet corner of North Yorkshire. Dating back some 200 years it has recently been taken over by a young but mightily-experienced family dedicated to restoring its ambience – and reputation for real ale. Chintzy lounge bar at the front, small public bar at the side. Equally handy for the business centres of Darlington and Teesside and the delights of rural North Yorkshire. The best overnight stop by far for Teesside Airport.

🛏 16 bedrooms
£ ££/£££
🍺 **Black Sheep Best Bitter, Theakston Best Bitter,** guest beer. A range of Belgian bottled beers are also available, served with the correct glass
🍴 Lunch, evening and snack menus
💳 Credit cards accepted

FOREST-IN-TEESDALE

High Force Hotel

High Force, Forest-in-Teesdale, County Durham DL12 0XH
T 01833 622222
E enquiries@highforcehotel.com
www.highforcehotel.com
Licensees: Gary Wilson and Shauna Harrison

Small, unpretentious, residential hotel popular with walkers and visitors to England's highest and most spectacular waterfall, High Force, which is secreted in woods just opposite. The core of the building was erected in the 18th century as a hunting lodge for the Duke of Cleveland, being extended and converted into a hotel in the 19th century. The stepped, two-roomed public bar is simply furnished and has a preponderance of panelling, exposed stone and well-used open fires – snow comes early 1,060 feet up in the Pennines.

A former stable behind the hotel became home to the pint-sized High Force Hotel Brewery in 1995 but due to the many pressures on the licensees' time ceased in 2001, with Darwin Brewery of Sunderland taking over production of the brands under licence.

🛏 Four double/twin, two single
£ £££
🍺 **Darwin Teesdale Bitter, Forest XB, Darwin Cauldron Stout**
🍴 Lunch, evening and snack menus
💳 Credit cards accepted

HOLWICK

Strathmore Arms

Holwick, Middleton-in-Teesdale, County Durham DL12 0NJ
T 01833 640362
E info@strathmorearms.co.uk
www.strathmorearms.co.uk
Licensees: Helen Osborne and Joe Cogdon

Beneath towering Holwick Scar this recently (and carefully) restored old inn takes its name from the noble family which owns most of the land on the south side of upper Teesdale, including much of this stone-built hamlet. The present Earl of Strathmore has been known to pop in for a pint when staying at his hunting lodge at the end of the road, Holwick Lodge. The building started life in the 1690s as a farmhouse, becoming a pub in the mid-1800s. But some of its most impressive elements are surprisingly recent – the stone flag floor in the beamed bar, for instance, is circa 2002. The beams, real fire and settles with scatter cushions and dartboard complete the perfect picture of a small, well-loved country inn. A small side-lounge has quarry-tiles, low-beams and a huge stone fireplace.

Somehow space has even been found to create a small new dining room (16 covers) tucked away behind the serving bar. Helen is a Cordon Bleu cook and Joe loves his real ale. Dogs are very welcome. Near the Pennine Way and Teesdale Way. Breathtaking views of Holwick Scars from the beer garden at the side. There is a camping field to the rear.

🛏 One twin, two doubles and one four-poster
£ ££/£££
🍺 **Ruddles Best**, **Jennings Cumberland Ale**
🍴 Lunch, evening and snack menus
💳 Credit cards accepted

SUNDERLAND

Shipwrights Hotel

Ferryboat Lane, North Hylton,
Sunderland, Tyne and Wear SR5 3HW
T 0191 5495139   **F** 0191 549 7464
Licensees: Maureen and Tony Atwill
Directions: off A19/Wessington Way

The Shipwrights is a 350-year-old coaching inn on the banks of the River Wear in the shadow of the Hylton Bridge. In its time, it has been a post office, a ships chandlers and the place where men were press-ganged in to the navy. It consists of two rooms – the main bar is dominated by a huge open fire and the ceilings are covered with an impressive collection of chamber pots. It is one of only a handful of pubs in the Sunderland area that have sold real ales continuously. In 2002, the pub marked 25 consecutive years in the Good Beer Guide – only the second pub in the North East to achieve this honour. Cask Marque accredited.

High quality home cooked food is served in the bars and the menu includes such delights as ostrich, crocodile and kangaroo. Nearby is the National Glass Centre in Sunderland, Penshaw Monument, Washington Old Hall the North East Aircraft Museum and Washington Wetlands Wildfowl Centre. Children welcome.

🛏 Two double, one twin, two single
£ £££
🍺 **Greene King Abbot**, **Jennings Cumberland Ale**,
Marston's Pedigree and a guest ale
🍴 Lunch, evening and snack menus
💳 Credit cards accepted

ROMALDKIRK

Rose & Crown Hotel

The Green, Romaldkirk, Barnard Castle,
County Durham DL12 9EB
T 01833 650213   **F** 01833 650828
E hotel@rose-and-crown.co.uk
www.rose-and-crown.co.uk
Licensees: Chris and Alison Davy

Built in 1733, the fine, upright sandstone Rose & Crown sits on the middle green overlooking the village stocks. Regular winner of country inn awards. The small, panelled front bar off the central corridor is a gem, its classy, country-casual style usually matched by its customers: shuttered window, polished wood ceiling, an abundance of copper and brass and an enormous stone fireplace. There is an oak-panelled restaurant and a comfortable lounge.

Look out for the footpath, picked out in dark cobbles, which runs in front of the fore-court and commemorates Queen Victoria's Diamond Jubilee in 1897. In scenic walking country – the Teesdale Way passes through the village. Seven bedrooms are in the main house (two with private sitting rooms); five modern courtyard rooms to the rear.

🛏 12 double/twin
£ ££££
🍺 **Black Sheep Best Bitter**, **Theakston Best Bitter**
🍴 Lunch, evening and snack menus
💳 Credit cards accepted

South East England

East and West Sussex
Kent
Middlesex
Surrey

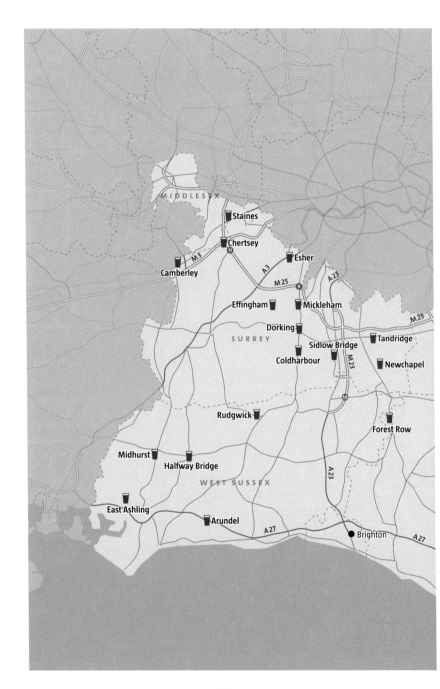

MIDDLESEX

Staines

Chertsey
11

Esher

M3

A3

Camberley

M25
9

A23

Effingham

Mickleham

Dorking

SURREY

Sidlow Bridge

Tandridge

M25

Coldharbour

M23

Newchapel

10

Rudgwick

Forest Row

Midhurst

Halfway Bridge

WEST SUSSEX

A23

East Ashling

Arundel

A27

Brighton

A27

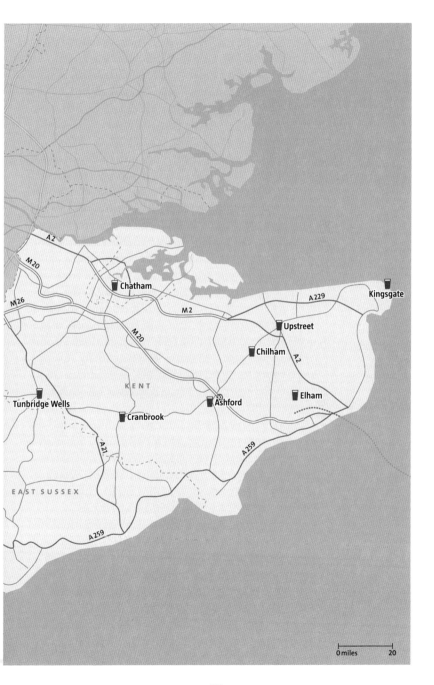

Picture yourself strolling through golden downland or enjoying a lively city break in the distinctive and beautiful counties of Kent, East and West Sussex and Surrey. Many people think only of the area as providing homes for commuters who travel into London as part of their daily grind.

But there is a hidden side to the region – away from the railway stations and the rumbling motorways – there is much beauty and tranquillity.

For visitors enjoying history and heritage, there's a feast of interesting places to see. Step back in time to the ages of Chaucer, Kipling and Churchill; discover 1066 Country where the Normans invaded and changed the history of England; or track down the secret coastal history of smugglers and pirates.

The South East has long been a favourite with great garden makers. The temperate climate and ideal growing conditions have produced world-famous gardens to delight every taste.

To the beer lover the greatest gardens must be the hop fields of Kent, many of which are still in existence, though the area has many former oast houses, where traditionally the hops used to be dried, which have been turned into luxury homes.

The region boasts over 500 miles of long distance footpaths and cycle routes through some of the best landscapes in England, through chalk downland, wooded valleys and dramatic cliff top walks, and over 250 miles of coastline offers some of the most beautiful pubs in the country.

The United Kingdom's oldest brewery can be found in the Garden of England, Kent. Shepherd Neame in Faversham is believed to be the oldest continuous brewer in the country since 1698, but records show brewing began on the site in the 12th century. The same water source is still in use.

A visitors' reception hall is housed in a restored medieval hall, and tours of the brewery can be made by arrangement. The brewery steam engines are still usable and the mash is produced in two teak tuns first used in 1910.

Lewes in Sussex is home to one of the most beautiful settings for a Victorian tower brewery in the country.

Harvey & Son was established in 1790 and this independent family brewery operates from the Bridge Wharf Brewery on the banks of the River Ouse.

The South East offers the chance to sample excellent cuisine in town, village and urban pubs serving traditional ale made from local hops. There is a wealth of theatres and outdoor venues providing live music, festivals and full dramatic productions, and London's lights are just a short journey away.

ARUNDEL

Swan Hotel

27–29 High Street, Arundel, West Sussex BN18 9AG
T 01903 882314   F 01903 883759
E swanhotel@accommodating-inns.co.uk
www.accommodating-inns.co.uk
Licensee: David Vincent

In the heart of enchanting Arundel, the Swan has been lovingly restored to its former Victorian elegance. A short stroll to the famous Arundel Castle and Cathedral, or perhaps take a boat trip along the River Arun which winds through this historic town.

- Eight double, three twin, two executive double, one single
- £ ££££
- Gales HSB, GB, Butser
- Lunch, evening and snack menus
- Credit cards accepted

ASHFORD

Pilgrims Rest Hotel

Canterbury Road, Kennington,
Ashford, Kent TN24 9QR
T 01233 636863   F 01233 610119
E pilgrims.rest@fullers.co.uk
www.fullers.co.uk
Licensees: Stephen Killick and Justin Huber
Directions: Leave M20 J10 and head towards Canterbury on A28, on first large roundabout

The pub's licensees have recently been awarded Cask Marque accreditation for the quality of its real ale. The pub is within 16 miles of Canterbury and close to Leeds, Dover and Hever castles – all are within a 20 mile radius. The McArthur Glen Designer Village is close-by as is some beautiful Kent countryside. It is a great stopping off point for the continent, whether travelling there by ferry or the tunnel.

- 34 double and twin
- £ ££££
- Fuller's London Pride, ESB and seasonal ales
- Lunch, evening and snack menus
- Credit cards accepted

CAMBERLEY

Cambridge Hotel

121 London Road, Camberley, GU15 3LF
T 01276 26488   F 01276 26558
Licensee: Sarah lion
Directions: On A30, High St junction

Close to the Sandhurst Military Academy the Cambridge Hotel was built in 1862 and is named after the old town name of Cambridge Town. A somewhat startling blue and yellow exterior belies a spacious comfortable interior with a warm welcome. Six well kept real ales and draught Hoegaarden should satisfy any thirst. Good, well-cooked food is served at sensible prices. A regular live blues night on Wednesday is popular with the locals. Children welcome in rooms but cannot use the bar area.

- Five singles, 10 doubles
- £ Single £££ double ££
- Fuller's London Pride, Flowers Original, Timothy Taylor's Landlord, Hook Norton Old Hooky, Wadworth 6X, Brakspear Bitter
- Lunch, evening and snack menus
- Credit cards accepted

CHATHAM

The Ship & Trades

Maritime Way, Chatham Maritime,
Chatham, Kent ME4 3ER
T 01634 895200   F 01634 895201
www.shepherd-neame.co.uk

Close to Chatham's historic dockyard the Ship & Trades is part of dockyard history. Although recently opened, it was built in the original 1875 structure that housed the dockyard's ship and trades offices as well as an engineering shop. This unusual pub,

The Ship & Trades, Chatham

complete with a waterside seating area, also features 11 en suite bedrooms, and bars on two floors. An excellent base for visiting the many local attractions and local towns of Gillingham and Rochester.

🛏 14 double/twin
£ £££
🍺 **Shepherd Neame** range
🍴 Lunch, evening and snack menus
💳 Credit cards accepted

CHERTSEY

The Crown

7 London Street, Chertsey, Surrey KT16 8AP
T 01932 564657   F 01932 570839
E crownhotel@youngs.co.uk
www.youngs.co.uk
Licensees: Mr and Mrs D Fiddes
Directions: Minutes from M25 J11

A 19th century coaching inn with an excellent friendly bar. One of an ever-increasing number of Young's pubs offering a high standard of modern hotel facilities. Efficient but friendly at all times, the beer is kept to a very high standard. It is conveniently located for Heathrow and Gatwick airports and many tourist attractions including Windsor Castle, Eton, Legoland and Thorpe Park.

🛏 30 rooms
£ ££££
🍺 **Young's Bitter** and **Special** plus seasonal beer
🍴 Lunch, evening and snack menus
💳 Credit cards accepted

CHILHAM

The Woolpack Inn

High Street, Chilham, nr Canterbury Kent CT4 8DL
T 01227 730351   F 01227 731053
E woolpack@shepherdneame.co.uk
www.shepherd-neame.co.uk

The Woolpack has been welcoming visitors for more than 600 years. Built around 1422, this ancient inn has inglenook fireplaces and an oak beamed restaurant whose extensive menu features local produce. Newly refurbished with 14 en suite bedrooms it is in a rural and picturesque part of Kent. It is a popular place for touring and conveniently close to Canterbury and Ashford.

🛏 14 double/twin
£ £££
🍺 **Shepherd Neame** range
🍴 Lunch, evening and snack menus
💳 Credit cards accepted

COLDHARBOUR near Dorking

The Plough Inn

Coldharbour Lane, Coldharbour,
Dorking, Surrey RH5 6HD
T 01306 711793   F 01306 710055
www.ploughinn.com
Licensees: Rick and Anna Abrehart
Directions: 3.5 miles south of Dorking off A25, OS TQ152441

Coldharbour is the highest village in Surrey, on the side of Leith Hill. Anstiebury Camp, an Iron Age fort on the eastern edge of the village, is a scheduled ancient monument. Originally a 17th century coaching inn, The Plough nestles among the Surrey Hills in good walking country, with the St George's Cross flying outside, and is a gem of a rural brew-pub. The cosy bar, well used by locals, features eight handpumps, one being devoted to Biddenden Cider.

Excellent homemade meals are served at all sessions, both in the dining room and, in the summer, in the large garden at the rear. The pub is the home of the two-barrel capacity Leith Hill Brewery, located at the rear. Landlord Rick Abrehart is also the brewer and has developed three distinctive beers: Crooked Furrow, a well rounded and fruity best bitter, Tickety-Boo, an amber ale, and Tallywhacker, which is a strong, dark ale with subtle overtones of roasted barley. Not suitable for children.

🛏 One single, five double
£ ££
🍺 Own brews **Leith Hill Crooked Furrow, Tickety-Boo** and **Tallywhacker** plus guests including **Badger Tanglefoot, K&B Sussex, Ringwood Old Thumper, Timothy Taylor Landlord**
🍴 Lunch and dinner menu
💳 Credit cards accepted

The Woolpack Inn, Chilham

George Hotel

Stone Street, Cranbrook, Kent TN17 3HE
T 01580 713348   **F** 01580 715532
E georgehotelkent@aol.com
www.georgehoteluk.co.uk
Licensee: Sue Latchford
Directions: On A229

Historic hotel, in a tranquil Weald town, dating back to the 14th century, although much of the interior is 15th century. In 1573 Queen Elizabeth I was entertained in what is now the function room. The high-ceilinged main lounge bar is uncluttered with comfy sofa and armchairs blending with simple tables and chairs. A 34-place restaurant with an impressive fireplace adjoins the bar. There is also a small informal bar with Sky TV which provides a contrast to the peaceful bar. Close to Kent and East Sussex Steam Railway and Sissinghurst Castle. Children welcome.

🛏 Four double – some four-poster, four twin/single, some with Jacuzzi
£ ££££
🍺 **Harveys Best Bitter** plus three guests
🍴 Lunch, evening and snack menus
💳 Credit cards accepted

DORKING

Pilgrim

Station Road, Dorking, Surrey RH4 1HF
T/F 01306 889951
Licensee: John Bateman
Directions: 50 yards from south platform of
Dorking West station

Close to Denbies Vineyard, the largest in
England, Ranmore Common and Box Hill
this is very much a drinker's pub – although
you won't go hungry here either. It offers
reasonably priced accommodation within
an easy walk of Dorking's renowned antique
centre, West St. The single bar has a pool
table and darts down a couple of steps at one
end, and a restaurant area off to the side at
the other end. There is also a large garden.
The occasional guest beer will probably be
from one of the larger independent
breweries. The poet Keats finished writing
his Endymion while staying nearby.

🛏 Four single, one double
£ £
🍺 **Adnams Bitter, Fuller's London Pride,
Ringwood Old Thumper**
🍴 Lunch dinner and snack menus
💳 Credit cards accepted

EAST ASHLING

Horse and Groom

East Ashling, nr Chichester, West Sussex, PO18 9AX
T 01243 575339   F 01243 575560
E horseandgroomea@aol.com
www.horseandgroom.sageweb.co.uk
Licensee: Michael Martell
Directions: Take B2178 north west of Chichester.
Pub is about three miles from Chichester in the
village of East Ashling on the lefthand side

A building full of character, this 17th century
inn has separate oak-beamed en suite accommodation in a converted flint barn. The pub
has a flagstone floor, old settles and half panel
walls and is heated by a fine old commercial
range. Situated in a quiet rural setting, it is
only five minutes from Chichester and 10
minutes from Goodwood and the Downs.
Superb cuisine and wide selection of real ales.

🛏 Range of double/twin
£ £££
🍺 **Draught Bass, Harveys BB, Hop Back Summer
Lightning, Young's Bitter**
🍴 Lunch, evening and snack menus
💳 Credit cards accepted

EFFINGHAM

Sir Douglas Haig

The Street, Effingham, Surrey KT24 5LU
T 01372 456886   F 01372 450987
E sirdouglashaig@accommodating-inns.co.uk
www.accommodating-inns.co.uk
Licensee: Dorothy Randles

Situated in the pleasant village of Effingham
with easy access to the M25 and London,
this local inn offers pleasant accommodation
and good pub fare. Guildford, Epsom
Racecourse, Thorpe Park and Chessington
World of Adventures are all close-by.

🛏 Two double, four twin
£ ££££
🍺 **Gales HSB, GB, Butser**
🍴 Lunch, evening and snack menus
💳 Credit cards accepted

ELHAM

Rose and Crown

High Street, Elham, Canterbury, Kent, CT4 6TD
T 01303 840226   F 01303 840141
E info@roseandcrown.co.uk
www.roseandcrown.co.uk
Licensees: Mr and Mrs G McNicholas
Directions: B2065 – five minutes from M20, 10
minutes Channel Tunnel

The Rose & Crown is a free house offering a
range of cask ales, supplemented by an
extensive bar and à la carte menu offered in
the lounge bar or non smoking restaurant.
It is a cosy village pub popular with walkers
and diners, with real beams and comfortable
sofas. A preference for keeping locally
brewed beers, such as Hopdaemon, adds to
the attraction of this pub which is off the
beaten track. Log fires make it a warming
place on winter evenings. It is ideally placed
to visit Canterbury Cathedral, Dover Castle,

Ashford International (Eurostar) Station and John Aspinall's Wildlife Parks.

It offers six en suite guest bedrooms in the newly refurbished stable block.

🛏 Four double, one twin, one family
£ £££
🍺 **Hopdaemon Golden Braid, Greene King IPA** plus guests
🍴 Lunch, evening and snack menus
▭ Credit cards accepted

ESHER

Bear Inn

71 High Street, Esher, Surrey KT10 9RQ
T 01372 469786   **F** 01372 468378
E bearinn@youngs.co.uk
www.youngs.co.uk
Licensee: Roger Stern
Directions: Junction of A307/A244

An 18th century inn, the oldest in Esher, handy for Sandown Park racecourse and Hampton Court Palace and Claremont. Chessington World of Adventures is only 10 minutes drive away. One central bar serves this large pub, which still has the feel of several separate areas. The range of food is good and the quality excellent. There is a regular bus service outside to Claygate, Surbiton and Kingston-upon-Thames. There is a token operated car park for residents and pub-goers spending over £5, alongside the patio area.

🛏 Four double, two twin one single
£ ££££
🍺 **Young's Bitter, Special, Triple A** and seasonals
🍴 Lunch, evening and snack menus
▭ Credit cards accepted

FOREST ROW

Brambletye Hotel

The Square, Forest Row, East Sussex RH18 5EZ
T 01342 824144   **F** 01342 824833
E brambletyehotel@accommodating-inns.co.uk
www.accommodating-inns.co.uk
Licensees: Belinda Bradshaw and Janet Sladden

Situated in the centre of the picturesque village of Forest Row offering an historical atmosphere steeped with old world charm and hospitality. Recently undergone a complete refurbishment and can include amongst its list of many famous visitors, Sir Arthur Conan Doyle. Black Peter's Bar is the villagers' favourite meeting and eating place with its renowned lunchtime carvery, extensive à la carte menu and a range of award winning real ales. The Deerstalker restaurant has an excellent Table d'Hôte menu and an interesting selection of wines.

🛏 Nine doubles, nine twin, three single, one family
£ ££££
🍺 **Gales HSB, GB, Butser**
🍴 Lunch, evening and snack menus
▭ Credit cards accepted

Roebuck

Wych Cross, Forest Row, East Sussex RH18 5JL
T 01342 823811   **F** 01342 824790
E 6499@greeneking.co.uk
Directions: On A22 between East Grinstead and Eastbourne – close to J10 M23

A former 17th century country inn that has certainly not fallen from grace. Recently refurbished, it has a beautiful garden and patio areas where barbecues are held on balmy summer evenings. The Beagle bar has a deserved reputation for the quality of the Real Ale it sells. Forest Row is on the edge of the Royal Ashdown Forest, which is home to Winnie the Pooh. Brighton and its unforgettable lanes, and Royal Tunbridge Wells with its renowned antique shops are an easy drive away. Close by is the Bluebell Steam Railway and the exquisite Sheffield Park Garden and Hever Castle.

🛏 30 rooms
£ £££ single ££££
🍺 **Greene King IPA, Speckled Hen** occasional guests
🍴 Lunch, evening and snack menus
💳 Credit cards accepted

HALFWAY BRIDGE, Petworth

Halfway Bridge Inn

Halfway Bridge, Petworth, West Sussex GU28 9BP
T 01798 861281
E mail@thesussexpub.co.uk
www.thesussexpub.co.uk
Licensees: Simon and James Hawkins
Directions: On A272 midway between Medhurst and Petworth

You will never be hurried as you sit back and enjoy life in this almost perfect pub with its five open fires. There is no blaring music, no video games cacophony or one-armed bandit irritation. Just the gentle art of conversation, good food, great company and beers from several local brewhouses. There are eight en suite bedrooms in the newly converted Sussex barn. The menus are changed monthly and the blackboard specials daily. Everything is prepared freshly on the premises with ingredients sourced as locally as possible. Children over 10 are welcome in the restaurant and well-behaved dogs are welcome in the bar.

There are always four real ales to choose from at the Halfway Bridge Inn. There are three regular favourites and one guest which is normally chosen from one of the local independent brewers. There is a real cider on hand pump and a locally produced methode champenoise cyder, Gospel Green, by the champagne glass or by the bottle.

🛏 One twin, five double and two king-sized
£ £££
🍺 **Cheriton Brewhouse Pots Ale, Fuller's London Pride, Gales HSB** plus guests

🍴 Lunch, evening and snack menus
💳 Credit cards accepted

KINGSGATE

The Fayreness Hotel

Marine Drive, Kingsgate, Broadstairs, Kent CT10 3LG
T 01843 861103   **F** 01843 608750
E fayreness@thorleytaverns.com
www.thorleytaverns.com
Licensee: Mr Ross Coles
Directions: A299 Thanet Way, A28

Situated on the cliff's edge it has stunning views over Botany Bay, and its bar is the ideal place to enjoy it. Close-by is the North Foreland Lighthouse, Dreamland and Canterbury is a short drive away. Golfers can try a round at the Royal St George's Golf and North Foreland Golf Clubs before buying a round in the bar. Children welcome.

🛏 25 double, three twins, one single
£ Between ££-££££ depending on facilities
🍺 **Draught Bass, Webster's, Charles Wells Bombardier, Courage Directors, Young's Special**
🍴 Lunch, evening and snack menus
💳 Credit cards accepted

MICKLEHAM

Running Horses

Old London Road, Mickleham, Surrey RH5 6DU
T 01372 372279   **F** 01372 363004
E info@therunninghorses.co.uk
www.therunninghorses.co.uk
Licensees: Josie and Steve Slayford
Directions: on the B2209, off the A24 between Leatherhead and Dorking, five minutes from the M25 J9

Set in the picturesque village of Mickleham, Surrey. The Running Horses has been providing traditional English hospitality for over 400 years. Whilst retaining its 16th century character. The Running Horses boasts five recently refurbished rooms, named after famous racecourses, all well equipped with all the modern conveniences associated with a quality establishment.

It is ideally situated for touring the local countryside of Surrey and Kent and visiting many of the finest examples of historic castles, country homes and gardens, including many National Trust and English Heritage properties. Within a short drive one can see the "breath of fresh air" that is Boxhill with its outstanding views in all directions. The pub has two traditional bar areas, the main one dominated by a large inglenook. Meals can be taken there or in the restaurant which offers an extensive, high quality menu. The pub is convenient for Gatwick (20 minutes by car) and Heathrow (35 minutes).

🛏 Three double, one twin, one four-poster
£ ££££
🍺 **Fuller's London Pride, Adnams, Young's Bitter, Greene King Abbot**
🍴 Lunch, evening and snack menus
💳 Credit cards accepted

MIDHURST

The Swan Inn

Red Lion Street, Midhurst, West Sussex GU29 9PB
T/F 01730 812853
Licensees: Graham and Jenny Staveley
Directions: Village centre next to Spread Eagle Hotel

The small market town has many interesting features, including the Midhurst Walk, a fascinating collection of little shops, antiques, arts and crafts. One of the oldest pubs in Sussex, the Swan Inn stands in the Market Square. It is a friendly 16th century village centre pub with three double en suite rooms furnished to a high standard. Food is available every lunchtime and most evenings. Situated near Cowdray Park polo fields and golf course and only a 10 minute drive for horse racing and motor sport.

🛏 Three double
£ ££
🍺 Various real ales
🍴 Lunch, evening and snack menus
💳 Credit cards accepted

NEWCHAPEL

Blacksmiths Head

Newchapel Road, Newchapel,
Near Lingfield, Surrey RH7 6LE
T 01342 833697
Licensees: Cecelia Hall and David French
Directions: B2028 – east of A22

Within easy driving distance of Lingfield racecourse and near the imposing Mormon Temple, this pub was purpose built in 1924 on the site of a smithy. The Head in the name comes from the name of brothers who once owned it. The L shaped bar has a non smoking restaurant area off to the side. The restaurant menu and bar snacks are available in the main bar area and the garden.

The accommodation has recently been created above the pub and so has been decorated to a high standard. The plant lover's garden, created with a pond from wasteland at the back of the pub, is a testament to the owner's previous occupation as a landscape gardener. The pub is shut on Sunday evenings.

There are various attractions within 30 minutes such as Chartwell, Hever Castle, Penshurst Place, Chiddingstone Castle, Wakehurst Place, Nymans Gardens and the Bluebell Railway.

🛏 Two twins, one with private bathroom all other rooms, four double
£ ££
🍺 **Fuller's London Pride, Harveys BB**, guest beer (regularly changing guest, usually from a small independent brewery)
🍴 Lunch and evening menu, separate snack menu
💳 Credit cards accepted

RUDGWICK

Mucky Duck Inn

Tismans Common, Loxwood Road,
Rudgwick, West Sussex RH12 3BW
T 01403 822300
www.mucky-duck-inn.co.uk
Directions: From the A281, Horsham Road, take the turning to Loxwood adjacent to the BMW garage and the Fox Public House

A traditional Sussex country free-house pub /restaurant with superior en suite accommodation in a separate building. Family garden with children's play area and adult beer garden with giant chess board. A Cask Marque pub, it is open all day, every day for a wide selection of real ales, which are normally sold on a single barrel basis. It has one of the largest selections of single malt whiskeys in West Sussex to go with an extensive range of Havana cigars for those who are feeling extravagantly comfortable. Dogs on leads are welcome.

Only twenty-five minutes from Gatwick, the Mucky Duck Inn is ideally suited for an overnight stay prior to your morning flight, or to relax following a long day's travel. Recently built are six superior en suite rooms for overnight accommodation. Two rooms have bathrooms suited for wheelchair users. An infant's travel cot is available at a nominal fee.

🛏 Six twin/double
£ £££
🍺 Regular guests
🍴 Lunch evening and snack menus
💳 Credit cards accepted

SIDLOW BRIDGE

Three Horseshoes

Ironsbottom, Sidlow, Reigate, Surrey RH2 8PT
T 01293 862315   F 01293 862257
E shoes@sidlow.com
www.sidlow.com
Licensee: Brian Ridge
Directions: Off the A217 by the garage at Sidlow (between Reigate and Horley)

The Three Horseshoes Inn is a friendly, family owned and managed free house located in the quiet hamlet of Sidlow less than 10 minutes drive due north of Gatwick Airport. The Inn offers a virtually permanent beer festival with beers from Fuller's, Young's and Harvey's. The pub slogan is "best beers for miles around". It is a comfortable and traditional country inn. There are no electronic machines, just the noise of people talking. The landlord is,

rightly, extremely proud of his beer with the Fuller's London Pride being regarded as a local legend. As well as accommodation, a function room is also available.

🛏 Three double rooms
£ £££
🍺 **Fuller's London Pride**, **ESB**, **Harvey's Best**, **Young's Bitter** plus regular guest beers
🍴 Snack and full menu
💳 Credit cards accepted

STAINES

The Swan Hotel

The Hythe, Staines, Middlesex TW18 3JB
T 01784 452494   F 01784 461593
E swan.hotel@fullers.co.uk
www.fullers.co.uk
Licensee: Kevin Lole
Directions: Just south of Staines Bridge on the south bank overlooking the Thames, off the A308

On the banks of the Thames the Swan can offer budget or deluxe bedrooms, single, double/twin or family rooms. In the bar there are two roaring log fires in winter months. The River Suite, with its canopied bed, decor of pale yellow and blue and magnificent bay window overlooking the river, is perfect for a romantic break. It has two large comfortable bars, conservatory overlooking shaded river terrace and a large restaurant. The hotel is only minutes from the M25, M4 and M3, 12 miles west of London and only five miles from Heathrow. Nearby is Runnymede where the Magna Carta was signed, Windsor with its castle and parks and Eton. Three rooms have balconies where you can sit out and look out over the river.

🛏 Seven double, two twin, two family
£ ££££
🍺 **Fuller's London Pride**, **ESB** and seasonal ales
🍴 Lunch, evening and snack menus
💳 Credit cards accepted

Barley Mow

Tandridge Lane, Tandridge, Surrey RH8 9NJ
T 01883 713770
Licensees: Paul and Louise Hewett
Directions: ¾ mile South of the A25 between Godstone and Oxted

Hever Castle and Chartwell are within striking distance (just over the Kent border) of this welcoming country inn. Situated on the Greensand Way it has a wooden-floored bar catering for dogs and walkers. There's also a large restaurant area. The current licensees have been at the pub since November 2001 and are planning to expand their range of entertainment – quiz nights are already very popular.

🛏 One twin with shared bathroom and one double
£ £££
🍺 **Badger Best**, **Tanglefoot**, **King & Barnes Sussex** plus seasonal beers including **King & Barnes Mild** and **Badger Golden Champion**
🍴 Lunch, evening and snack menus
💳 Credit cards accepted

The Beacon

Tea Garden Lane, Rusthall,
Tunbridge Wells, Kent TN3 9JH
T 01892 524252   **F** 01892 534288
E beaconhotel@btopenworld.com
www.the-beacon.co.uk
Licensees: John and Di Cullen

Described as a comfortable and relaxing home from home which is set in Happy Valley. It has 17 acres of its own land and offers superb views of the Kent countryside. It is close to Hever Castle and Penshurst Place. The house Beacon was built in 1895 as the country home of Sir Walter Harris, a former Lieutenant of the City of London.

🛏 Four double, two single
£ £££
🍺 **Harveys Best Bitter**, **Timothy Taylor Landlord**
🍴 Lunch, evening and snack menus
💳 Credit cards accepted

The Grove Ferry Inn

Upstreet, Nr Canterbury, Kent CT3 4BP
T 01227 860302   **F** 01227 860929
E groveferry@shepherdneame.co.uk
www.shepherd-neame.co.uk

Famous for its location, the Grove Ferry is situated by the side of the Great River Stour and is so named because there used to be a

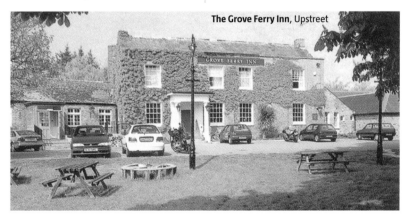
The Grove Ferry Inn, Upstreet

hand drawn ferry until it was replaced by a bridge in the 1960s. The pub has recently been refurbished and has six en suite bedrooms. Upstreet is a popular area for fishing, walking and bird watching and it is also conveniently close to the cathedral city of Canterbury and the coastal towns of Margate, Ramsgate and Broadstairs.

🛏 Six double/twin
£ £££
🍺 **Shepherd Neame** range
🍴 Lunch, evening and snack menus
💳 Credit cards accepted

Harveys Brewery, Lewes (old and new brewery towers 1881 and 1985)

South of England

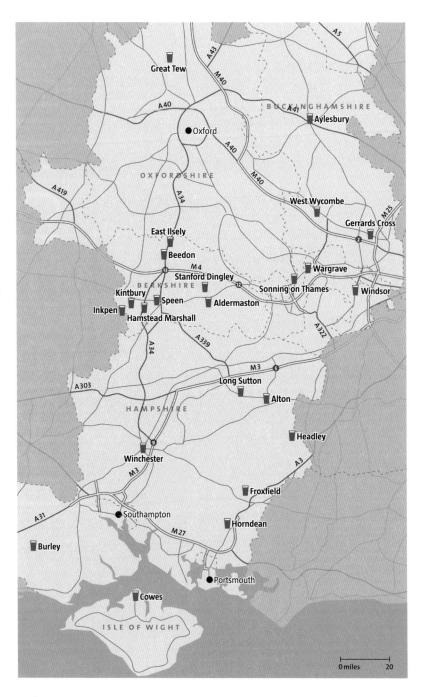

The region is divided into three British Tourist Authority areas – Thames and Chilterns Country, Rural Southern England and the South Coast.

Each is different and each will offer the beer lover a journey of taste and experience.

Thames and Chilterns Country, just on London's doorstep is dominated by the Royal River Thames and the Chiltern Hills. Royal pomp and tradition abound – Windsor with its famous Castle, Eton College and the Dreaming Spires of Oxford's colleges will delight lovers of history and heritage. Some of the most famous pubs in Britain are to be found in Thames and Chilterns Country – as are many stately homes linked to a host of celebrated names in the country's history

Real ale travellers should seek out beers from the West Berkshire Brewery and marvel at the skill of one of the country's burgeoning number of microbrewers.

Rural Southern England is renowned for its history and heritage connections; from the medieval cities of Winchester and Salisbury with their famous cathedrals to stately homes and houses; from the grand Highclere Castle, near Newbury and Wilton House, near Salisbury to the smaller properties with their literary connections such as Jane Austen's House, in Chawton near Alton and Thomas Hardy's cottage, near Dorchester. Explore the World Heritage site of Stonehenge, near Salisbury.

On the South Coast you are never far away from England's maritime heritage in Portsmouth, Southampton and Gosport. Portsmouth is the flagship of maritime England, home to some of the nation's most famous historic ships, and the story comes right up to date in the newest museum – Action Stations. Ancient forts and castles line the coastline, many with royal connections such as Portchester Castle near Portsmouth, Carisbrooke Castle on the Isle of Wight and Portland Castle near Weymouth. Also on the Isle of Wight is Queen Victoria's holiday home, Osborne House. Relive the golden era of the transatlantic liners Queen Mary and Queen Elizabeth in Southampton or discover the history of Naval Firepower and Submarines at Gosport.

Many glorious beers can be found too. Gales in Horndean,

Hampshire has been brewing good honest ale for more than 150 years, and it is possible to tour the brewery on selected days during the summer months.

Visitors to the New Forest can try beers from one of the country's most successful newcomers to brewing the delightful Ringwood Brewery, Ringwood, Hampshire. It is only just over 25 years old but has moved from being a mini to being a major regional player in the brewing industry.

ALDERMASTON

Hinds Head

Wasing Lane, Aldermaston, Berkshire RG7 4LX
T 011 8971 2194   F 011 89/1 4511
E hindshead@accommodating-inns.co.uk
www.accommodating-inns.co.uk
Licensees: Peter and Colleen Cook

Nestled in old Aldermaston village. Dating back to the 17th century, the brewery which closed in 1912 is now a feature of great interest having been sympathetically restored during recent renovations.

🛏 11 doubles, one twin, two singles
£ ££££
🍺 Gales HSB, GB, Butser
🍴 Lunch, evening and snack menus
💳 Credit cards accepted

ALTON

French Horn

The Butts, Alton, Hampshire GU34 1RT
T 01420 832669
Licensee: Colin Dennis
Directions: Close to A31 junction, west of town centre

Consistently popular historic pub, renowned for its food. It overlooks the medieval archery butts, now a public open space. A warming, roaring fire on winter nights lights up a tankard collection on the beams. There is an unusual fish tank and outside several grassed drinking areas. A skittle alley is adjacent and an annual old fashioned cricket match is held on Father's Day.

Regulars corner near the fire is a welcoming and eccentric spot. No children under 14 allowed in main building. The garden boasts good views of steam trains on the Watercress Line, a 10 mile rail line that links Alton with Alresford. Opened in 1865 it originally carried watercress for sale in London. The train stops at Four Marks the highest station in southern England.

🛏 Two double
£ £££
🍺 Gales HSB, Young's Bitter, Courage Best, Ushers seasonal beers, Bass
🍴 Lunch, evening and snack menus
💳 Credit cards accepted

AYLESBURY

Aristocrat

1–3 Wendover Road, Aylesbury, Buckinghamshire HP21 7SZ
T 01296 415366
Directions: On the gyratory system at the end of Walton Street, A413

A Fuller's pub within walking distance of the the town centre, the Aristocrat has a good atmosphere which makes it popular with all ages. There is a lot of social activity here: regular pub games, discos, karaoke and live music. It is also a frequent stop for business people, who enjoy the hearty, traditional breakfasts and other meals which are very good value and include vegetarian options. A full English breakfast is provided. For tourists, it is convenient for the National Trust's splendid Waddesdon Manor and the Chiltern Brewery at Terrick (both 15 minutes drive). The latter has a small museum and shop selling its own beer-related products. The comfortable bedrooms have tea/coffee making facilities, TV and share two bathrooms. Children can be accommodated. There is a public car park behind the pub.

🛏 Two twin
£ ££
🍺 Fuller's London Pride, ESB, seasonal beers
🍴 Snacks and meals daily, lunchtime and Monday-Thursday evening
💳 Credit cards accepted

BEEDON

Langley Hall

Oxford Road, World's End,
Beedon, Newbury RG20 8SA
T 01635 248332   **F** 01635 248571
Licensees: Simon Liquorish
Directions: West of A34, M4 J13

Once a small roadhouse on the former main road, the pub has undergone several name and management changes in recent years, but has now settled down as a busy local. The large single bar is furnished with a modern minimalist décor. Set away from the clamour of the M4 and Chieveley Services it is a perfect place to enjoy a pint of the locally brewed West Berkshire Good Old Boy. It has three comfortable, clean bedrooms and in the style of the bar, they are simply furnished. The pub is ideally placed to visit Donnington Castle, Newbury Showground and the Berkshire Ridgeway.

🛏 Three double
£ ££
🍺 **West Berkshire Good Old Boy**
🍴 Lunch, evening and snack menus
💳 Credit cards accepted

BURLEY

White Buck Inn

Bisterne Close, Burley, Hampshire BH24 4AT
T 01425 402264   **F** 01425 403588
E whitebuckinn@accommodating-inns.co.uk
www.accommodating-inns.co.uk
Licensees: David and Lynn Reed

Large, detached country inn set within the heart of the New Forest on the outskirts of Burley. Close to all local amenities, the White Buck Inn offers the guest a very good location for walking and touring together with excellent food and accommodation with a friendly and inviting atmosphere. Ample seating at the bar to relax where a wide selection of bar meals are available along with a variety of meals to choose in the dining room.

🛏 Seven double, two twin
£ ££££
🍺 **Gales HSB, GB, Butser**
🍴 Lunch, evening and snack menus
💳 Credit cards accepted

COWES

The Fountain

High Street, Cowes, Isle of Wight PO31 7AW
T 01983 292397**T**   **F** 01983 299554
www.oldenglish.co.uk
Licensee: Andrew McCullagh
Directions: On the High Street, overlooking the Solent at the mouth of the Medina, adjacent to the High Speed Cat passenger ferry terminal, in the heart of Cowes

The Fountain is a traditional period inn located in the heart of West Cowes. It overlooks the Medina and has beautiful harbour views from the patio. Recently refurbished, the inn is a haven for yachting enthusiasts, especially during Cowes Week and one resident has described the beer as always being perfect. All 20 comfortable en suite bedrooms have full facilities including a CD player. Large feature rooms are also available. The Fountain Hotel is an ideal base to explore the sights of the Isle of Wight. The Needles and Blackgang Chine are nearby as is Queen Victoria's Osborne House.

🛏 10 single, six double, three twin and one executive
£ £££ ££££ single
🍺 **Greene King Abbot, IPA**
🍴 Lunch, evening and snack menus
💳 Credit cards accepted

EAST ILSLEY

Star Inn

High Street, East Ilsley, Berkshire RG20 7LE
T 01635 281215   **F** 01635 281107
E kimrichstar@aol.com
www.starinnhotel.co.uk
Licensees: Kim and Richard Vellender
Directions: ½ mile off A34, seven miles north of Newbury

A basic, simple, split level bar, popular with the locals. The Star likes to offer the visitor comfortable shelter and cosy hospitality as it has done for centuries. The bar offers refreshment and a chance to unwind next to the cosy log fire, and a good night's sleep is assured in the comfortable accommodation. The Star is an ideal spot for the business person and visitor alike, positioned in the heart of the rolling Berkshire Downs; the commercial centres of Reading, Newbury and Swindon are within very easy distance. If it is a break from the stresses and strains of modern life that you seek, then this is the perfect spot for a getaway. Peace and tranquillity can be found on the ancient Ridgeway and along the banks of the meandering River Thames.

- 🛏 Three single, two twin, four double
- £ ££ ££££ single
- 🍺 **Fuller's London Pride** and guest ales
- 🍴 Lunch, evening and snack menus
- 💳 Credit cards accepted

FROXFIELD

Trooper Inn

Alton Lane, Froxfield, Hampshire GU32 1BD
T 01730 827293   F 01730 827103
E info@trooperinn.com
www.trooperinn.com
Licensee: Mr H Matini
Directions: From the A32, five miles south of Alton, take the turning for Froxfield and High Cross

If the best part of travelling is getting there then this remote free house is worth the trip. Situated at the highest point in Hampshire, in the heart of the countryside, the Trooper is one of the county's finest pubs. The first

bricks of this charming inn are reputed to have been laid in at the beginning of the 17th century, and in the 400 years since, the building has had a chequered history. At the turn of the last century, it was a busy stopover on what was then the main route to London, as well as the inn of choice for local hunting parties. At the outset of the First World War it is said that the pub was used as a recruiting centre for troops, although it is not known whether this was the source of the Trooper name. Since the end of the Great War, the Trooper has been home to a friendly ghost. Local folklore tells that he rides across the fields opposite the inn. A hotel has been recently built alongside the pub.

Each of the eight en suite rooms has its own individual character – they are each named after a local village or landmark, and feature paintings specially commissioned by local artist Sally Maltby.

- 🛏 Seven double, one twin – with disabled access
- £ £££
- 🍺 **Ringwood Best** plus three guests
- 🍴 Lunch, evening and snack menus
- 💳 Credit cards accepted

GERRARDS CROSS

The Ethorpe

Packhorse Road, Gerrards Cross, Buckinghamshire SL9 8HX
T 01753 882038   F 01753 887012
Licensee: Peter Perpetuini
Directions: M40 J2

Traditional inn with log fires, a short drive from the M40. Extensive menu including snacks, fresh fish, and chef's daily specials. On a sunny day it is possible to sit out in the terraced garden. Ideal base for anyone visiting the Hell Fire caves at Wycombe or Cleveden. Children welcome providing they are well-behaved. Unusually for a pub so far south it sells Harviestoun Schiehallion a Scottish cask lager, brewed using a lager yeast and Hersbrucker hops.

🛏 34
£ ££££
🍺 **Harviestoun Schiehallion**, **Courage Directors** and **Best**
🍴 Lunch, evening and snack menus
💳 Credit cards accepted

GREAT TEW

Falkland Arms

Great Tew, Nr Chipping Norton, Oxfordshire OX7 4BD
T 01608 683653   **F** 01608 683656
E sjcourage@btconnect.com
www.falklandarms.org.uk
Licensees: Paul Barlow-Heal and Sarah-Jane Courage

The once derelict Great Tew now stands proud again, with weekenders clamouring to buy the cottages in this classic Cotswold village. This award winning, idyllic 16th century pub is built with golden Cotswold stone and swathed with roses and wisteria. Inside simple wooden furniture and flagstones create a comfortable atmosphere with drinkers and diners squeezing into the comfortable settles, warmed on colder days by the roaring fire in an inglenook fireplace. The food is good, the beer even better and if you like malt whiskies – get a friend to drive you home or even better book into one of the bedrooms. Clay pipes and snuff are on sale at the bar. It has eight hand pumps and one real cider.

🛏 Five double including two four-posters
£ £££
🍺 **Wadworth Henry's IPA**, **6X** and seasonal plus guests
🍴 Lunch and evening menus, snack lunchtime only
💳 Credit cards accepted

HAMSTEAD MARSHALL

White Hart

Kintbury Road, Hamstead Marshall, Newbury RG20 0HW
T 01488 658201   **F** 01488 657192
E info@thewhitehart-inn.co.uk
Licensee: Mr Aromando
Directions: On Kintbury Road, four miles from Newbury

Originally attached to the Craven Estate, this 18th century inn has a single, comfortable oak-beamed bar. Most customers are there to enjoy the highly praised restaurant which specialises in real Italian food. The pub has a tranquil, walled garden which is beautiful on summer evenings. The six bedrooms are in a converted barn.

🛏 Two single, one twin, three double
£ ££££
🍺 **Wadworth 6X, Hook Norton Best Bitter**
💳 Credit cards accepted

HEADLEY

Hollybush

High Street, Headley, Hampshire GU35 8PP
T 01428 712211   **F** 01428 714889
E thehollybush@aol.com
Licensee: Tony Bishop
Directions: Between A325 and A3

Close to the Devils Punchbowl, this superb rural inn is off the beaten track but worth seeking out through the country lanes. A warm welcome is assured at the one central bar which is surrounded by four contrasting areas, designed to suit all tastes. The long lounge is decorated with sporting trophies, water jugs above the bar and Victorian pictures on the walls. There is a bar billiards table in another area and a dining area to the rear which serves good value food. Barbecues are held in the garden during summer months. All a good village pub should be! Children welcome in bars until 9pm.

🛏 One twin, one single
£ ££
🍺 **Greene King IPA, Courage Best, Gales HSB**
🍽 Lunch, evening and snack menus
💳 Credit cards accepted

HORNDEAN

Ship & Bell

London Road, Horndean, Hampshire PO8 0BZ
T 023 9259 2107   **F** 023 9257 1644
E shipandbell@accommodating-inns.co.uk
www.accommodating-inns.co.uk
Licensees: Paul and Sarah Marshall

Located in the centre of Horndean next to Gales Brewery, which is also Victorian in origin, this pub takes great pride in personal service, offering guests a friendly atmosphere in which to stay combining comfort with the many facilities on offer. It is 20 minutes from Portsmouth and 25 minutes from Chichester.

🛏 Eight doubles, four twins, one family, one single
£ ££££
🍺 **Gales HSB, GB, Butser, Festival Mild**
🍽 Lunch, evening and snack menus
💳 Credit cards accepted

INKPEN

Crown & Garter

Inkpen Common, Hungerford, Berkshire RG17 9QR
T 01488 668325
www.crownandgarter.com
Licensees: Gillian Hern
Directions: Three miles south of A4 Kintbury

Friendly village local, given a fresh lease of life by new owners, who incorporated an excellent restaurant offering an interesting and thoughtful menu at pub prices. The bedrooms are in a newly built, single story quadrangle surrounding a beautiful garden complete with a fish pond. There is a thriving local trade, and the bar is still the central part of the business selling a full range of West Berkshire beers. It is the West Berkshire CAMRA Branch Pub of the Year for 2002. The pub is close to Coombe Gibbet, Walbury Hill and Hungerford Antiques. Children welcome.

🛏 Eight rooms, single, double and twin to order
£ £££ ££££ single
🍺 **West Berkshire Mr Chubbs Lunchtime Bitter, Good Old Boy** and seasonal ales
🍽 Lunch, evening and snack menus – no food Sunday, Monday evenings
💳 Credit cards accepted

The Swan Inn

Craven Road, Lower Green, Inkpen,
Hungerford, Berkshire RG17 9DX
T 01488 668326   **F** 01488 668306
E enquiries@theswaninn-organics.co.uk
www.theswaninn-organics.co.uk
Licensees: Bernard and Mary Harris

Situated in an area of outstanding natural beauty and good walking country. It is approximately one mile from Coombe Gibbet which is said to be the highest point in Southern England. The Swan is a very attractive 17th century inn, with old beams, which has been extended by Mr and Mrs Harris and now consists of a pub, with accommodation, an organic butchery and an organic farm shop. Outside there is a terraced area with tables and bench seats. The Swan has a warm, welcoming atmosphere with two bar areas (one non-smoking). At each end of the main bar there is a fireplace and another in the second bar area. These open fires give the pub a cosy and inviting atmosphere on cold, dismal winter days.

A good selection of organic bar meals is available. There is also a games/darts room off the main bar area. They have a restaurant, The Cygnet Restaurant, which serves a varied à la carte, mostly organic, menu. The licensees also run an organic beef farm nearby and use beef from the farm in the restaurant and bar meals. The licensees are members of the Campaign for Real Food. The hotel has 10 en suite bedrooms including family rooms and a bridal suite.

One single, four double, three twin, two family
£ £££ single ££££
Butts, Hook Norton, Blackguard
Lunch, evening and snack menus
Credit cards accepted

Dundas Arms

53 Station Road, Kintbury, Berkshire RG17 9UT
T 01488 658263   **F** 01488 658568
E info@dundasarms.co.uk
www.dundasarms.co.uk
Licensee: David Dalzell Piper
Directions: Off A4, by Kintbury Railway Station

A canal side pub, which overlooks Kintbury lock at the point it joins the River Kennet, it is named after the first chairman of the Kennet and Avon Canal, Lord Dundas. The white-painted, late Georgian pub is relaxing even on busy sunny days when the waterside tables soon fill up.

The Dundas Arms offers a balanced mix of a late 18th century village pub with comfortable rooms, all en suite and a fine restaurant with an extensive wine list. It has just five rooms, all of them spacious and comfortable with telephones and en suite bathrooms. Every one of them looks out onto the River Kennet, and the trees beyond. The rooms are on the ground floor in the old stable block where the barge horses were originally housed.

Tranquillity rules here, less than an hour and a half from London. The restaurant is like a French auberge, a comfortable setting in which to enjoy local produce imaginatively cooked and enjoy beers from Butts and West Berkshire. Children welcome.

🛏 Five double
£ ££££
🍺 **Butts Barbus, Greene King Morland Original, West Berkshire Good Old Boy**
▭ Credit cards accepted

LONG SUTTON

Four Horseshoes

The Street, Long Sutton, Hampshire RG29 1TA
T 01256 862488   F 01256 862488
E tony.brooks@bun.com
www.fourhorseshoes.com
Licensee: Tony Brooks
Directions: Three miles south of junction 5 M3

Wonderful rural retreat, just east of the attractive village centre, next to Lord Wandsworth College and looking out on open downland. It stands on an ancient trackway, the Harroway; the landlord found iron-age remains whilst laying the petanque terrain. The bar is open plan but retains all the traditional elements you might expect from a good country pub: a good atmosphere, cosy warmth of an open fire in winter with rustic beams and brasses. The landlord's cooking has a good reputation. The guest beers always include a mild (the landlord's favourite tipple). Camping at the pub by arrangement or en suite accommodation available. Children welcome in the conservatory.

🛏 Two twins, two singles
£ ££
🍺 **Gales Butser, Gales HSB**, two/three guest ales – one always a mild
🍴 Lunch, evening and snack menus
▭ Credit cards accepted

SONNING ON THAMES

Bull Inn

High Street, Sonning on Thames, Berkshire RG4 6UP
T 011 8969 3901   F 011 8969 1057
E bullinn@accommodating-inns.co.uk
www.accommodating-inns.co.uk
Licensees: Dennis and Christine Mason

A delightful country inn located in a picture postcard setting in Sonning village. This 16th century timbered property boasts oak beams, winter log fires and a recommendation from Jerome K Jerome who mentioned the pub in his novel *Three Men in a Boat*. Henley on Thames, Reading, Maidenhead, Windsor are all close-by.

🛏 Seven doubles including one four-poster
£ ££££
🍺 **Gales HSB, GB, Butser**
🍴 Lunch, evening and snack menus
▭ Credit cards accepted

SPEEN, Newbury

Hare & Hounds

Bath Road, Speen, Newbury, Berkshire RG14 1QY
T 01635 521152   F 01635 47708
Licensee: Tony Turner
Directions: on A4, two miles from M4 J13

A 17th century, former coaching inn now a hotel with bar open to non-residents. It has a single split level bar with adjacent dining room. Beer from the local award winning Butts Brewery is always available. Conveniently located two miles from M4 Junction 13 it offers easy access to London, Bath and Windsor. An ideal place to stay, if visiting Newbury Racecourse or Donnington Castle. Children welcome to stay but not in bars.

🛏 Three single, three twin, two triple, 21 double, one family
£ £££ ££££ single
🍺 **Butts Traditional Bitter, Arkells 3B, Fuller's London Pride**
▭ Credit cards accepted

STANFORD DINGLEY

The Bull

Stanford Dingley, Reading, Berkshire RG7 6LS
T 01189 744409 **F** 01189 745249
E admin@thebullatstanforddingley.co.uk
www.thebullatstanforddingley.co.uk
Licensees: Robert Archard and Robin Walker
Directions: M4 J12, two miles north of A4

A creaky, low-ceilinged pub, which is sadly
one of a dying breed. This 12th-century two-
bar pub is in an idyllic village. The pub was
recently threatened with closure, but now
under a new owner it is expanding and a
restaurant and letting rooms have been
added. The bars have tiled and wooden
floors and simple wooden furniture. One
bar displays ancient wattle and daub walls.
It was the West Berkshire CAMRA Pub of the
Year in 1999 and is known for being one of
the few places in England where the ancient
game of Ring the Bull can still be played.
It is close to the Pang Valley and Wyld Court
Rainforest. Children welcome.

- Three twin, two double, one family
- £ £££
- **West Berkshire Skiff**, **Good Old Boy** and seasonals
- Lunch, evening and snack menus
- Credit cards accepted

WARGRAVE

Bull

High Street, Wargrave, Berkshire RG10 8DD
T 0118 940 3120 **F** 0118 940 1362
E jw@thebullatwargrave.co.uk
www.thebullatwargrave.co.uk
Licensee: Jayne Worrall
Directions: on the A321 by the central traffic lights

A large, unspoilt, genuine 15th-century
former coaching inn with a wealth of
exposed oak beams and two inglenooks.
Traditionally furnished, with an abundance
of brasses, the Bull attracts customers from
far and wide for its meals which are served
in the bar or the more intimate restaurant.

The beer is so popular that an extra set of
handpumps had to be installed. Only one of
the bedrooms has en suite facilities, but each
has a hand basin, plus colour TV and tea/
coffee making facilities. An extra bed can be
put in one of the double rooms for a child.
Residents can enjoy the secluded, vine-clad
patio and walled garden to the rear.

Wargrave is a pleasant Thameside village
and there are plenty of tourist attractions
within easy reach, such as formal gardens,
stately homes, Legoland and of course
Windsor Castle is only about 10 miles away.

- Two single, two double, twin
- £ £££
- **Brakspear Bitter**, **Special**, seasonal beers
- Snacks and meals daily, lunchtime and evening
- Credit cards accepted

WINCHESTER

Wykeham Arms

75 Kingsgate Street, Winchester,
Hampshire SO23 9PE
T 01962 853834 **F** 01962 854411
E Doreen@thewykehamarms@freeserve.co.uk
Licensee: Peter Miller
Directions: Between the college and cathedral –
M3 J9, via St Cross Street

The pub's Nelson's and Bishop's bars are a
cornucopia of memorabilia including a
mitre, old school canes, beer tankards and a

multitude of framed pictures and prints. Its attractive old furniture, much of it passed on from Winchester College, adds to its appeal. The food, which has won many accolades, is superb and imaginative, and the service is excellent.

Above the pub are some small but stylish bedrooms; opposite is a 16th-century annexe which includes a double suite and overlooks Winchester College Chapel. All the rooms (in both buildings) have en suite bathrooms, colour TV, mini bar and tea/coffee making facilities. It also has a secluded rear garden and a delightful courtyard. Parking can be difficult. Close-by is the home of Jane Austen, Winchester Cathedral and the ruins of Wolvesey Palace

🛏 Two single, two twin, six double, one double suite in annexe
£ ££££
🍺 **Gales HSB**, **GB** and **Butser** plus seasonal ales
🍴 Lunchtime meals
💳 Credit cards accepted

Trooper

97 St Leonards Road, Windsor, Berkshire SL4 3BZ
T 01753 670123   **F** 01753 670124
E trooper@accommodating-inns.co.uk
www.accommodating-inns.co.uk
Licensee: Joanne Richardson and Stuart Bailey

A 19th century coaching inn full of charm and character. Ideally situated in the centre of Windsor within walking distance of the castle and other attractions

🛏 Five double, one triple, one family, one single
£ ££££
🍺 **Gales HSB**, **GB**, **Butser**
🍴 Lunch, evening and snack menus
💳 Credit cards accepted

George & Dragon

West Wycombe, Buckinghamshire HP14 3AB
T 01494 464414   **F** 01494 462432
Licensee: Mr P. Todd
Directions: In the village centre

The substantial brick-built George and Dragon is owned by the National Trust – as is the whole village! Overlooking the village is West Wycombe Park (also NT), a Palladian house, set in landscaped gardens, designed in the 18th century for Sir Francis Dashwood. Another nearby attraction (not NT) are the West Wycombe caves. Also within easy reach are Marlow (5 miles), Henley (12 miles) and Bekonscot Model Village (a favourite with children, 6 miles).

The former coaching inn mainly dates from the 18th century, but some parts of the building are nearly 600 years old, so it is not surprising that it is said to be haunted. This doesn't deter most visitors who consider it just adds to the charm of an already characterful hotel.

Each of its eight en suite rooms is furnished differently, and two have four-poster beds; all rooms have tea/coffee making facilities and colour TV. Special weekend rates apply. Pets can be accommodated. The food is recommended.

🛏 One single, five doubles, one twin-bedded, one family room
£ ££ (single ££££)
🍺 **Courage Best Bitter**, guest beer
🍴 Snacks and meals daily, lunchtime and evening
💳 Credit cards accepted

South West England

Bath
Bristol
Cornwall and The Isles of Scilly
Devon
Dorset
West Gloucestershire
Somerset
Wiltshire

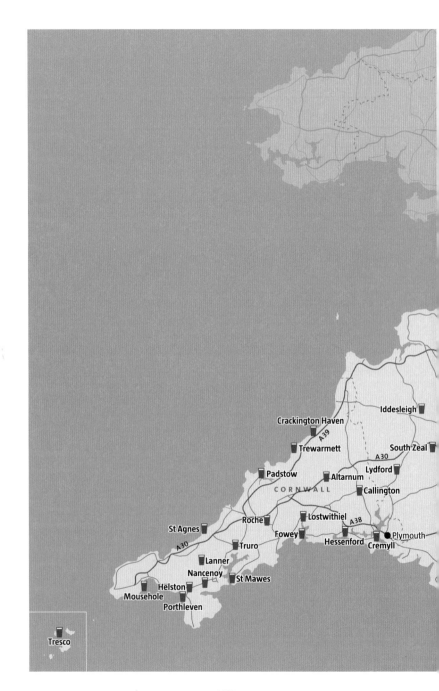

THE SOUTH WEST OF ENGLAND is a beer-lover's paradise with more independent breweries than any other part of the country. It stretches from Gloucestershire and the Cotswolds down to Dorset in the south, and west along the south west peninsula as far as Lands End in Cornwall.

It includes the wide open spaces of Dartmoor and Exmoor, picturesque villages with thatched cottages nestling in amongst rolling hills, the Roman city of Bath, Stonehenge, and a magnificent and varied coastline dotted with fishing villages, seaside resorts, and 600 miles of coastal footpath.

The World Heritage Site of Bath is home to Abbey Ales, the first brewery in the city for more than 40 years, and the beers from it are only sold within a 20-mile radius. The nearby harbourside city of Bristol is famous for superb architecture, museums, festivals, fine dining, great shopping and the city centre Smiles Brewery. A traditional tower brewery, which was founded in 1977, it has a brewery shop and offers tours by arrangement.

The Eden project in Cornwall has turned the county into a year-round place for tourists to visit. Nearby is the St Austell Brewery Visitor Centre which offers twice daily tours and a chance to buy the company's bottle conditioned beer.

Newton Abbot, Devon is the home of Tuckers Maltings, England's only traditional floor maltings open to the public. Tours of the maltings and the Teignworthy Brewery happen every day from Easter to October

Dorset and the New Forest offer an oasis of rural tranquillity, breathtaking heritage coastline, a wealth of thriving market towns and idyllic villages, and a handful of lively resorts and busy maritime harbours. The old Devenish Brewery in Weymouth, Dorset has been turned into the Brewers Quay and Timewalk. It contains speciality shops and a museum with the old brewing vessels still in place. The Quay micro-brewery can also be seen.

The Cotswolds is famous for its coloured stone villages, idyllic pubs and the Donnington Brewery near Stowe on the Wold, which is rarely open to the public. Its beers can be found in 15 tied pubs and some freehouses in the area.

The Wiltshire town of Devizes is the home of the Wadworth Brewery and its award winning Shire horses which can be seen in their stables opposite the brewery most weekday afternoons. The horses are still used to deliver beers locally including Henry's Original IPA, 3.6 per cent ABV, a beer rarely found outside Wadworth's own pubs.

ALTARNUN

Rising Sun

Altarnun, Launceston, Cornwall PL15 7SN
T 01566 86332
Directions: Seven miles west of Launceston on the A30, turn off at sign for Altarnun and continue on this road for one mile towards Camelford. The inn is in view 400 yards after the T junction

Originally a farmhouse dating from the 16th century, this friendly pub retains many original features; there are two small rooms off the main bar area for pool players and diners. It is 600 metres from the nearest building making it a pleasant retreat from modern urban life There are generally four ever-varying ales, with five at weekends and up to six in summer. Legend has it that the front wall collapsed when a previous landlord dug out the pub cellar.

Camping is in the pub grounds. Dogs are welcome but look out for the pub cat! There is a very limited bus service to/from Launceston in daytime, Mon-Fri, from Altarnun village, nearly 2km/20+ min walk away. Tintagel Castle and coastal walks are nearby. Children are welcome.

🛏 Two double, one twin, one family (sleeps three)
£ £
🍺 Range of guest ales
🍴 Lunch, evening and snack menus
💳 Credit cards accepted

AYLBURTON

The George Inn & Millingbrook Lodge

High Street, Aylburton, Lydney,
Gloucestershire GL15 6DE
T 01594 842163
www.millingbrooklodge.com/TheGeorgeInn.htm
Licensees: Gillian Dennis and Derek Smallman
Directions: Centre of village on A48

Situated on the main road of the village, this old, established inn retains a two-bar layout. Popular with local and visiting CAMRA members for its four real ales – two ever present and two regularly changing guest ales – it has a comfortable restaurant with an interesting menu of good pub food and daily specials.

The well appointed en suite accommodation of seven doubles and seven twin rooms – two of which have disabled facilities – is situated in a beautifully refurbished building of traditional local stone next to the pub. Facilities include TV and tea/coffee making equipment. Children are most welcome.

On the edge of the ancient primeval Forest of Dean, the pub makes an ideal base for visiting the many nearby castles, the beautiful Wye valley and the Forest of Dean Railway which has a regular steam passenger service.

🛏 Seven double, seven twin
£ Price band: ££
🍺 **Cotswold Way** and **Charles Wells Bombardier** and two guests
🍴 Lunch, evening and snack menus
💳 Credit cards accepted

BECKINGTON

The Woolpack Inn

2 Warminster Road, Beckington,
Nr Bath, Somerset BA11 6SP
T 01373 831244   F 01373 831223
www.oldenglish.co.uk
Licensee: John Farrell
Directions: A36 from Bath, turn right at junction with A361. Follow road into village. Hotel is on left

In the heart of the historic Somerset village of Beckington you can find The Woolpack

Inn. Just ten miles south of Bath, this is a perfect place to stay if you want to explore Somerset and North Wiltshire but also offers a superb restaurant providing excellent food and a marvellous quality of service.

The 16th century stone-built coaching inn has a friendly main bar, complete with roaring fire in winter months and offers a relaxed atmosphere in which to sample traditional English beers or perhaps choose a bottle from the carefully selected wine list. The pub has 11 en suite bedrooms including two four-posters and a family room. The surrounding area is steeped in history providing a host of attractions that include stone circles and ancient barrows.

🛏 11 including two four-posters and a family room
£ £££ ££££ single
🍺 **Greene King IPA** and **Abbot**
🍴 Lunch and evening menus
💳 Credit cards accepted

BEER

The Anchor Inn

Beer, Nr Seaton, Devon EX12 3ET
T 01297 20386 **F** 01297 24474
www.oldenglish.co.uk
Licensees: Dennis & Julie Kerswell and Graham king
Directions: From A3052 take B3074 into Beer. Inn is on the sea front

Down in Devon, there's a little village and the angels call it Beer. The Anchor Inn, which has been refurbished during the winter, overlooks the sea in this pretty seaside village built around a small cove on the south coast of East Devon. The bars and the restaurant specialise in local seafood but offer a wide range of other dishes too.

The cosy bars have open fires on cooler days, and the cliff top beer garden is an ideal place to enjoy a glass of real beer.

The eight bedrooms are all attractively decorated and several have sea views. Superb cliff-top walks surround the village and fishing trips are available from the beach – a natural sun-trap. Golf and horse riding are all offered locally.

🛏 Eight
£ £££ ££££ single
🍺 **Greene King IPA** and **Abbot**
🍴 Lunch, evening and snack menus
💳 Credit cards accepted

The Dolphin Hotel

Beer, Nr Seaton, Devon EX12 3EQ
T/F 01297 20068
Licensee: L Gibbs

The couple who recommended the Dolphin so liked it that they extended their stay from one night to 13 and they plan to go again. A one room bar very popular with locals, which has delicious food and great beer. The freehouse is contained in a Grade II listed building that is situated 100 yards from the beach. As part of the complex there is an antique centre including Beer Collectables and Courtyard Curios, catering for all tastes from bric-a-brac to quality antiques.

Stone from the local quarry has been prized for centuries. Soft and easy to carve when newly quarried it hardens quickly on exposure to air. Beer Head, a magnificent chalk promontory, can be easily reached by footpath.

🛏 20 rooms
£ £
🍺 **Draught Bass**, **Cotleigh Tawny** and **Barn Owl**
🍴 Lunch, evening and snack menus
💳 Credit cards not accepted

BOURTON

White Lion Inn

High Street, Bourton, Dorset SP8 5AT
T 01747 840866 **F** 01747 841529
E whitelioninn@bourtondorset.fsnet.co.uk

Licensees: Michael and Scarlett Senior
Directions: Just off A303

Built in 1723, a traditional English pub with beams, flagstone floors and inglenook fireplace set in a low stone building. Three bar areas served by a central bar, there is a separate non-smoking dining area. Well-behaved children and dogs welcome – but no children's room, juke boxes or fruit machines. There is a lovely mature garden with tables and chairs for summer eating. Both bedrooms are en suite.

🛏 One double, one four-poster
£ ££
🍺 **Young's Bitter, Fuller's London Pride** plus guests
🍴 Lunch and evening menus, snacks lunchtime only
💳 Credit cards accepted

BOVEY TRACEY

The Cromwell Arms Hotel

Fore Street, Bovey Tracey,
Newton Abbot, Devon TQ13 9AE
T 01626 833473   **F** 01626 836873
E reservations@westcountryhotelrooms.co.uk
www.staustellbrewery.co.uk
Licensee: Nick Evans
Directions: Just off the A38 Devon Expressway

Bovey Tracey is often referred to as the gateway to the moors nestling on the edge of Dartmoor National Park. The Cromwell dates from the 1600s, its old charm remains but facilities have been bought up to the 21st century. There is a lounge area and restaurant for which the chef has created a range of traditional and unique dishes to suit all tastes – this includes an 18th century Lobster loaf, Beef Wellington, Pupton (terrine) of pigeon with a Cumberland sauce and Scallops of venison in liqueur and mushroom sauce. In the hotel cottage there are two larger rooms which are ideal for families and those with dogs.

🛏 Six double, four twin, two family
£ £££
🍺 **St Austell HSD, Tribute, Dartmoor Best**
🍴 Lunch, evening and snack menus
💳 Credit cards accepted

CALLINGTON

Coachmaker's Arms

Newport, Callington, Cornwall PL17 7AS
T 01579 382567   **F** 01579 384679
Licensee: Mr L Elliot

Close to the Tamar Valley and Morwellham Quay this traditional 300-year old coaching inn offers a warm atmosphere. The popular small bar is low-ceilinged with wooden beams, furnished with settles and decorated with local memorabilia and horse brasses. Note also the beautiful and unusual Wedgewood handpumps. One or two guest beers are offered in summer. Meals 12.00–14.00 and 19.00–21.30; there is a separate dining area.

🛏 Three double, one family – sleeps three
£ £
🍺 **Bass, St Austell Dartmoor Best Bitter** plus guests
🍴 Lunch, evening and snack menus
💳 Credit cards accepted

CRACKINGTON HAVEN

Coombe Barton Inn

Crackington Haven, Nr Bude, Cornwall EX23 0JG
T 01840 230345   **F** 01840 230788
E info@coombebartoninn.com
www.coombebartoninn.com
Licensees: Mr John and Mr Nicholas Cooper
Directions: Off A39, south-west of Bude

Spacious bar set in a 300 year old hotel with an excellent view over the beach and out to sea; the inn was originally built for the captain of the local slate quarries. This free house stocks beers from the Cornish breweries and regularly features guest ales in summer. Skittles are played but for the outdoor types there is surfing, beaches and cliff walks. Children are welcome and will enjoy the beach with its rock pools. The family room sleeps two adults and two/three children in one double bedroom and one bedroom with two single beds. It has a private bathroom, TV, lounge and kitchen with a microwave, fridge and electric cooker. Pets can be accommodated.

🛏 Four double, one twin and one family
£ £ (££ en suite)
🍺 **St Austell Dartmoor Best Bitter,**
Sharp's Doom Bar and guests
🍴 Lunch, evening and snack menus
💳 Credit cards accepted

CREMYLL

The Edgcumbe Arms

Cremyll, Nr Torpoint, Cornwall PL10 1HW
T 01752 822294   F 01752 822014
E reservations@westcountryhotelrooms.co.uk
www.staustellbrewery.co.uk
Licensees: Tony O'Dowd and Alex Patterson

The Edgcumbe is a beautifully refurbished
inn set in an 800 acre country park. Now
with a civil wedding licence, many have
celebrated a special day with a wedding
breakfast and idyllic views across the River
Tamar. It is only a short walk from the
delightful Mount Edgcumbe Gardens
where formal gardens meet beautiful
coastal walks. With plenty of opportunities
for fishing, river trips run from the slip just
outside the pub door. Children welcome.

🛏 Four double, two family
£ ££
🍺 **St Austell Tribute, IPA**
🍴 Lunch, evening and snack menus
💳 Credit cards accepted

CROWCOMBE

Carew Arms

Crowcombe, Taunton, Somerset TA4 4AD
T 01984 618631
E info@thecarewarms.co.uk
www.thecarewarms.co.uk
Licensees: Reg and Simon Ambrose
Directions: just off the A358, ten miles from Taunton

An unspoilt gem of a pub, that is worthy of
its entry in the CAMRA National Inventory
of Heritage Pubs which lists only those that
have been little altered over their history
and which need protection for future
generations. It is highly recommended by
What's Brewing's editor Ted Bruning as a
fine example of a 17th century building. It

retains its flagged stone floors, original
windows and three open fireplaces.

The bedrooms, as one might expect, are
not en suite, and are described as cosy, the
only modern concessions being the provision
of a TV and tea/coffee making facilities.
Children are welcome to stay and pets can be
accommodated. The pub boasts a skittle alley
and an untamed garden. Good quality food
is available, including a full English breakfast.

Crowcombe is a lovely village at the southern edge of the Quantocks, in a good area for
walking, cycling and horse riding. The West
Somerset railway, which runs between Bishops
Lydeard and Minehead for most of the year,
stops at Crowcombe Heathfield Station.

🛏 Two double, one twin-bedded room
£ £
🍺 **Exmoor Ale** plus local guest, **Lanes Cider**
🍴 Lunch evening and snack menus
💳 Credit cards not accepted

DITTISHAM

Red Lion

The Level, Dittisham, Dartmouth, Devon TQ6 0ES
T 01803 722235
E info@redliondittisham.co.uk
www.redliondittisham.co.uk
Licensee: Mr Ian Hill
Directions: In centre of village

Set in the heart of one of Devon's most
tranquil villages which borders on the 11 mile
estuary of the River Dart. This beautiful
region, part of Devon's South Hams, enjoys
the mildest climate in mainland Britain,
where the Old Red Lion has been offering
generous hospitality since 1750. The dining
room serves good food using local produce.
Superior guest accommodation is provided
in six en suite rooms plus two cottages in
the grounds. The single bar, with open fires,
admits dogs on leads. There is a children's
room and patio garden.

🛏 Five double, one twin
£ ££
🍺 **Butcombe Bitter, Palmers IPA**
🍴 Lunch, evening and snack menu
💳 Credit cards accepted

DODDISCOMBSLEIGH

Nobody Inn

Doddiscombsleigh, Nr Exeter, Devon EX6 7PS
T 01647 252394   **F** 01647 252978
E nick@nobodyinn.co.uk
www.nobodyinn.co.uk
Licensee: Nick Borst-Smith
Directions: Five miles south-west of Exeter, from the A38 at Haldon Hill, take the road to Dunchideock and follow signs to Doddiscombleigh

This isolated 16th century inn, close to Lawrence Castle, that once had a reputation for turning away visitors, is now famous for its hospitality. The bar area has exposed beams, flagged floors, wooden furniture, brass and copper artefacts, a large open fire and subdued lighting.

The Branscombe Vale house beer and two guests are complemented by Heron Valley and Brinblecombe's cider plus more than 250 whiskies and 800 wines. It offers over 40 West Country cheeses mainly from Devon, for which it has won many awards. One local describes the food as 'the best I have ever tasted in a pub'.

The accommodation needs to be booked well in advance to avoid disappointment. There are four letting rooms in the pub, two with a private shower; additional more spacious rooms are available at Town Barton, a 15th century Georgian manor house in the grounds of the parish church which has the largest amount of medieval stained glass in any church in Devon. Here a continental breakfast is served but guests may pay a supplement for the full English option in the pub. No children under 14 can be accommodated and horses can be stabled nearby.

🛏 Two double, one twin (with only a wash hand basin) and one small double with no facilities plus three rooms in the manor house close to the pub, comprising of two double and one twin rooms
£ £££ single occupancy or £70 for a double room
🍺 **Own Ale** brewed by **Branscombe Vale** and two guests
🍴 Lunch, evening and snack menus
💳 Credit cards accepted

FOWEY

King of Prussia

Town Quay, Fowey, Cornwall PL23 1AT
T 01726 833694   **F** 01726 834902
E reservations@westcountryhotelrooms.co.uk
www.staustellbrewery.co.uk
Licensees: Mark and Maria Montgomery

Originally a 15th century building which was rebuilt in 1887, now a welcoming community pub offering pleasant views across the river and harbour from the upstairs bar. An extra St Austell real ale may appear in summer. Separate restaurant at ground level; meals available 12.00–14.30 and 18.00–20.30 (21.00 Sun). All bedrooms have been refurbished, are en suite, non-smoking and have views over the Fowey Estuary. Fowey's church, built in 1336, is one of the highest in Cornwall.

🛏 Six double, one family
£ ££
🍺 **St Austell Tinner's**, **Tribute**, **HSD** plus guest
🍴 Lunch, evening and snack menus
💳 Credit cards accepted

The Ship Inn

Trafalgar Square, Fowey, Cornwall PL23 1AZ
T 01726 832230   **F** 01726 834935
E reservations@westcountryhotelrooms.co.uk
www.staustellbrewery.co.uk
Licensees: Nick and Hannah Rogers

The Ship was built in 1570 and is one of the oldest buildings in the area. It retains much of its original character including oak beams in the bar, a stained glass window in the dining room and the principal bedroom still has the original 16th century oak panelling. The Ship is based in the ancient port of Fowey, and is a short distance from the Eden Project and the Lost Gardens of Heligan. Children welcome.

🛏 One double, one family, two twin
£ £
🍺 **St Austell Tinners, Tribute, HSD**
🍴 Lunch, evening and snack menus
▭ Credit cards accepted

HALSE

The New Inn

Halse, Nr Taunton, Somerset TA4 3AF
T 01823 432352   **F** 01823 432363
E mark@newinnhalse.co.uk
www.newinnhalse.co.uk
Licensee: Mark Leadeham
Directions: Brown Inn signpost from A358 Taunton-Minehead Road

Run by a CAMRA member, this deliberately old-fashioned and comfortable 17th century freehouse is designed to appeal to the discerning. The bar has a unique elm servery counter and a wood-burner; there is a quiet snug and a separate non-smoking dining room plus a children's room and skittle alley.
    The New Inn is a haven for lovers of traditional pub games, who dislike piped music and do not want to watch television in the bar. It is close to the West Somerset Railway, the Quantock Hills and Exmoor National Park. Halse is a quintessential picture postcard English village. Five bedrooms – two of which can be made up to family rooms. Children welcome. A micro-brewery is planned for next year.

🛏 Two twin, three double
£ ££
🍺 **Bishops Somerset Ale**, plus two or three guests, bottle conditioned beers and real cider
🍴 Lunch, evening and snack menus
▭ Credit cards accepted

HALWELL

Old Inn

Halwell, Totnes, Devon TQ9 7JA
T 01803 712329
Licensees: Brian and Crispina Crowther
Directions: A381 on Totnes-Kingsbridge road

Friendly, family run pub with a warm village atmosphere, which specialises in oriental food. Situated next to a beautiful Norman church, the present inn was built in 1874 after the original Old Inn was destroyed by fire. There is a single bar with seating and dining tables in the bar area and a separate dining room. Eight miles from Dartmouth. Three en suite rooms, children welcome.

🛏 Two double, one family
£ ££
🍺 **RCH PG Steam, East Street Cream**
🍴 Lunch, evening and snack menus
▭ Credit cards accepted

HELSTON

Blue Anchor

50 Coinagehall Street, Helston, Cornwall TR13 8EU
T 01326 562821
Licensee: Kim Corbett
Directions: Town centre

A flagship among pub breweries, this is a rambling, unspoilt 15th century granite building with thatched roof and its own brewery at rear, and now with garden and accommodation. There is no distracting jukebox or bandits, only good conversation in the two small bars. There is also an indoor skittle alley out the back with its own bar, which can be activated during group functions.
    The occasional seasonal beer may be a winter warmer or some other commemorative brew – a bragget or honey and herb based beer appeared in 2001 to commemorate the 800th anniversary of Helston's town charter. The pub is only one of 16 to have appeared in every edition of the CAMRA Good Beer Guide. Good home-cooked food is served 12.00–16.00. The pub enjoys good bus connections with the Lizard, Penzance and

Truro, as well as the railway at Redruth, including services late at night.

🛏 Two twin, two double
£ £
🍺 **Blue Anchor IPA, Middle, Best, Special**
🍴 Lunch and snack menu
💳 Credit cards accepted

HESSENFORD

The Copley Arms

Hessenford, Torpoint, Cornwall PL11 3HJ
T 01503 240209   **F** 01503 240766
E reservations@westcountryhotelrooms.co.uk
www.staustellbrewery.co.uk
Licensees: Mike and Di Bradburn
Directions: on A387 five miles from Looe

Five miles from Looe with the historic fishing village of Polperro close by. The pub is set in a picturesque village which itself is steeped in history and in which the pub remains an essential part of village life. The Copley is a charming inn and restaurant with five superb en suite rooms set in the lovely village of Hessenford. The pub has an extensive patio and tables alongside the stream. Several riding stables are close by and it is a good base for walking trips

🛏 Three double, one twin, one family
£ ££
🍺 **St Austell Tribute, Tinners**
🍴 Lunch evening and snack menus
💳 Credit cards accepted

HOLNE

Church House Inn

Holne, near Ashburton, Devon TQ13 7SJ
T 01364 631208   **F** 01364 631525
www.churchhouse-holne.co.uk
Licensee: Tony Skerritt
Directions: Off the A38 Plymouth-Exeter road in the centre of the village

Grade II listed 14th century inn in an unspoilt village in the Dartmoor National Park. The pub has two bars, one by the dining area and the other just for drinkers. Excellent local fresh food cooked to order. Dogs, children and walkers are all welcome. As well as a choice of real ales, good cider is available at the bar.

🛏 Four double, two single
£ ££
🍺 **Butcombe Bitter** plus guest ales
🍴 Lunch, evening and snack menus
💳 Credit cards accepted

IDDESLEIGH

Duke of York

Iddesleigh, Devon EX19 8BG
T 01837 810253   **F** 01837 810253
Licensees: Jamie Stuart and Pipa Hutchinson
Directions: On B3217 10 miles north of Okehampton

The CAMRA member who nominated this pub says it has the best breakfast he has had for ages. This remote village pub is not as old as the hill it nestles on but dates from the 12th century; it was CAMRA's North Devon Pub of the Year for 1999 and serves Adnams and local ales from the barrel. Very friendly, rooms with amazing character. The white-painted and thatched exterior leads into a comfortable bar with rocking chairs and scrubbed oak tables in front of a log fire. The landlord likes real food as well as real beer and much of the produce for the kitchen comes from his own farm. No juke box but fiddlers welcome to play by the fire.

🛏 Seven rooms – some can sleep three

£ £

🍺 **Adnams Broadside, Cotleigh Tawny** plus guest beers from local breweries including **Sharps, Exe Valley** and **Jollyboat** and local cider from Winkleigh

🍴 Lunch, evening and snack menus

IDMISTON near Salisbury

The Earl of Normanton

Tidworth Road, Idmiston,
Salisbury, Wiltshire SP4 0AG
T 01980 610251   F 01980 619231
Licensees: Alan and Nicola Howe
Directions: On A338, six miles north east of Salisbury

An idyllic rural pub with wonderful views over the Bourne Valley. The pub is renowned for the excellence of its beer, Cheriton Pots Ale and Hop Back Summer Lightning, which are well regarded by discerning drinkers. A perfect stop for anyone wanting to visit Salisbury, Stonehenge or Woodhenge. The pub has two bars and a terraced garden for wiling away sunny afternoons. Three bedrooms all en suite with TV and tea/coffee making facilities.

🛏 Two double, one single

£ £££

🍺 **Cheriton Best** and **Pots, Hopback Summer Lightning** plus one guest

🍴 Lunch, evening and snack menus

💳 Credit cards accepted

KNOWSTONE near South Molton

The Masons Arms Inn

Knowstone, South Molton, North Devon EX36 4RY
T 01398 341231
T Masonsarmsinn@aol.com
www.masonsarmsinn.com
Licensees: Paul and Jo Stretton-Downs
Directions: Turn north off the A361 (North Devon Link Road) about 11 miles west of Tiverton and follow signs. It's about 18 miles from M5 J27

A 13th century thatched building in the southern foothills of Exmoor. Originally housing the masons who built the village church, it became a pub the 15th century.

A traditional small, old, main bar with inglenook fireplace (always alight), oak beams. and a lower, small lounge bar. A recent extension provides a family/dining room plus a patio area and garden. The Masons is within half an hour's drive of Exmoor and then the North Devon coast and about one hour's drive of Dartmoor. There are several National Trust gardens and houses within easy driving distance. Also many visitors come down to the area in the winter for the shooting and fishing.

The pub itself does not have rooms but the owners have bought a tiny cottage, beautifully furnished and very romantic, about 50 yards away, The Hunters Lodge. Just one up and one down, none-the-less the double bedroom has en suite facilities, albeit the bath (but not the loo which is separate!), is just behind a curtain in the bedroom. The downstairs lounge, with fireplace, has a large sofa-bed that can sleep two more. There is a small kitchenette just off the sitting room and the makings of breakfast are provided in the fridge so the guests can serve themselves when ready. As the guests are frequently young couples this can often be just before midday!

🛏 One double, one double sofa bed

£ £££

🍺 **Cotleigh Tawny, Exmoor**

🍴 Lunch, evening and snack menus

💳 Credit cards accepted

LACOCK

The Red Lion

High Street, Lacock, Chippenham,
Wiltshire SN15 2LQ
T 01249 730456
Licensees: Christopher and Sarah Chappell
Directions: Off A350 between Chippenham and Melksham

The Red Lion, a public house dating from the early 1700s, lies opposite the 14th century beamed Tithe Barn dominating the High Street of this National Trust village of mellow medieval cottages, built with the wealth created by the woollen industry. It is sited on the old cloth road from London to Avonmouth. Lacock was well placed to benefit from this trade and from the introduction of wide looms in the 15th century; and examples of jettied first storied houses built to take these wide looms can still be seen in the village.

The Red Lion, refurbished recently to an exceptionally high standard to echo its Georgian past, offers bed and breakfast to a superior standard. Four rooms, each of a very different character offer private facilities. After a peaceful night's rest in this historic setting you will be welcomed by a full Wiltshire English Breakfast to set you up for the day. Lacock has been the setting

for a number of films including Harry Potter and more recently the classic television series Pride and Prejudice had scenes that were in Lacock and the Red Lion.

🛏 Four double
£ ££££
🍺 **Wadworth 6X, Henry's IPA**
🍴 Lunch, evening and snack menus
💳 Credit cards accepted

The Red Lion, Lacock (above and below)

LANNER

Lanner Inn

The Square, Lanner, Redruth, Cornwall TR16 6EH
T 01209 215611
E lannerinn@btconnect.com
Licensees: John and Sue Wilson
Directions: On A393 Redruth-Falmouth road

Busy if small community pub, whose keen landlord varies the guest beer regularly on the advice of his locals. An extra gravity-fed beer may be provided on the bar on special occasions. This is not a food-orientated pub; the only way to get fed is to stay for bed and breakfast! The emphasis is on real ale, conversation, and games such as darts, euchre, pool, dominoes and quizzes, while the good-value accommodation is especially welcoming for Real Ale enthusiasts.

A delightful orchard doubles as the beer garden and children's play area in summer. Nearby buses run to Truro, Falmouth and Camborne until late evening. Nearby is Falmouth, Pendennis Castle and the National Maritime Museum.

🛏 Four double and families can be accommodated. New rooms may be added soon

£ £

🍺 Sharp's Cornish Coaster

🍴 Breakfast only

💳 Credit cards accepted

LOSTWITHIEL

Royal Oak

Duke Street, Lostwithiel, Cornwall PL22 0AG
T 01208 872552
Licensee: Mr M G Hine
Directions: Just off A390 (Queen Street)

A 17th century listed building with beamed ceilings and stone floors, with public bar, lounge bar and separate restaurant. The cellar is reputedly connected to Restormel Castle, which was used as an escape route by smugglers. The castle is the best preserved of its type in Cornwall. Ideal for anyone visiting the Eden Project, the pub is close to the River Fowey, noted for its salmon fishing and good sailing facilities; there is a golf course nearby. Opposite the pub is the outstanding 13th century lantern spire of its village church.

Children are welcome and even pets can be accommodated. Situated just off the main road, in what was the former capital of Cornwall, it is a busy pub well known for its food. It specialises in guest beers mainly from small independent breweries and has a good range of bottled beers.

🛏 Six double rooms, five with tea making facilities and TV, one with a separate bathroom

£ £££

🍺 Six real ales always available including **Sharps Own** and beers from the local **Keltek Brewery**

🍴 Lunch, evening and snack menus

💳 Credit cards accepted

LYDFORD

The Castle Inn

Lydford, Nr Oakhampton, Devon EX20 4BH
T 01822 820241   F 01822 820454
Licensees: Richard Davies

Sherlock Holmes fans will enjoy staying in this 12th century inn, as it features in the Hound of the Baskervilles. With a castle next door and a fine beer garden where real ale can be enjoyed on sunny afternoons and warm evenings, the Lydford Inn is certainly worth a visit, especially if you fancy a visit to the impressive Lydford Gorge nearby. The pub has a granite floored public bar, an acclaimed restaurant and a comfortable lounge with many antiques and interesting artefacts. Traditional ales, often from local brewers, are available.

🛏 Nine double

£ ££

🍺 **Otter Bitter, London Pride**

🍴 Lunch, evening and snack menus

💳 Credit cards accepted

MONKTON COMBE

The Wheelwright's Arms

Mill Lane, Monkton Combe, Bath BA2 7HB
T 01225 722287   F 01225 723029
Licensee: Jacqueline Gillespie
Directions: Off A36 – Bath/Warminster Road

In the heart of England's glorious West Country, the Wheelwright's Arms was first licensed in 1871. Today, with the excellent accommodation in a separate converted barn and stables, it is a fascinating place in which to stay or just spend a pleasant hour or so. Once owned by a Viscount and at one time in competition with the local monastery which brewed its own ale. The Wheelwright's Arms stands in the lovely Midford Valley and is only three miles from glorious Bath. In winter, the evening's chill is taken away by a roaring log fire and the company of a glass of Butcombe Bitter. The pub is a perfect base for walking, riding, fishing or just relaxing. Only children over 14 and no dogs.

🛏 Two twin, six double
£ ££
🍺 **Wadworth 6X, Butcombe Bitter, Adnams Southwold Bitter**
🍴 Lunch, evening and snack menus
💳 Credit cards accepted

MOUSEHOLE

The Ship Inn

South Cliff, Mousehole, Cornwall TR19 6QX
T 01736 731234 **F** 01736 732259
E reservations@westcountryhotelrooms.co.uk
www.staustellbrewery.co.uk
Licensees: Tim and Jenny Hibbert
Directions: Follow the A30 to Penzance and then
the signs to Mousehole

Situated on the Harbour Edge, on the western tip of Cornwall, the Ship Inn lies at the heart of a very friendly local community. It has a 30-cover restaurant off an old traditional local community bar. Overlooking the harbour, some of the rooms have views of St Michael's Mount. The Ship is on the Great West Way coastal walk. With the sea on the doorstep the opportunity for fishing is unlimited. Children welcome.

🛏 Seven double, one family
£ ££
🍺 **St Austell Tinners, Tribute, HSD, IPA, Duchy**
🍴 Lunch, evening and snack menus
💳 Credit cards accepted

NANCENOY

Trengilly Wartha Inn

Nancenoy, Constantine, Falmouth,
Cornwall TR11 5RP
T 01326 340332
Licensee: Nigel Logan
Directions: Off Falmouth-Gweek road, near
Constantine

A well-organised and versatile inn with extensive grounds, including a lake and boules piste, in a steeply-wooded valley. Real Ale is limited in winter but two or three guest beers are usually available in summer. An imaginative selection of fresh food is

prepared and presented with flair, but there are no bar snacks. An extension at the front serves as a conservatory and family room, and a large and pleasant garden may offer barbecues on warm summer evenings. The pub is close to Flambards theme park, Gunwalloe Church Cove and the Lizard. Six bedrooms are in the pub with two family rooms in the annexe, which overlook the lake.

🛏 Five double, one twin, two family – each
sleeps four
£ ££
🍺 **Sharp's, Cornish Coaster** and guests
🍴 Lunch and evening menus
💳 Credit cards accepted

NETTLECOMBE

Marquis of Lorne

Nettlecombe, Bridport, Dorset DT6 3SY
T 01308 485236 **F** 01308 485666
E Julie.woodroffe@btinternet.com
www.marquisoflorne.com
Licensees: David and Julie Woodroffe
Directions: Turn off the A3066 one and a half miles
north of Bridport; go through West Milton village
and past the Powerstock turn; the inn is a little
further uphill on the left

A CAMRA award winning, idyllic 16th century country inn. It is surrounded by unspoilt countryside in the quiet, rural location of Nettlecombe, a tiny village hamlet of old stone cottages just half a mile away from the picturesque village of Powerstock and four miles northeast of Bridport, a bustling small market town with the coast and

fishing village of West Bay a further two miles away.

Two cosy bars with log fires in winter ensure a relaxing atmosphere to sample a local Real Ale, often served straight from the wood, while studying the blackboards which have a wonderful selection of homemade dishes. The large well kept gardens have superb views all around, making them a perfect place to eat, or for a peaceful drink before dinner.

🛏 Eight double, two twin-bedded rooms
£ ££
🍺 **Palmers BB, IPA, 200**
🍴 Lunch, evening and snack menus
💳 Credit cards accepted

NEWTON ABBOT

Dartmouth Inn

63 East Street, Newton Abbot, Devon TQ12 2JP
T 01626 353451
Licensee: Frank McBride
Directions: Opposite hospital

This 17th century freehouse has been locally described as the village pub in the town. The warm and friendly three-roomed pub has open fires and a good selection of South West micro brewed beer, real cider and fruit wines. Well-prepared traditional pub food of excellent value is served weekday lunchtimes at the frequent South Devon Pub of the Year.

There is a discount to CAMRA members.

🛏 Two twin
£ ££
🍺 **Princetown Dartmoor IPA** plus local guest
🍴 Lunch weekdays only
💳 Credit cards not accepted

NORTON ST PHILIP

The George Inn

High Street, Norton St Philip,
Bath, Somerset BA2 6LH
T 01373 834224   F 01373 834861
E info@thegeorgeinn-nsp.co.uk
www.thegeorgeinn-nsp.co.uk
Licensees: David and Tanya Tatchell
Directions: On A366 in centre of village about six miles south-east of Bath

Norton St Philip is a former wool village, famous for one of England's oldest medieval inns, reputed to be one of the oldest continuously licensed houses in England. The George began life in 1230 as a guesthouse for Hinton Priory and at the dissolution in 1539 it became an inn. The Duke of Monmouth, who was mounting a rebellion against the Crown, stayed here in 1685 after the decision not to attack Bristol. It is even said that Samuel Pepys slept here. This Grade One listed building, with its fine half-timbered and oriel-windowed upper two stories, has offered hospitality to travellers and locals for over 700 years.

In the 1990s its owner, the family brewer Wadworth & Co., decided to undertake the huge and complex task of restoring the building to its former glory. During the restoration work, wall paintings dating from the 15th century were uncovered and preserved. The restoration also created eight luxury letting rooms, three of which have hand-carved four-poster beds in a period setting. The George Inn has been seen as a setting in such films as The Remains of the Day, Tom Jones, and The Canterbury Tales. It has also been used in the television serialisations of Persuasion by Jane Austen and Daniel Defoe's Moll Flanders.

🛏 Five double, three four-poster
£ £££
🍺 **Wadworth 6X, Henry's Original IPA** and **JCB**
🍴 Lunch, evening and lunchtime snack menus
💳 Credit cards accepted

OGBOURNE ST GEORGE

The Old Crown

Marlborough Road, Ogbourne St George,
Wiltshire SN8 1JQ
T 01672 841445   F 01672 841056
E theinnwiththewell@compuserve.com
www.theinnwiththewell.com
Licensees: Megan and Mike Shaw
Directions: On A436 leave M4 at J15 and head south

The Old Crown is known by regulars as the Inn with the Well. There are few such examples in Britain where you can stand on the glass top and look down into the well, 90ft deep, when entering the restaurant. Set in the midst of the Ridgeway path (one of Europe's oldest highways), the Old Crown has been a village local for more than 300 years as well as a coaching inn during the 17th century. The inn is also a dropping off point for horse riders and cyclists who are using the old railway track or the Ridgeway to explore the Og Valley. The bar is small and comfy and despite the handpumps every pint is drawn from the barrels in the cellar. A separate accommodation block houses six rooms, all en suite and with TVs.

🛏 Three double, one family
£ £
🍺 **Wadworth 6X** plus guests
🍴 Lunch, evening and snack menus
💳 Credit cards accepted

PADSTOW

Old Custom House

South Quay, Padstow, Cornwall PL28 8BL
T 01841 532359   F 01841 533372
E reservations@westcountryhotelrooms.co.uk
www.staustellbrewery.co.uk
Licensee: Linda Allen

The Old Custom House, now a listed building, has been recently refurbished to provide an intimate and stylish hotel and an ideal place to watch boats come into the harbour. The Pescadou restaurant is the jewel in the crown, fashionably blending ancient with modern design. Using fresh local produce and fish straight from the quay on the doorstep, it offers an extensive menu of fish and seafood dishes complemented by a fine selection of wines. Nearby is Polzeath beach and Tintagel castle where King Arthur was allegedly born. Children welcome.

🛏 15 double, one twin, eight family
£ £££
🍺 **St Austell Tinners, Tribute, HSD, IPA**
🍴 Lunch, evening ad snack menus
💳 Credit cards accepted

PORTHLEVEN

The Harbour Inn

Commercial Road, Porthleven, Cornwall TR13 9JB
T 01326 573876   F 01326 572124
E reservations@westcountryhotelrooms.co.uk
www.staustellbrewery.co.uk
Licensees: Mr and Mrs A. Lee
Directions: On A39

The Harbour is a lively pub situated on the harbour of Porthleven, a small Cornish village and the UK's most southerly working port. It is ideal as a base for a holiday. The beach is only 150 yards away and the pub is situated on the Coastal Path. Ten bedrooms –

many are suitable for families, some are en suite and several have views of the harbour.

🛏 One single, four double, three doubles with additional put ups, one twin, one family
£ ££
🍺 **St Austell Black Prince**, **IPA**, **Tribute**, **HSD**
🍴 Lunch, evening and snack menus
💳 Credit cards accepted

ROCHE

Victoria Inn & Lodge

Victoria, Roche, St Austell, Cornwall PL26 8AQ
T 01726 890207   **F** 01726 891233
Licensees: Adrian and Jacky Bradbury
Directions: On A30

An old coaching inn incorporating a modern accommodation lodge, which nowadays is the first actual roadside pub on the way into Cornwall by the A30. The Victoria Inn prides itself on quality cuisine, offering a large range of innovative bar food, daily specials and an à la carte restaurant. Recently completely refurbished, the emphasis is on food which is available every day 12.00–21.00. The licensee is a Cask Marque holder. A good place to stay if visiting the Eden Project which is only 15 minutes away.

🛏 28 rooms in total including double rooms, family rooms and disabled twin rooms
£ ££
🍺 **St Austell Tinner's**, **Tribute**, **HSD**
🍴 Lunch, evening and snack menus
💳 Credit cards accepted

ST AGNES

Driftwood Spars

Quay Road, Trevaunance Cove,
St Agnes, Cornwall TR5 0RT
T 01872 552428   **F** 01872 553701
E driftwoodspars@hotmail.com
Licensees: Gordon and Jill Treleaven
Directions: Off B3285, near St. Agnes

A former 17th century mine warehouse and sail loft, now a fine family-run hotel and friendly public house with a micro-brewery. The pub is built of granite, slate and enormous ships' spars, hence the name.

The three-bar interior with beamed ceilings, lead light windows and granite fireplaces is cosy and atmospheric. The décor is nautical, with a fine collection of ships' clocks; a wreckers' tunnel is also visible. The pub is warm and welcoming, family and pet-friendly, and popular with locals and tourists alike, with easy access to cliff walks and surfing. Excellent meals for all, on an extensive, varied menu including authentic Cornish pasties. Entertainment includes live theatre and music at weekends. Buses are 10 minutes walk away.

🛏 15 bed rooms including double, twin and family
£ ££
🍺 **Driftwood Spars Cuckoo Ale**, **St Austell HSD**, **Sharp's Own**, and **Draught Bass**
🍴 Lunch, evening and snack menus
💳 Credit cards accepted

St Agnes Hotel

Churchtown, St Agnes, Cornwall TR5 0QP
T 01872 552307   **F** 01872 553114
E stagnesinn@aol.com
www.st-agnes-hotel.co.uk
Licensees: Ben and Emma Hough
Directions: In centre of village opposite the church

An ideal base from which to explore the area. St Agnes is a thriving village, which has avoided many of the tawdry trappings of over-commercialised tourism and remains a thriving Cornish community. There is a strong emphasis on art too, with several delightful galleries selling Cornish art and crafts. The whole area is deemed to be an area of outstanding natural beauty. The Eden Project and Lands End are 45 minutes drive away. There are six en suite rooms, all with good facilities.

🛏 Four double, one twin, one family
£ ££
🍺 **St Austell Tinners**, **Tribute**, **HSD**
🍴 Lunch, evening and snack menus
💳 Credit cards accepted

Rising Sun

The Square, St Mawes, Cornwall TR2 5DJ
T 01326 270233   **F** 01326 270198
Licensee: John Milan
Directions: At end of A3078

Situated on the unspoilt Roseland Peninsula in the heart of St Mawes, The Rising Sun maintains the traditions of a real Cornish inn. All eight bedrooms are stylishly decorated and are charmingly individual. It is a luxury pub/hotel that encompasses perfect food, seaside accommodation and a warm atmosphere. The hotel lounge bar is decorated in light pastel shades, dedicated to conversational drinking, and there is a large patio for summer drinking. A third St Austell beer appears during the summer. Food is available either as bar snacks or in the à la carte restaurant; locally-caught sea food is a speciality of Chef Ann Long, the only female Master Chef in the West Country.

🛏 Four double, two twin, one family suite –
     sleeps four, one single
£ £££
🍺 **St Austell HSD** plus guest
🍴 Lunch, evening and snack menus
💳 Credit cards accepted

Oxenham Arms

South Zeal, Devon EX20 2JT
T 01837 840244   **F** 01837 840791
E oxhenhamarms@aol.com
Licensee: Paul Lucas
Directions: Situated just off the A30 the main Exeter-Okehampton road

An ancient inn in an ancient village in the Dartmoor National Park. First licensed in 1477, The Oxenham Arms is a unique inn with romantic associations. It lies in the valley on the old coaching road, in the quiet and peaceful atmosphere of South Zeal, midway between the north and south coasts of Devon. There's a standing stone in one of the rooms and the theory of the archaeologists is that the monastic builders placed their house around this prehistoric stone-shaped by man 5,000 years ago. Beers from Sharpe and other local brewers, very friendly, log fires in book lined room, dogs and children welcome, good food.

🛏 Seven double and twin including one four-
     poster and three family rooms, one double
     with bathroom only
£ ££

🍺 **Princetown Breweries Dartmoor IPA, Jail Ale**
🍴 Lunch evening and snack menus
💳 Credit cards accepted

White Horse Inn

Stogumber, Somerset TA3 3TA
T 01984 656277   **F** 01984 656277
Licensee: John Trebilcock
Directions: Take turn off the A358, 12 miles north of Taunton, pub is two miles down lane to Stogumber

With easy access to the Quantock Hills, Minehead and Dunster Castle/Village and beaches, the White Horse is a traditional pub in the conservation village of Stogumber. Standing opposite a 12th century church, the pub has one bar plus a small games room and a small patio area at the rear with tables and chairs (in summer months). The pub has three bedrooms comprising one twin, one double and one family room which sleeps four. All are en suite with tea making facilities and TV.

Set in open countryside, it is an ideal base for walkers who wish to be challenged by some strenuous hill walking as well as those who like something gentler. A mile out of the village is Stogumber Station, a small and secluded country stop on the West Somerset Railway.

🛏 One twin, one double and one family room, which sleeps four
£ £
🍺 **Cotleigh Tawny**, plus ever changing guest ales from local breweries including **Exmoor**
🍴 Lunch, evening and snack menus
💳 Credit cards accepted

The Bell House

High Street, Sutton Benger,
Chippenham, Wiltshire SN15 4RH
T 01249 720401   **F** 01249 720301
Directions: M4 J17, follow signs – the hotel is opposite the Saxon Church

The Bell is a delightful 500 year old hotel which is full of character. It offers an extensive restaurant menu and a fine range of ales. There are 14 en suite bedrooms, two of which are on the ground floor. The hotel's large English garden is often used for marquee weddings. Nearby is the village of Lacock, where some of Harry Potter was filmed and the Cotswolds are a short drive away. Bath and its Roman baths are approximately 20 miles away. The Badminton Horse Trials are a popular local attraction.

🛏 14 rooms
£ ££££
🍺 **Greene King** range plus guests
🍴 Lunch, evening and snack menus
💳 Credit cards accepted

The Crown Inn

73 Ermin Street, Stratton St Margaret,
Swindon, Wiltshire SN3 4NL
T 01793 827530   **F** 01793 831683
Licensees: Ian Blake and Tina Smith
Directions: At the junction of Highworth Road and Ermin Street, near city centre

The Crown Inn is well situated for access to Swindon town centre, M4, the Cotswolds, Cirencester, Gloucester and Oxford. With its major refurbishment, The Crown has come full circle, returning to its former function as an inn – even if its new customers will no longer find accommodation for their horses!

The 13 en suite bedrooms, sumptuous 40-seater restaurant and bar are all furnished and decorated to a high standard, yet still remain in keeping with the historical background of the property. With the exception of the Tudor and Forge dining areas, every room has a name that is related to the brewing process – thus reflecting Swindon's brewer Arkells' proud heritage and their long association with The Crown that dates back to 1868.

- 🛏 Eight double, 11 twin, one single
- £ ££££
- 🍺 **Arkells 2B**, **3B** and **Kingsdown Ale**
- 🍴 Lunch, evening and snack menus
- 💳 Credit cards accepted

TARRANT MONKTON

Langton Arms

Tarrant Monkton, near Blandford Forum, Dorset DT11 8RX
T 01258 830225   **F** 01258 830053
Licensee: Barbara Cossins
Directions: off the A354, north east of Blandford Forum

This is Thomas Hardy country, and this picturesque village has changed little since he wrote his novels. Surrounded by the spectacular countryside of the Tarrant Valley, it makes an ideal base for visiting Wessex, particularly the nearby towns of Shaftesbury, Salisbury, Sherborne and Poole. Voted Pub of the Year by local CAMRA in 1997, the delightful Langton Arms, thatched like many of the houses here, is at the heart of the village and the CAMRA member who nominated it says nothing could be too much trouble for the staff.

The pub dates back to the 17th century, but the guest rooms, built in rustic brick around an attractive courtyard, are a more recent addition. These are all on the ground floor, which makes them accessible to wheelchair-users. Children are welcome to stay – an extra bed can be provided – and pets can be accommodated. A free house, the pub offers a wide range of Real Ales. Bar meals are available and a bistro-style restaurant, situated in a converted stable and conservatory, is open Wednesday to Saturday evenings

- 🛏 Three doubles, three twin-bedded rooms
- £ ££ (single occupancy £££)
- 🍺 **Ringwood Best Bitter**, plus four regularly changed guest beers
- 🍴 Lunch, evening and snack menus
- 💳 Credit cards accepted

TAUNTON

Mason's Arms

3 Magdelene Street, Taunton, Somerset TA1 1SG
T 01823 288916
E jjmax@jleyton.freeserve.co.uk
www.masonsarms.freeuk.com
Licensee: Jeremy Leyton
Directions: By St Mary's Church

The Mason's Arms stands in the shadow of one of the finest church towers in the south west, the jewel that is St Mary Magdalene. A Traditional English pub in the heart of Taunton, serving English ale in a quiet relaxing atmosphere. It was voted Somerset CAMRA pub of the Year in 2002. A speciality of the house is the Grillstone Concept – your hot meal served at just the right temperature for your taste, courtesy of a preheated stone tray. This releases heat for up to 40 minutes allowing you to cook the meat to your liking or keep it warm. There is a charming, luxuriously furnished, self-contained flat – available all year round for those seeking the convenience of its central location, perhaps whilst on business in the area, or as a well deserved holiday. The flat, which is normally let on a weekly basis, has its own separate entrance and comprises a twin bedded and a single bedroom; a spacious lounge with sofa, easy chairs, colour TV, and own telephone.

- 🛏 Self-contained flat – sleeps three
- £ ££
- 🍺 **Draught Bass**, **Exe Valley Bitter**, **Otter Bitter** plus guest beers
- 🍴 Lunch, evening and snack menus
- 💳 Credit cards accepted

TOTNES

Steam Packet Inn

St Peters Quay, Totnes, Devon TQ9 5EW
T 01803 863880
E steampacket@buccaneer.co.uk
www.thesteampacketinn-totnes.co.uk
Licensees: Phil and Ester Young

Beautifully situated on the banks of the
River Dart, just five minutes walk from the
centre of historic Totnes, the Steam Packet
Inn offers a warm and intimate location for
any occasion. Three 18th century cottages
were converted many years ago into this
atmospheric pub. Recently refurbished
both upstairs and down, its décor combines
vibrant colours, exposed bricks and leather
settees. It has a striking conservatory and
restaurant. Children welcome.

🛏 One double, one twin, one family, one single
£ ££
🍺 **Courage Best**, **Draught Bass** and guests
🍴 Lunch, evening and snack menus
💳 Credit cards accepted

TRESCO

New Inn

Townshill, Tresco, Isles of Scilly TR24 0QG
T 01720 422844   F 01720 423200
E newinn@tresco.co.uk
Licensee: Robin Lawson

The gentle Gulf Stream gives Tresco a mild,
frost-free climate in which plants from all
over the world flourish in the wild. Cars are
banned, and the tranquil way of life has not
changed for more than half a century.
So where better to stay on beautiful Scilly
than this pleasant pub near New Grimsby
harbour, a haven between demanding
coastal walks and the boat to St Mary's.

Recent extensions to the garden and
provision of a covered pavilion have added
to the attractions of this popular Real Ale
outlet. The beer range varies but look out
for beers from the local brewery, Ales of
Scilly, the most south-westerly brewery in
Britain. An Ale and Sausage festival is held

over the spring bank holiday weekend, with
a second beer festival early September.
Children welcome.

🛏 14 double
£ ££££
🍺 **Ales of Scilly Scuppered**, **St Austell Tribute** plus
guests
🍴 Lunch, evening and snack menus
💳 Credit cards accepted

TREWARMETT

Trewarmett Inn

Trewarmett, Tintagel, Cornwall PL34 0ET
T 01840 770460
Directions: On B3263, south of Tintagel

Until recently, just a hotel and restaurant, it
has now become a welcoming village pub,
parts of which date back 300 years. It is a
very traditional Cornish local, with low
beams, slate floors, stone walls and open
fireplace. There are two drinking rooms and
a separate dining area, all the food being
home-made, while the raised beer garden
offers distant sea views. Folk music is very
much in evidence, with instruments
hanging from the walls and live sessions
Wednesday and Saturday evenings.
Children and dogs are welcome.

🛏 One twin, three double, one family
£ ££ single, £
🍺 **Sharp's Doom Bar**
🍴 Lunch, evening and snack menus
💳 Credit cards accepted

TRURO

City Inn

Pydar Street, Truro, Cornwall TR1 3SP
T 01872 272623
Licensees: Graham and Jackie Hill
Directions: Just off city centre, on B3284
Perranporth road

A busy 2-bar community pub away from
the shopping centre, and popular with local
residents. The Skinner's beers are regularly
varied, as is the guest ale; real Cornish cider
from Haye Farm is also usually on offer on

gravity, brought straight from the cellar. The comfortable lounge bar has several drinking corners and sports an impressive collection of water jugs, while the bar is more spartan and sports-orientated. The beer garden at the back is a summer sun-trap, while a new covered drinking area to the side provides shelter when needed. The pub is about 10 minutes walk from the main bus station, 15 minutes from the railway station.

🛏 One single, four double

£ £

🍺 **Sharp's Doom Bar**, **Skinner's Betty Stogs**, **Courage Best Bitter**, guest beer

🍴 Lunch, evening and snack menus

💳 Credit cards accepted

TUCKENHAY

The Maltsters Arms

Tuckenhay, Nr Totnes, Devon TQ9 7EH
T 01803 732 350   **F** 01803 732 823
E pub@tuckenhay.demon.co.uk
www.tuckenhay.com
Licensees: Denise and Quentin Thwaites
Directions: Off 381, 10 minutes drive from Totnes

If every pub was like the Maltsters we would never go home. An idyllic waterside pub overlooking the peaceful, wooded Bow Creek. In the summer months a real barbecue is held on the quayside. The menu always includes fresh fish, rump steaks, good sausages and something vegetarian. Inside the narrow bar links to two rooms – one with a big log fire with two large tables (The Dart Cabin) and another (The Map Room) has charts of South Coast Waters and The Channel Islands all over the walls.

There are loads of games – dominoes, Jenga, Scrabble, chess, Monopoly, shove-halfpenny, a library of pub guides, cookery books, wine and drink books, and grown ups are allowed to read licensee Quentin Thwaites back copies of the Beano. Mooring is available, children and dogs are welcome and CAMRA members are given a 10 per cent discount. The letting rooms are wonderfully idiosyncratic and comfortably furnished. The pub also serves as the village shop.

🛏 Seven double

£ £££

🍺 **Princetown Dartmoor IPA**, plus regular guests from **Teignworthy**, **Blackawton**, **Exmoor**, **St Austell**

🍴 Lunch, evening and snack menus

💳 Credit cards accepted

WELLS

The Crown at Wells

Market Place, Wells, Somerset BA5 2RP
T 01749 673457   **F** 01749 679792
E reception@crownatwells.co.uk
www.crownatwells.co.uk
Licensees: Adrian and Sarah Lawrence
Directions: In the heart of Wells, follow signs for hotel and deliveries to bring you into the Market Place

Situated in the medieval Market Place, overlooked by Wells Cathedral and the Bishop's Palace, the Crown dates back to 1450 when it was built as a coaching inn. Originally divided into two public houses, the Royal Oak and The Crown, it now has one bar, The Penn Bar, named after William Penn who preached to a crowded Market Place in 1685, for which he was promptly arrested. He was later reprieved by the Bishop and returned to The Crown to preach again.

The pub has a lunchtime carvery-style buffet seven days a week in the Penn Bar; light meals and snacks are also available in the early evening. In addition is has a separate, popular restaurant, Anton's Bistro, serving a table d'hôte and à la carte menu. The Crown has been awarded two stars by the English Tourism Council and the AA. Close by are Wookey Hole Caves, Cheddar, Glastonbury, Street, the Mendip Hills and Somerset Levels. Children welcome.

- Two single, four twins, four doubles and four four-posters
- £ £££
- Butcombe, Smiles and Oakhill beers
- Credit cards accepted

WINKTON

Fisherman's Haunt

Winkton, Christchurch Dorset BH23 7AS
T 01202 477283   F 01202 478883
E fishermanshaunt@accommodating-inns.co.uk
www.accommodating-inns.co.uk
Licensees: Peter and Shirley Palmer

A haven for the country-lover, the Fisherman's Haunt stands a stone's throw away from the River Avon. Excellent country pursuits nearby and a good shopping centre at Bournemouth. Winkton is an ideal centre for those who like walking or leisurely motoring. Bournemouth, New Forest, Highcliffe and Mudeford are all within easy motoring distance.

- 13 doubles, four twins
- £ ££££
- Gales – HSB, GB, Butser
- Lunch, evening and snack menus
- Credit cards accepted

WOODLAND

Rising Sun

Woodland, Ashburton, Newton Abbot,
Devon TQ13 7JT
T 01364 652544   F 01364 654202
E mail@risingsunwoodland.co.uk
www.risingsunwoodland.co.uk
Licensees: Heather Humphries and Jed Cafferty
Directions: Village signed from the Plymouth-bound A38, pub on left after 1.5 miles

A spacious rural free house in beautiful countryside between Torbay and Dartmoor. The long single bar serves a large open plan bar and dining area where small screens offer some privacy. There is an additional children's area off the main bar. A large collection of keys hang from the ceiling. Outside are extensive grounds with seating and a play area. The Rising Sun is well known for its home made pies and holds a 'pie' evening every month on the first Tuesday and Thursday of the month. Children welcome.

- One double, one twin
- £ ££
- Princetown Jail Ale plus guests
- Lunch, evening and snack menus
- Credit cards accepted

Yorkshire and Northern Lincolnshire

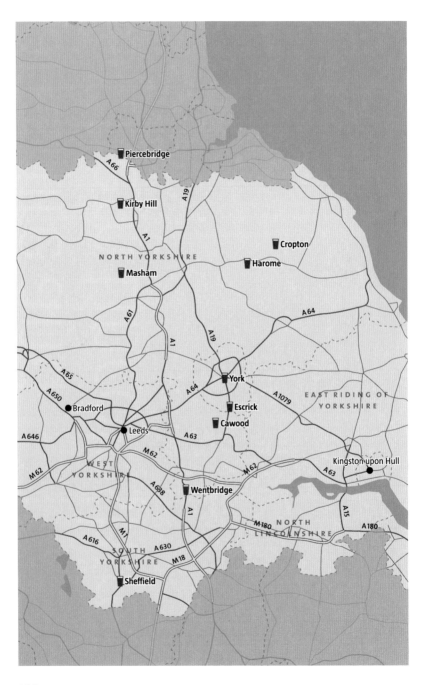

For more than 2,000 years YORKSHIRE has dared to be different.

Many of its beers are different too, with many brewers still using the traditional slate Yorkshire Square in which to ferment their beers.

Once a kingdom in its own right, England's biggest county has never lost that sense of being special. A grandeur you don't get anywhere else, the power of its history and pride of its people make this a place where 'ordinary' simply won't do.

Yorkshire together with Northern Lincolnshire is most sublimely beautiful: ruined abbeys and castles, great houses and gardens are framed by high moors, wooded hills and lush farming country. Three National Parks: the Yorkshire Dales, the Peak District and the North York Moors protect more than 1,000 square miles of matchless walking country.

Masham is a small, beautiful town high in the Yorkshire Dales and it is home to two marvellous real ale breweries, Theakston and Black Sheep, which both have visitors' centres.

The Theakston Brewery is owned by the mighty Scottish and Newcastle, founded in 1827. More than £1 million has been invested in recent years in the brewery and in developing its museum.

Its famous beer is Old Peculier, a full-bodied, rich dark brown, strong ale. In Medieval times the town grew rich from the sale of wool, and the town was given a "peculier" status independent of the local archdeacon after which the beer is named.

Visitors can see the brewing process, which still uses the state of the art, tower brewery equipment which was installed in 1875. A cooper is employed on site, who continues to craft the wooden casks still used to supply local pubs.

The Black Sheep Brewery was set up in 1992 by Paul Theakston, a member of the town's famous brewing family, in the former Wellgarth Maltings.

The Black Sheep complex includes video shows of the brewing process, a brewery shop and a bistro.

There is so much to see in the area. The National Museum of Photography, Film and Television in Bradford is the most visited museum outside London.

The National Railway Museum in York is the European Museum of the Year.

Watch live combat at the Royal Armouries in Leeds, the world's premier collection of armaments. Prepare to invade the new Viking city of Jorvik in York, re-opened after a multi million investment. Go down a mine shaft at the National Coal Mining Museum near Wakefield which is linked by a Yorkshire Discovery Trail to Yorkshire Sculpture Park and historic Elsecar at Barnsley.

CAWOOD

The Ferry

2 King Street, Cawood, North Yorkshire YO8 3TL
T 01757 268515
E lynnmoore@theferry.fsnet.co.uk
www.ferryinn.f9.co.uk
Licensees: Lynn Moore and Phil Daggitt
Directions: South side of river, near swing bridge

The Ferry Inn, standing on the banks of the River Ouse, is situated in Cawood, a small village between Selby and the historic city of York. The Ferry as it is known to the locals has often appeared on TV after many near encounters with the floods in the Vale of York and has gained many new customers who came to witness the events. The Ferry has a wooden sign displaying the menu of a medieval banquet hailed "the greatest feast ever recorded" in the village castle in 1464. Customers should not mistake this exotic menu which includes porpoises, 400 mallards and teals, 12 seals and 104 peacocks for the pub's more traditional menu.

- One double, one double, one triple
- **£** £ £10 supplement for single
- **Marston's Pedigree, Timothy Taylor Landlord** plus guests often from micros
- Lunch, evening and snack menus
- Credit cards accepted

CROPTON

The New Inn

Woolcroft, Cropton, Nr Pickering, YO18 8HH
T 01751 417330   **F** 01751 417582
E info@croptonbrewery.co.uk
www.croptonbrewery.co.uk

The New Inn has had more nominations from CAMRA members than any other pub in this book and is said to offer one of the finest pints in North Yorkshire with food to match. It is right on the very edge of the North York Moors National Park and is home to the Cropton Brewery, famed for its additive free beers which are suitable for

Cropton Brewery, The New Inn, Cropton

The New Inn, Cropton

vegans and vegetarians. Food is served in the delightful Victoria restaurant. Accommodation is 10 en suite rooms – nine are doubles in the pub itself, two with an additional single bed, one double is in a separate cottage. The pub organises a beer festival every November.

🛏 Eight doubles, two triple
£ ££
🍺 **Cropton's** full range of additive free beers
🍴 Lunch, evening and snack menus
💳 Credit cards accepted

ESCRICK

The Black Bull

Main Street, Escrick, York YO19 6JP
T 01904 728245   F 01904 728154
E blackbullhotel@btconnect.com
www.yorkblackbullinn.co.uk

Traditional cottage styled inn set in an idyllic village 15 minutes from Historic York centre. Blazing log fire in winter, magnificent flower baskets in summer. Close to York Race Course. Excellent cuisine, member of Les Routiers 2003. No smoking dining room. Ten en suite beautiful bedrooms, colour TV, tea and coffee facilities, trouser press. Accommodation includes four-poster bed. Room with sunken bath. Children welcome and catered for. Special overnight breaks available.

🛏 Six double, two twin, two single
£ ££
🍺 **Tetley, John Smiths Beer**, plus regular guests
🍴 Lunch, evening and snack menus
💳 Credit cards accepted

HAROME

Star Inn

Harome, Helmsley, North Yorkshire YO62 5JE
T 01439 770397   F 01439 771833
Licensees: Andrew and Jackie Pern
Directions: From Helmsley take A170 towards Kirkbymoorside. After half a mile turn right for Harome

One of only three pubs in the UK to hold a Michelin Star, the food is influenced by the meals owner Andrew Pern ate as a farmer's son – pheasants, grouse and pigeon, complimented by the salmon his grandfather smoked and fresh fish from Whitby. This 14th-century thatched pub has just eight tables in the restaurant and six in the bar, unmistakeably English and distinctively pubby.

The accommodation on three-and-a-half acres opposite the pub comprises three suites in the Back Eagle cottage and eight bedrooms in the Cross House Lodge. The lodge has on-site cooking coming from an open plan kitchen and bakery, where a chef cooks fresh bread daily for sale in the pub and village shop. Pub customers can come in just for a beer and play dominoes or have a full meal. The menu is just a guideline as guests can ask the chef to cook whatever they want. The nearby Helmsley is one of the North Riding's prettiest market towns. Children welcome.

🛏 Three suites with own kitchens and eight double rooms
£ ££££
🍺 **Black Sheep Special** and regular guests
🍴 Snack and meals – very flexible
💳 Credit cards accepted

KIRBY HILL

Shoulder of Mutton

Kirby Hill, Richmond, North Yorkshire DL11 7JH
T 01748 822772   F 01325 718936
E info@shoulderofmutton.net
www.shoulderofmutton.net
Licensees: Mick and Anne Burns

An ivy-fronted country inn in a beautiful hillside setting overlooking lower Teesdale and the ruins of Ravensworth Castle. Just opposite the village church and the narrow entrance to the historic, enclosed village green. Carpeted and cosy throughout the linked spaces of the opened-out front bar, which is traditionally decorated with old brasses and plates on oak beams. Lounge bar and restaurant to the rear. An ideal base from which to explore the Yorkshire Dales National Park, the North York Moors National Park, the North Pennines and the coast.

🛏 Four double and one family

£ ££

🍺 **Black Sheep Best Bitter, Black Sheep Riggwelter, Jennings Cumberland Ale, John Smith's Cask Bitter**

🍴 Lunch, evening and snack menus

Kings Head

Market Place, Masham, Yorkshire HG4 4EF
T 01765 689295   F 01765 689070
E masham.kingshead@snr.co.uk
Licensees: Philip and Samantha Capon
Directions: Located on the Market Square

The King's Head is a fine Georgian building dating back to the 18th century, situated in the Market Square of the picturesque town of Masham. The town is a must for any beer lover as it is home to two of England's finest real ale breweries, Theakston and Black Sheep, both of which have visitor centres. From the outset The King's Head was always more than an inn. In its time it has been combined with a Posting House and,

Kings Head,
Masham

surprisingly, an Excise Office. It now offers a warm welcome with an excellent menu range and serves traditional Theakston's cask ales and an extensive wine list, making it a popular choice for both locals and visitors to the town.

The 10 stylish bedrooms are all individually designed and named, with some using a brewing theme. They offer the modern luxuries with beautiful antique furniture. Some of the rooms have four-poster beds and Jacuzzi baths, though anyone staying in the Head Brewers room has to be careful not to flood the bar below. Most rooms look out over the Market Square so you can watch the world go by!

- 🛏 10 doubles
- £ £££
- 🍺 **Theakson Cool Cask**, **Best Bitter**, **Black Bull** and **Old Peculier**
- 🍴 Lunch, evening and snack menus
- 💳 Credit cards accepted

PIERCEBRIDGE

George Hotel

Piercebridge-on-Tees, Darlington DL2 3SW
T 01325 374576
www.thegeorgehotel.activehotels.com
Directions: On B6275, Dere Street

A famous 16th-century coaching inn at the Yorkshire end of the 16th century wide-arched, sandstone Pierce Bridge over the River Tees. Home of a famous grandfather clock – the one that "stopped, never to go again, when the old man died". The wooden hanging sign over the main door is by Mousey Thompson – spot the trademark mouse. A choice of two cosy bars with welcoming real fires.

- 🛏 Nine twin, 25 double
- £ ££/£££
- 🍺 **Black Sheep Best Bitter**, **Taylor's Landlord**, **Adnams Broadside**
- 🍴 Lunch, evening and snack menus
- 💳 Credit cards accepted

SHEFFIELD

Hillsborough Hotel

54–58 Langsett Road, Sheffield S6 2UB
T/F 0114 2322100
E reception@hillsboroughhotel.com
www.hillsboroughhotel.com
Licensee: Del Tilling

A real ale paradise. Opened in 1999 following refurbishment, the Hillsborough is a recent CAMRA/English Heritage Design Award winner. It is a free house and English Tourist Board 2 Star hotel, situated between Sheffield Town Centre and Hillsborough. Ideally placed for visitors to Sheffield, being within easy reach of all the major attractions including The Ski Village, Crucible and Lyceum Theatres, Sheffield Arena/Don Valley Stadium and Meadowhall Shopping Centre. The Supertram runs directly from Sheffield Midland Station to the hotel. All rooms are en suite with TV and there is secure under-cover parking. Free Internet/data facilities.

Beers from the award winning on-site Crown Brewery are supplemented by a range of 15 guest beers, eight on handpull and eight from jugs direct from the cellar.

- 🛏 Three double, three twin
- £ £££
- 🍺 **Crown Brewery** beers plus at least 15 guests
- 🍴 Lunch, evening and snack menus
- 💳 Credit cards accepted

WENTBRIDGE near Pontefract

The Blue Bell

Old Great North Road, Wentbridge, Pontefract, West Yorkshire WF8 3JP
T 01977 620697
www.pub-explorer.com/thepubs/bluebellhotel pontefract
Licensees: Paul and Sue Stafford
Directions: On Old Great North Road just off modern A1

Situated in the picturesque village of Wentbridge on the old A1. A former coaching inn, it was rebuilt in 1633. An original sign hangs in the entrance. It stands at the head of the Brockadale, the smallest of the Yorkshire Dales in the valley of the tiny River Went, with nature reserve areas noted for magnesian Limestone flora and fauna, crag and woodland paths. A warm, friendly atmosphere, it is noted for its excellent range of food which includes several vegetarian options. It is comfortably furnished with Mousey Thompson chairs and tables. The pub is close to Castleford Freeport Designer Outlet Mall, one junction west on M62 and a short drive from the Mid Yorkshire Golf Club, Darrington. Not suitable for children.

🛏 Four doubles
£ ££
🍺 **Bass Bitter, Timothy Taylor Landlord, Tetley Bitter**
🍴 Lunch, evening and snack menus
💳 Credit cards accepted

YORK

The Carlton Tavern

140 Acomb Road, York YO24 4HA
T 01904 781181

Acomb, York's largest suburb lies to the east of the city centre. The pub is a smart conversion of a former hotel. A popular Sunday Carvery is served in the spacious,

no smoking, conservatory and outside the patio leads to extensive enclosed gardens. This family pub has full disabled facilities for guests and pub users and the accommodation is in separate chalets at the rear.

🛏 One double, two twin, one family
£ £ ££ single
🍺 **Marston's Pedigree, Camerons Creamy** and **Strongarm**
🍴 Lunch, evening and snack menus
💳 Credit cards accepted

The Victoria

1 Heslington Road, York YO10 5AR
T 01904 622295

Nice cosy pub, renovated by Old Mill Brewery whose splendid beers are on tap. It is one of the best pubs you will find on the outskirts of the city centre. Nice decor and good jukebox, although if it's left alone for too long it starts to choose its own songs! The only regular outlet for mild in York, it is handy for the Barbican Centre. Accommodation is five rooms, all en suite.

🛏 Two double, two twin and one single
£ ££ £££ single
🍺 **Old Mill Traditional Mild, Old Mill Guest Beers, Traditional Bitter, Bullion**
🍴 Lunch, evening and snack menu
💳 Credit cards accepted

Scotland

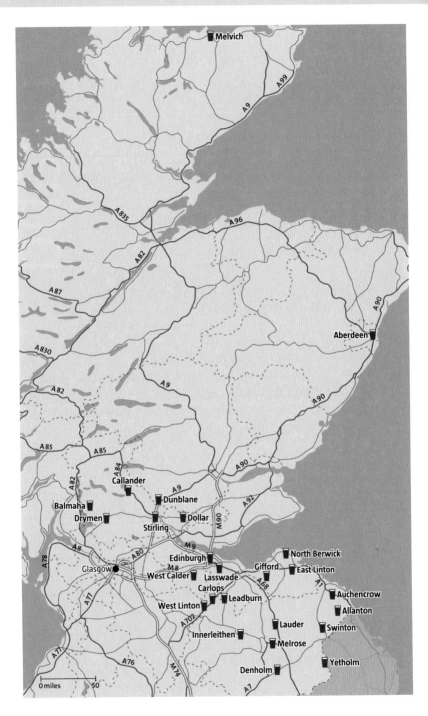

Think of SCOTLAND and you think of whisky – and yes the distillation of the malted grain does generate millions of pounds in exports.

But the truth is, if you think of Scotland you *should* think of beer.

There was a time when real ale was seldom seen, but a quiet revolution has taken place in recent years – brewers are taking cask conditioned beer to the Highlands and Islands, the lowlands and cities.

Space is too limited to list them all but the Traquair House Brewery in Innerleithen still uses the 18th century brewhouse in the wings of the 1,000-year old Traquair House, Scotland's oldest inhabited house, visited by Mary Queen of Scots.

Harviestoun Brewery in Dollar, Clackmannanshire has won many plaudits for the quality of its beers. Its golden session beer Brooker's Bitter and Twisted, a former Champion Beer of Britain, is one of the finest beers to be brewed north or south of the border.

And the Heather Ale Brewery in Strathaven, Lanarkshire produces Fraoch Heather Ale using flowering heather picked from the grounds around a stunning 18th century watermill which houses the brewery.

Edinburgh is home to the Caledonian Brewing Company, or the *Callie* as it is known to its friends and admirers worldwide.

Saved from closure by a management buyout in 1978, beer is brewed in three direct fired open coppers, the last of their type still used in Britain. Its Golden Promise Organic Ale is the original organic ale and the award winning Deuchars IPA was the Champion Beer of Britain in 2002.

And brewing has returned in force to the Highlands and Islands. The Isle of Skye on the Isle of Skye, Quoyloo on Orkney, Valhalla in the Shetlands and Hebridean on the Western Isles, all brew beers of great distinction.

The most northerly brew pub on the mainland, is the Far North in Melvich, Thurso. It originally brewed one cask a week for hotel guests working at the Dounray nuclear site but has recently expanded production.

The Valhalla Brewery on the island of Unst in the Shetlands has the distinction of being the most northerly brewery in Great Britain.

Think of Scotland and think of beer and think of the magnificent pubs where they can now be drunk, at a time that suits the beer drinker.

Scotland swept away its outmoded licensing laws in the 1970s making it much easier for drinkers to be able to go out and enjoy a drink at a time that suited them.

If only the legislators in England and Wales could have acted in such a foresighted way.

ABERDEEN

Globe Inn

13–15 North Silver Street, Aberdeen AB10 1RJ
T 01224 624258

The CAMRA member who recommended the Globe says it is a real gem for visitors to this northern Scottish city it is centrally located and offers excellent value for money. This Good Beer Guide listed pub has recently expanded to include seven letting rooms. A friendly, open pub with a single bar. Folk music evenings are frequently held, and musical instruments decorate the bar. Ideally located for both the theatre and music hall, it enjoys a substantial lunchtime food trade. Continental breakfast provided in the room.

- Seven double
- **£** £
- **Houston Peter's Well** plus guest
- Lunch, evening and snack menus
- Credit cards accepted

ALLANTON

Allanton Inn

Allanton by Duns, Berwickshire TD11 3JZ
T 01890 818260   **F** 01361 882014
Directions: On the B6437, one mile south of Chirnside off A6105

Traditional welcoming Borders coaching inn in a village surrounded by rolling farmland. The exterior still boasts hitching rings for horses. The front part of the bar is cosy and functional with stone flagstones around the bar. The back area has a juke-box and a pool table. An interesting variation of up to three real ales are on sale along with a traditional perry. The restaurant has a good varied menu which features local ingredients and it has won awards for its haggis. Children are welcome.

- Two double, one twin, two family
- **£** ££
- Beer range varies, but normally at least one Scottish ale
- Lunch, evening and snack menus
- Credit cards accepted

AUCHENCROW

Craw Inn

Auchencrow, Eyemouth, Borders TD14 5LS
T/F 01890 761253
Licensee: Trevor Wilson
Directions: On the B6438, signed from the A1 at Reston

The Craw Inn is a welcoming village pub not far from the coast. Built around 1680, the wooden beamed bar has bench seating at one end and wooden tables by the log-burning stove at the other. Two real ales are usually from smaller brewers and change regularly. The non-smoking rear of the inn has wonderful views of the surrounding countryside and is divided into a lounge cum-eating area and restaurant. The traditional furniture gives it a select feel. Local produce is used in the wide-ranging menu.

Children are welcome to stay and guests with disabilities can also be catered for. The three guest rooms are attractively decorated in country style and all offer en suite facilities. Pets can be accommodated by arrangement.

- One double, one twin, one family
- **£** ££
- Beer range varies
- Lunch, evening and snack menus
- Credit cards accepted

BALMAHA

Oak Tree Inn

Balmaha Road, Balmaha, Loch Lomond G63 0JQ
T 01360 870357 **F** 01360 870350
E info@oak-tree-inn.co.uk
www.oak-tree-inn.co.uk
Licensees: Lucy and Sandy Fraser
Directions: Close to Loch Lomond and the West Highland Way

Take a break from the well trodden tourist route and visit the Oak Tree Inn on the east shore of Loch Lomond. The Oak Tree Inn stands in the shade of a magnificent 500 year old oak tree, a focal point in the village and the perfect setting in which to relax. Every detail of design and construction has been meticulous in order to create a truly unique environment for visitors and guests. This is complemented by the impressive welcoming interior with its extensive use of natural oak which sets the mood perfectly.

Of special note is the bar area, constructed from a 300 year old oak tree. In a remarkable salvage operation, timbers and panelling were dismantled from a neighbouring country house dating from 1864. A local slate quarry was reopened for this one building and all the slates were reclaimed from the roof of Buchanan Castle. All this ensures its uniqueness in the area. The 1600 tons of slate extracted from the quarry was moved to site where it was painstakingly cut and constructed over a period of twelve months using traditional building methods to give the Oak Tree Inn its authentic rustic appeal. Child friendly, there is even a room for walkers to dry wet clothes.

- Four double, three twin. Two of the rooms have an adjoining door, which would be suitable for a family
- **£** ££
- One guest ale
- Lunch evening and snack menus
- Credit cards accepted

CALLANDER

Waverley Hotel

88–94 Main Street, Callander, Perthshire FK17 8BD
T 01877 330245 **F** 01877 331120
E enquiries@thewaverleycallander.com
www.thewaverleycallander.com
Licensees: Gordon and Margaret Scott

A haven for lovers of Real Ale it offers value for money and comfortable accommodation. All rooms are spacious and have hot and cold water and tea/coffee facilities. Most rooms have digital television but at present there are no en suite rooms – families can be accommodated. The Claymore bar stocks beers from Arran and Harviestoun breweries with guests from Houston and Heather. Situated at the gateway to the Trossachs, it is popular with visitors. Two beer festivals are held each year in September and December.

- Single, double and family
- **£** ££
- **Arran Dark, Light, Harviestoun Bitter & Twisted**, plus guest beers
- Lunch, evening and snack menus
- Credit cards accepted

CARLOPS

Allan Ramsay Hotel

Carlops by Penicuik EH26 9NF
T/F 01968 660258
E allanramsay@hotmail.com
www.allanramsayhotel.co.uk
Licensee: Linda Fraser

An attractive family-run hotel in a small village beside the Pentland Hills, originally a flax mill dating from 1792. Several rooms have been knocked through into a single area with many original features retained. The bar is inlayed with pre-decimal pennies. Carlops gets its name from the Gaelic for witches leap and local myth suggests witches leapt from two stones either side of the road near the pub. It is an ideal base for golfing, pony-trekking, hill-walking, cycling, and fishing. All rooms are tastefully decorated with en suite facilities, satellite TV, and a hospitality tray.

🛏 Three twin, one double, three single
£ ££
🍺 **Caledonian Deuchars IPA** plus guests
🍴 Lunch, evening and snack menus
💳 Credit cards accepted

DENHOLM

The Auld Cross Keys Inn

The Green, Denholm, Hawick,
Roxburghshire TD9 8NU
T 01450 870305   **F** 01450 870778
E enquiries@crosskeysdenholm.co.uk
www.crosskeysdenholm.co.uk
Licensee: Peter and Heather Ferguson
Directions: On the A698 Hawick to Kelso road

An 18th century inn by the village green. The Auld Cross Keys Inn has an exceptional reputation in the area for good food, excellent ales and topflight entertainment, with regular folk music and other concerts. The comprehensive menu ranges from dishes such as Creamy Mushroom Crepes to Denholm Beef Sausages which won the "Best Beef Sausages in Scotland" award in 1996. Those not wishing to dine are recommended to try the cheesy eggs or high teas. The hotel stocks a good range of ales, amongst them the local Broughton real ale and an ever-changing guest ale. Children welcome.

🛏 Two twin
£ £
🍺 **Broughton** ales plus guests
🍴 Lunch, evening and snack menus
💳 Credit cards accepted

DOLLAR

Castle Campbell Hotel

11 Bridge Street, Dollar,
Clackmannanshire FK14 7DE
T 01259 742519   **F** 01259 743742
E booking@castle-campbell.co.uk
www.castle-campbell.co.uk
Licensee: Mr Richard Nealon
Directions: In the middle of the town – half-an-hour's drive from Stirling, Falkirk, Grangemouth

The hotel dates back to 1822, when it was a coaching inn and staging post for travellers, overlooked by the Castle Campbell, itself, which was the chief lowland stronghold of the Earls of Argyll. Take a good pair of walking shoes if visiting as the hotel is situated at the foot of the Ochill Hills, with Dollar Glen a short walk away which leads to Castle Campbell at the top of the glen. It has a lovely bright bar, selling locally brewed Harviestoun Ale, two lounges and a restaurant. A basement bar does not sell real ale. Children welcome.

🛏 Six double/twin
£ £££
🍺 **Harviestoun, Orkney, Fuller's London Pride**
🍴 Lunch, evening and snack menus
💳 Credit cards accepted

DRYMEN

The Clachan Inn

The Square, Drymen, Stirlingshire G63 0BG
T 01360 660824
Licensee: Elizabeth Plank
Directions: Off A4811 close to Loch Lomond

Drymen was once a watering hole for roving cattle drovers and the Clachan is said to be Scotland's oldest registered licensed premise; once it had a thatched roof but it is now slated. The simple, white-painted

Castle Campbell Hotel, Dollar

cottage offers bar food and separate restaurant meals and also serves the divine Caledonian Deuchars IPA from Edinburgh, CAMRA's Champion Beer of Britain in 2002. An ideal stopping off point for walkers or those who are travelling further, it offers a warm atmosphere and two single and one double bedrooms.

🛏 Two single, one double
£ £
🍺 **Caledonian Deuchars IPA**
🍴 Lunch and evening menus
💳 Credit cards accepted

DUNBLANE

Dunblane Hotel

10 Stirling Road, Dunblane, Perthshire FK15 9EP
T 01786 822178

Dunblane's importance in history is principally due to its strategic geographical location. Situated where the main roads from the north, the south and the east converge, the parish saw many armies march both north and south, to and from battles. The parish itself however has a peaceful and largely uneventful history, the only battle within its boundaries being the Battle of Sheriffmuir in 1715. The hotel has a bright bar with views over the River Allan. A good

selection of frequently changing ales are served in the lounge bar of this comfortable hotel. It is very close to the railway station and convenient for Stirling, Perth and Gleneagles.

🛏 Four double/twin
£ £££
🍺 **Greene King Old Speckled Hen, Abbot, Tetley Burton Ale** plus guests
🍴 Lunch, evening and snack menus
💳 Credit cards accepted

EAST LINTON

Bridgend Hotel

3 Bridge End, East Linton,
East Lothian, Edinburgh EH40 3AF
T 01620 860202   F 01620 860571
www.thebridgendhotel.co.uk
Licensee: Les Orde
Directions: Off A1

Set in the charming East Lothian village of East Linton, just off the A1 and only 30 minutes drive from Edinburgh. The Bridgend Hotel is the perfect base during a visit to the area. The Bridgend is a village pub with a public bar and lounge. Ownership connections to the Hadrian and Border Brewery means that their beers normally feature in the bars. The stained glass windows and roof top statue hint that the pub was once called the Red Lion. There are six letting rooms all en suite.

🛏 Three double, two twin, one family
£ ££
🍺 **Hadrian** and **Border** beers plus guests
🍴 Lunch, evening and snack menus
💳 Credit cards accepted

Bruntsfield Hotel

69 Bruntsfield Place, Edinburgh, Lothian EH10 4HH
T 0131 229 1393   **F** 0131 229 5634
Licensee: Gary Field
Directions: on A4702 the main road between Tollcross and Morningside

The Kings Bar at the Bruntsfield Hotel is a comfortable, if basic, hotel cellar lounge bar, but it serves good Real Ale normally the award winning Caledonian Deuchars IPA and 80/-. This large town house hotel overlooks one of Edinburgh's many golf courses and is close to Edinburgh castle. Depending upon the season the rates for rooms vary. Children and families are welcome and pets can be accommodated.

🛏 15 single, 23 double, 10 twin, two family
£ £££
🍺 **Caledonian Deuchars IPA**, 80/-
🍴 Lunch, evening and snack menus
💳 Credit cards accepted

Hampton Hotel

14 Corstorphine Road, Edinburgh EH12 6HN
T 0131 337 1130   **F** 0131 313 3621
E info@hampton.hotel.co.uk
Directions: Near Murrayfield Stadium

Situated close by Murrayfield Stadium – the home of Scottish Rugby and only a short distance from Edinburgh's historic city centre – the Hampton Hotel is ideally located for a short stay in Scotland's capital city. The two resident chefs use only the finest, fresh ingredients to prepare daily lunch and dinner menus and the bar offers a wide selection of cask conditioned ales.

The hotel's six well appointed, comfortable bedrooms offer versatile accommodation with single, twin, double or family rooms available. The Hampton is situated on the main route into the city

centre if travelling from the airport, and only a short five minute taxi journey from Haymarket railway station. Ample off-street parking is also available. Children welcome.

🛏 Three double, one twin, one single, one family
£ ££££
🍺 **Belhaven 80/-**, plus three guests
🍴 Lunch, evening and snack menus
💳 Credit cards accepted

Royal Ettrick Hotel

13 Ettrick Road, Edinburgh EH10 5BJ
T 0131 228 6413
Directions: Behind Merchiston tennis and bowling club

Dating from 1860, the Royal is a large suburban villa with a well-appointed lounge bar offering up to seven real ales in what was originally the grand town house of a rich Edinburgh barrister. The house was converted into a hotel in the 1940s, and today it is one of Edinburgh's finest small hotels in a quiet, residential country setting, less than one mile from Princes Street.

🛏 Seven rooms — various formats
£ ££££
🍺 **Caledonian Deuchars IPA**, 80/- plus five guests
🍴 Lunch, evening and snack menus

Goblin Ha' Hotel

Main Street, Gifford, Haddington, East Lothian EH41 4QH
T 01620 810244   **F** 01620 810718
Licensee: Douglas Muir
Directions: 4½ miles south of Haddington, on the B6369 and B6355

Nestling at the foot of the Lammermuir Hills, the charming village of Gifford was mostly laid out in the 1700s. At the heart of the village stands the Goblin Ha' Hotel. Since 1960, the hotel has been in the ownership of the Muir family who like to think that the atmosphere is exceptionally friendly, that the table consists of the best of food, well cooked, with home baking and their own garden produce being a speciality of the hotel.

Guests have a choice of seven rooms, six with full en suite and one with shower only. A golf course is nearby, and Edinburgh is a 20-mile drive away. The beer garden is popular with families in the summer.

🛏 Two double, three twin, two single
£ ££
🍺 **Caledonian Deuchars IPA, Timothy Taylor Landlord, Hop Back Summer Lightning** plus guests
🍴 Lunch, evening and snack menus
▭ Credit cards accepted

INNERLEITHEN

Traquair Arms Hotel

Traquair Road, Innerleithen, Peebleshire EH44 6PD
T 01896 830229   **F** 01896 830260
E traquair.arms@scottishborders.com
www.traquair-arms-hotel.co.uk
Licensee: Gig Johnston
Directions: On the B709, off the A72, six miles south of Peebles

Elegant 18th century family run hotel situated in the picturesque village of Innerleithen, close to the River Tweed which meanders through one of the most beautiful and unspoilt areas of countryside in Britain.

Traquair Arms Hotel, Innerleithen

The plush lounge is decorated with prints of local and historical interest and has a tank of goldfish to provide a relaxing atmosphere. The log fires in the lounge and adjacent dining room provide a cosy, traditional Border atmosphere. Good home-cooked food from local produce is on offer.

The guest beer is often from the local Traquair brewery, situated in the oldest inhabited house in Scotland, which dates from the 18th century and was pressed back into use by the late 20th Laird of Traquair, Peter Maxwell Stuart. Tours of the brewery can be arranged but no one can go in by the main gates as according to tradition these will remain firmly shut until a Stuart is safely back on the throne.

🛏 Three single, five double, five twin, two family
£ £££
🍺 **Broughton Greenmantle Ale, Traquair Bear Ale**
🍴 Lunch, evening and snack menus
▭ Credit cards accepted

LASSWADE

The Laird & Dog Hotel

5 High Street, Lasswade, Midlothian EH18 1NA
T/F 0131 663 9219
www.lairdanddog.btinternet.co.uk
Licensee: Frederick Mehlson
Directions: On A768 near river bridge

The Laird & Dog Hotel is an old inn set in the middle of the village of Lasswade close to the River Esk. It is a comfortable village local catering for all tastes, from the music-loving pool player to those who enjoy a quiet drink or meal. The pub oozes local life with historical pictures and horse brasses. The food is good and plentiful with an extensive conservatory menu, daily specials and cheaper bar options. An interesting bottle-shaped well, a real fire surrounded by arm chairs and two real ales usually from smaller breweries complete the picture.

- Three double, four twin, one family, one single
- £ ££
- Two guest beers, usually one brewed in Scotland
- Lunch, evening and snack menus
- Credit cards accepted

LAUDER

Eagle Hotel

1 Market Place, Lauder, Peeblesshire TD2 6SR
T 01578 722225　**F** 01578 722426
Licensee: Ron Dick
Directions: On the A68

A friendly, rambling hotel dating from 1665 in this small market town on the A68. The stone wall surrounding the fireplace and the ornate bar are features of the comfortable lounge. The more functional bar has an interesting mirrored-backed gantry and a real fire. The bar can be a crowded jostle when big rugby games are played, and much rugby memorabilia hangs on the walls.

The Eagle offers a good range of Real Ales, with at least one guest cask a week, plus an occasional traditional cider. The bar menu offers options for children as well as vegetarians. Children are welcome to stay overnight as well as in the family room. Two other rooms can accommodate an additional child's bed.

- One single, one double, one twin, two family
- £ £
- **Caledonian Deuchars IPA** plus guests
- Lunch, evening and snack menus
- Credit cards accepted

LEADBURN

Leadburn Inn

Leadburn, Nr Penicuik, West Linton, Peeblesshire EH46 7BE
T 01968 672952　**F** 01968 676752
E info@Leadburninn.com
Licensee: Adrian Dempsey
Directions: On A701 at A701/A703/A6904 junction

The Leadburn is one of the oldest inns in Scotland, established in 1777. Bonnie Prince Charlie was still alive and Napoleon only a schoolboy, when the Thomson family were given "the privilege and liberty of brewing, baking, vending and retailing ales, spirits bread and others". The brewing no longer takes place but traditional cooking, Real Ales and hospitality abound. A railway coach has been converted into a function room. The functional public bar overlooks the Pentland Hills. A conservatory, with a massive grape vine, links the bar to a plush lounge. The beer range usually includes beers from the smaller Scottish micros. All the letting rooms are en suite.

- Two double, two single, two family
- £ £
- Four regularly changing guest ales
- Lunch, evening and snack menus
- Credit cards accepted

MELROSE

Burts Hotel

Melrose TD6 9PN
T 01896 822285　**F** 01896 822870
E burtshotel@aol.com
www.burtshotel.co.uk
Licensee: Graham Henderson
Directions: In main square

An elegant family run hotel almost in the shadow of the three peaks of the Eildon Hills, at the very heart of the Scottish Borders, in the picturesque 18th century setting of Melrose Market Square. Built in 1772, Burts retains and reflects the period charm of that time. Its elegant restaurant offers à la carte and table d'hôte menus skilfully

Burts Hotel, Melrose

prepared by Head Chef Gary Moore and his dedicated brigade using the best of produce from Scotland's Natural Larder.

Activities near Burts Hotel include sightseeing, castles, gardens, stately homes, golf, shooting, fishing, rambling and walking. It is an area of myth and legend, of beautiful and contrasting scenery, the inspiration for Sir Walter Scott's historic novels whose descriptions brought 18th century visitors from around the world to experience the splendour at first hand. Close-by is Melrose Abbey, where the heart of Robert the Bruce lays buried, and the Teddy Bear museum. Children welcome.

🛏 Four double, six twin, seven single, three family
£ ££££
🍺 **Caledonian Deuchars IPA, 80/-** plus guests
🍽 Lunch, evening and snack menus
💳 Credit cards accepted

MELROSE

The Kings Arms Hotel

High Street, Melrose TD6 9PB
T 01896 822143   F 01361 823812
E enquiries@kingsarmsmelrose.co.uk
www.kingsarmsmelrose.co.uk
Licensees: Mike and Helen Dalgetty

One of Melrose's best loved inns is The Kings Arms in the High Street. A former coaching inn which dates back almost 300 years, it was used as the original meeting place of the Melrose Rugby Football Club, the founders of Sevens Rugby. The bar has a wooden floor, church pew seating, wooden tables and is decorated with a rugby theme.

There are seven en suite bedrooms which are comfortably furnished with a traditional feel and offer all the usual facilities for the weary traveller. Lovers of good food will enjoy the traditional Scottish dishes using only the finest quality beef and game. This 17th century coaching inn provides guests with a warm welcome to this lovely area and comfortable surroundings in which to spend a delightful holiday.

🛏 One single, one double, three twin, two family
£ £££
🍺 **Tetley Bitter**, **Burton Ale** plus guest
🍽 Lunch, evening and snack menus
💳 Credit cards accepted

MELVICH

Melvich Hotel

Melvich by Thurso, Caithness KW14 7YJ
T 01641 531206   F 01641 531347
E melvichtl@aol.com
Licensee: Peter Martin

The home of Far North, the mainland's most northerly brewery, it is the antithesis of frenetic urban life. Situated on Scotland's northern seaboard, 18 miles west of Thurso on the A836 and 40 miles north of Helmsdale on the A897. A comfortable but informal country hotel with a cliff top position overlooking Melvich Bay to the Island of Hoy and the Orkney mainland beyond.

Melvich Hotel, Melvich

The hotel has 14 en suite modern bedrooms. These are fully equipped with colour TV, coffee/tea making facilities, radio alarms, and shower with WC. The lounge bar with its peat fire has wonderful views over the bay to Orkney. There is also a games room with a pool table adjacent to the public bar where you can experience true highland spirits. The large garden allows guests to take in the breathtaking sight and sound of the surf from the bay.

- 14 bedrooms
- £ £ £ single
- **Far North Real Mackay, Split Stone Pale, Fast Reactor**
- Lunch, evening and snack menu
- Credit cards accepted

NORTH BERWICK

Nether Abbey Hotel

20 Dirleton Avenue, North Berwick,
East Lothian EH39 4BQ
T 01620 892802   F 01620 895298
E bookings@nether-abbey.freeserve.co.uk
www.netherabbey.co.uk
Licensee: Stirling Stewart
Directions: On A198, one kilometre west of town centre

Sitting on the Scottish (eastern) Riviera, North Berwick is a charming seaside town with sandy beaches, a picturesque harbour and a bustling high street surrounded by beautiful countryside. The area provides some of the best golf courses in Scotland. Muirfield, North Berwick, Dunbar and Gullane are only some of the twenty courses within a twenty minute drive, all offering a different challenge and attracting golfers from around the world. The Nether Abbey, a family run hotel in a Victorian villa, boasts a comfortable bar and bistro. An annual real ale festival is held in February. Children welcome, cheaper rates during winter months. The rooms have recently been refurbished.

- Four double, three twin, five family, one single
- £ ££
- **Caledonian Deuchars IPA** plus three guests
- Lunch, evening and snack menus
- Credit cards accepted

STIRLING

The Portcullis

Castle Wynd, Stirling, Stirlingshire FK8 1EG
T 01786 472290   F 01786 446103
E theportcullis@aol.com
www.theportcullishotel.com
Directions: Beside Stirling Castle in the Old Town of Stirling

The Wheatsheaf has many accolades for its food and hospitality. Excellent examples of local game and seafood are served with the added flavour of the chef's innovative flair. Menus are extensive with extra dishes of the day. It has eight bedrooms all of which are en suite. There are three large comfortable dining and lounge areas. A small dimly lit snug bar has an oak topped counter, church pews and photos of local legend racing driver Jim Clark. The bar offers a taste of Scotland with beers from Caledonian and Broughton breweries often on sale. Children welcome.

🛏 Five double, three twin
£ £££
🍺 **Caledonian 80/-**, plus guests
🍴 Lunch, evening and snack menus
💳 Credit cards accepted

The hotel is small, friendly and family run. At present there are four rooms which are all en suite and are equipped with central heating, tea and coffee making facilities, telephone and television. The rooms to the front of the building have wonderful views over the town and to the Ochill Hills beyond. The hotel itself was built in 1787 and its original purpose in life was to serve the community as a school for boys. It stands on the site of the previous school which was demolished when it became too small. Indeed within the walls of the former building, King James VI of Scotland was educated – more than five centuries ago.

🛏 Four double/twin
£ £££
🍺 **Orkney Dark Island** plus guest
🍴 Lunch evening and snack menus
💳 Credit cards accepted

SWINTON

The Wheatsheaf

Swinton, Berwickshire TD11 3JJ
T 01890 860257   **F** 01890 860688
E reception@wheatsheaf-swinton.co.uk
www.wheatsheaf-swinton.co.uk
Licensees: Julie and Alan Reid

WEST CALDER

Railway Inn

43 Main St, West Calder, West Lothian EH55 8DL
T 01506 871475
Licensee: George Stark

Well kept bar and lounge with a large island bar and very attractive central gantry, window screens, corniced ceiling and wooden detail around archways and doors. There is a collection of liquor on top of the gantry and whisky jugs, beer mugs, miner's lamps and horse brasses below. Children welcome. The three letting rooms offer basic and clean accommodation.

🛏 Two double, one single
£ £
🍺 Range of guests
🍴 Lunch, evening and snack menus
💳 Credit cards accepted

WEST LINTON

Gordon Arms Hotel

Dolphinton Road, West Linton,
Peebleshire EH46 7DR
T/F 01968 660208
Licensee: John and Debbie Cleary

Directions: On the A702, about 17 miles south of Edinburgh

Close to the Pentland Hills the pub is situated in a village from where many people commute into Edinburgh. The public bar is L-shaped with stone walls and an interesting cornice. A homely feel is created with a collection of sofas and chairs. The restaurant has a continental feel with wooden floors and a neatly arranged dining area. Outside is a small beer garden. Children welcome.

- One single, three double, one family
- £ ££
- **Caledonian Deuchars** plus guest
- Lunch, evening and snack menu
- Credit cards accepted

Plough Hotel

Main Street, by Kelso, Yetholm,
Roxburghshire, TD5 8RF
T 01573 420215
Licensee: John Darling
Directions: On B6352

A friendly village local dating from 1710. It is set in idyllic surrounds near the end of the Pennine Way and at the midway point of the St Cuthbert's Walk. The tastefully modernised public bar has wood panelling around the fireplace. A separate functional games room has a pool table and video machine. The small, tastefully decorated, dining room is non-smoking. Memorabilia of the gypsy king and queen adorn the walls.

- Two double, one twin, one family
- £ ££
- **Greene King Old Speckled Hen**
- Lunch, evening and snack menus
- Credit cards accepted

Wales

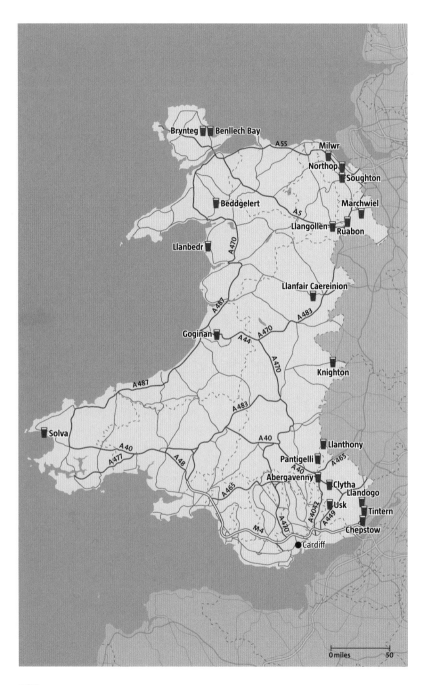

When a lot of people think of WALES they think of mountains, or rivers, valleys or seascapes. Yes, Wales has all those things – plenty of them. But it's also a fun and entertaining country to visit – with some fabulous pubs and ales.

It also has a rich brewing heritage, as long before the English could boast about Burton beer and London porter, Welsh ale was famous – with every household expected to brew its own beer.

Wales has a distinct culture all of its own. The National Eisteddfod dates back to the 12th century and is staged at a different venue each year.

It has the Urdd Eisteddfod, Europe's largest youth arts festival which attracts 100,000-plus visitors annually. There is also the annual International Musical Eisteddfod, when the town of Llangollen hosts singers and dancers from all over the world.

The Bryn Terfel Faenol Festival – set against the backdrop of the mountains of Snowdonia – takes place on the August bank holiday weekend and is fast becoming a must-see each year. And of course, there's Brecon Jazz. It's now one of the great international festivals on the jazz circuit and always features some of the top names from the jazz world.

Travel in the south and experience the joys of a pint of Brains or Tomos Watkin but also look out for beer from some of the country's micros. Wales is known as the land of song and the Bryn Celyn Brewery in Swansea names one of its beers after Buddy Holly.

The beers from Cwmbran Brewery on the slopes of Mynydd Maen in Upper Cwbran in Gwent's Easter Valley are brewed with water from a mountain spring.

Visitors to the West of Wales should try and seek out beers from the famous Felinfoel Brewery, now the oldest brewery in Wales. Its present building built in the 1870s is Grade II listed.

Travellers should also try brews from Bragdy Ceredigion Brewery in Pentre-Gat, Coles Brewery in Llanddarog and the Nag's Head in Abercych.

In the north beer lovers will find many English Ales, but any visitor to Anglesey should seek out beers from the Bragdy Ynys Mon Brewery in Talwm, especially its bottled beers which are filled on site, unfiltered straight from the cask.

And with the help of the CAMRA Good Beer Guide, ale travellers should look for beers from the Plassey Brewery in Eyton and the Snowdonia Brewery in Waunfawr.

ABERGAVENNY

Somerset Arms

Victoria Street, Abergavenny,
Monmouthshire NP7 5DT
T 01873 852158
www.powellsomerset@aol.com
Licensees: Ray and Alison Powell
Directions: Situated on the junction with Merthyr Road, just out of the town centre

Abergavenny is often described as the gateway to Wales and is situated on the edge of the Brecon Beacons National Park. With good train and road links to Cardiff, Hereford and Bristol. The Somerset Arms is a thriving example of a town street-corner pub – often vibrant and never dull, with separate public bar and lounge. In summer the exterior features colourful floral hanging baskets. There is always a guest beer from an independent brewery on tap. The public bar, which certainly does not have a male only feel, is a great place for those who like TV sport, with a large screen for big soccer games, and excellent music from the landlord's extensive CD collection – or he may even start playing himself! The lounge is more sedate, and is also used as the dining room for the popular good value meals and is home to the popular quiz which is held every Sunday night. The pub is just a short distance outside the town centre and makes an ideal venue – a warm welcome awaits all visitors who like to stay in traditional public houses. The big breakfasts are legendary!

🛏 Two twin rooms
£ Price is per room – £45.00
🍺 **Draught Bass** (winter), **Worthington Bitter**, Regular guest beer (usually from local independents)
🍴 Lunch, evening and snack menus
💳 Credit cards not accepted

BEDDGELERT

Tanronnen Inn

Beddgelert, Gwynedd LL55 4YB
T 01766 890347   **F** 01766 890606
www.frederic-robinson.com
Licensee: Alun Hughes
Directions: A498/A4085

Situated in the heart of Snowdonia National Park with some of the most magnificent and unspoiled countryside, not just in Wales, but in Britain. The Tanronnen is in the heart of the village and has seven en suite bedrooms, together with a beautiful restaurant. It is quiet, relaxing and comfortable. There are two lounge bars and a separate coffee lounge with a large open fire. The ideal spot to enjoy a glass of Frederic's after a day's hill walking. Children welcome.

🛏 Five double, one twin, one double with single
£ £££
🍺 **Frederic Robinson Cumbria Way**, **Best Bitter**
🍴 Lunch, evening and snack menus
💳 Credit cards accepted

The Prince Llewelyn

Smith Street, Beddgelert, Gwynedd LL55 4LT
T 01766 890242   **F** 01766 890808
E kay@princellewelyn.fsnet.co.uk
Licensee: Mrs Kay Kislingbury
Directions: On A498

Situated in the heart of the Snowdonia Mountains the Prince seeks to offer peaceful accommodation, good home cooked fare and real ale. Activities such as climbing, hill

walking, golf, fishing, sail boarding and pony trekking are all available nearby. The hotel has 11 bedrooms with single, double, twin and family rooms – some of which are en suite. Children welcome.

🛏 Seven double, three single, two family
£ £
🍺 **Robinson's Best Bitter** plus guest
🍴 Lunch, evening and snack menus
💳 Credit cards accepted

BENLLECH BAY

Breeze Hill Hotel

Benllech Bay, Anglesey, Gwynedd LL74 8TN
T/F 01248 852308
E contact@breezehill.co.uk
www.breezehill.co.uk
Licensee: Mr A J Hargreaves

Recently refurbished there are now four en suite bedrooms, most with a view over the sea. Children are welcome at the Breeze Hill which is an ideal base for exploring the island. Walking, fishing, golf and boating are all available nearby.

🛏 Two double, one twin, one family
£ ££
🍺 **Robinson's Best Bitter** plus seasonal ales
🍴 Lunch, evening and snack menus
💳 Credit cards accepted

BRYNTEG

California

Bryntech, Nr Benllech, Anglesey, Gwynedd LL78 8JR
T 01248 852360   F 01248 853547
Licensee: Barbara Walton

Near several main tourist attractions and opposite a golf course, the California is ideal for families wishing to explore the area. There is a large lounge bar, separate restaurant and function room and a family room conservatory plus a beer garden. Children welcome. Flexible room rates are available for longer stays. All rooms are en suite.

🛏 Three double, two family
£ £
🍺 **Robinson's Best Bitter**
🍴 Lunch, evening and snack menus
💳 Credit cards accepted

CHEPSTOW

Castle View Hotel

16 Bridge Street, Chepstow, Gwent, Wales NP16 5EZ
T 01291 620349   F 01291 627397
E info@hotelchepstow.co.uk
www.hotelchepstow.co.uk
Licensees: David and Tacilia Jones
Directions: Near old Wye Bridge and castle

Aptly named residential hotel on the doorstep of the famous castle (used in several film sets), the oldest stone castle built in Europe. The hotel is an attractive whitewashed ivy-clad building, originally a private house built circa 1700 and extended about 150 years ago. 18th century wall paintings are still visible in some rooms. The tastefully decorated lounge bar, giving views of the magnificent castle, is adjoined by a small dining room offering Egon Ronay recommended food. There is a pleasant garden at the rear. A short stroll from the old iron bridge spanning the River Wye that gives access to England. The pub is an ideal base for anyone wanting to explore Chepstow Castle, Chepstow museum, Chepstow Racecourse, St Pierre golf course, Wye Valley and Tintern Abbey.

🛏 Two single, three double, one twin, seven family
£ ££
🍺 **Wye Valley HPA**, guest beer
🍴 Lunch, evening and snack menus
💳 Credit cards accepted

CLYTHA near Abergavenny

Clytha Arms

Clytha, Abergavenny, Monmouthshire NP7 9BW
T 01873 840206   **F** 01873 840206
E one.bev@lineone.net
www.clytha-arms.com
Licensees: Andrew and Beverley Canning
Directions: On the B4598 the Abergavenny-Raglan old road

Multi-award winning, high quality pub, restaurant and accommodation – Gwent CAMRA Pub of the Year on more than one occasion. A visit to the Clytha is not to be missed – an event to savour, particularly if it coincides with one of the Welsh beer, or cider/perry festivals that also feature local Welsh ham and cheeses. Extensive grounds around the pub, which was once the dower house to next door Clytha Hall. Regular beers are complemented by a range of guests, usually from independent brewers, and always in first class condition – after all, the landlord and his wife are life-members of CAMRA.

The food is inventive, satisfying all tastes and the family tradition of excellent cuisine is being maintained by the eldest daughter joining the culinary team – you may have caught them on the Radio 4 Father and Daughter series. The décor is comfortable, the welcome sincere and the experience one that will be remembered. The pub has four individually styled bedrooms including one with as four-poster bed.

🛏 One twin, two doubles, one four-poster double
£ ££
🍺 **Hook Norton Best Bitter, Felinfoel Double Dragon, Draught Bass** plus a wide range of guest beers, a draught cider and often a draught perry
🍴 Lunch, evening and snack menus
💳 Credit cards accepted

GOGINAN

Druid Inn

High Street, Goginan, Nr Aberystwyth, Ceredigion SY23 3NT
T 01970 880650
Licensees: John and Margaret Howell
Directions: On A44, seven miles East of Aberystwyth

A friendly, family run freehouse which has been gradually but consistently improved over the years by its hardworking licensees. The provision of B&B is the latest phase of improvements in the pub which has been in every Good Beer Guide since 1976. Close by is the Llwernog silver and lead mining museum. Two of the three bedrooms have splendid views over the Melindwr Valley. The guest beer, available during the summer months and other busy times is often from a Welsh or Borders micro. Children welcome.

🛏 Two double, one double with single
£ £
🍺 **Brains Bitter, Banks's Bitter** plus occasional guest
🍴 Lunch, evening and snack menus
💳 Credit cards not accepted

KNIGHTON

The George and Dragon

Broad Street, Knighton, Powys LD7 1BL
T 01547 528532
Licensees: Peter and Angela Vretos
Directions: On the main street, Knighton is situated approx 16 miles west of Ludlow on the Powys/Shropshire border

The George & Dragon is a Grade II listed, 17th century coaching inn located in the centre of Knighton, a small borders market town nestling in the Teme Valley.

It is ideal for anyone wanting to walk on Offa's Dyke Path. The building bears a date of 1637 and the small lounge contains benches which were originally the bow pews removed from the parish church in 1876. The pub has bags of character and attractive restaurant offering home-cooked food Accommodation is in the renovated stables to the rear of the inn.

- Three twins, two double
- £ £££
- John Smith Cask, Woods Woodcutter plus a range of guests
- Lunch, evening and snack menus
- Credit cards accepted

LLANDOGO

Sloop Inn

Llandogo, Monmouthshire NP25 4TW
T 01594 530291   F 01594 530935
Licensees: Eddie and Julie Grace
Directions: Situated on the A466 between Monmouth and Chepstow

A pleasant roadside pub situated alongside the local parish church, set back off the road, in a small rural community nestling between steep wooded hills and the meandering River Wye. The Sloop takes its name from the sailing vessels which plied their trade to and from Bristol. The traditional front bar is characterised with wooden beams, and massive old masts that seem to prop up the ceiling. A welcoming large log fire warms in colder weather. The lounge/restaurant at the rear offers splendid views down river and across to the Forest of Dean. There is an outdoor play area. The comfortable rooms help make the Sloop a good base from which to explore the delights of the picturesque Wye Valley.

- One four-poster + single bed, two doubles, one twin. Additional cot/single available
- £ ££
- Wye Valley Dorothy Goodbody Bitter plus guest beers
- Lunch, evening and snack menus
- Credit cards accepted

LLANBEDR

Victoria Inn

Llanbedr, Gwynedd LL45 2LD
T 01341 241213   F 01341 241644
E jbarry@currentbun.com
www.frederic-robinson.com

Situated on the banks of the River Artro with its large beer garden and children's play area, the Vic is at the centre of the village

community. The main lounge bar is warmed by a large open log fire which permeates down into the Settle bar area. The restaurant is open all year round and non-residents can also enjoy a full breakfast in comfortable surroundings. Meals are mainly served with vegetables and salad grown from the pub's own market garden. It is ideally based for visiting Harlech Castle and the seaside resort of Barmouth. Children welcome. All rooms are en suite.

- Three double, one twin, one single
- £ £££
- Frederic Robinson's Best Bitter
- Lunch evening and snack menus
- Credit cards accepted

LLANFAIR CAEREINION

Goat Hotel

High Street, Llanfair Caereinion,
Welshpool, Powys SY21 0QS
T 01938 810428
E thegoathotel@aol.com
Directions: On A458

For almost 300 years The Goat Hotel has provided lodging for travellers. Originally a coaching inn, at the junction of the Shrewsbury to Aberystwyth and Cardiff to Chester routes, today's travellers still arrive to find traditional hospitality, excellent food and fine beers. often from Welsh breweries, in this delightful beamed inn. The comfortable lounge has leather armchairs and settees. From the Goat, there are innumerable excursions to the lovely mountains and lakes of Snowdonia, the West Wales coast, historic borderlands or the interesting towns and villages of Mid Wales. Llanfair Caereinion is the terminus of the Welshpool and Llanfair Light Railway and many fine walks can be made around the town and riverside. In winter when snow caps the hills, a brisk walk can be followed by a hearty bowl of homemade soup beside a roaring fire.

- Three double, one twin, one family
- £ £
- Brains Rev James plus guests
- Lunch, evening and snack menus
- Credit cards accepted

Wynnstay Arms Hotel

Bridge Street, Llangollen, Denbighshire LL20 8PF
T 01978 860710

This 16th-century pub stands on the old London Holyhead coaching road; the former stable yard now forms a spacious enclosed garden, overlooking the river, and has a grassy area. Inside, the pub has a traditional wood-panelled bar warmed by an open log fire, a snug, a lounge, and a restaurant, although meals can be taken in the bar. The menu, offering home-cooked dishes, caters for children who are welcome to stay overnight. The three guest rooms are all en suite. Llangollen nestles within the beautiful Dee Valley in the North East of Wales. It offers amenities for angling and canoeing, and the pub provides a convenient base for visitors to the area. Llangollen itself, at the heart of the mountains, is famous for its little steam railway and the delightful canal that passes through; it also has a ruined medieval castle. The room rate does not include breakfast, which is available as a supplement.

- Two double, one twin-bedded room
- **Greene King Abbot** and **Old Speckled Hen** plus guest beers
- Snacks and meals daily, lunchtime and evening
- Credit cards not accepted

Half Moon Hotel

Llanthony, Nr Abergavenny,
Monmouthshire NP7 7NN
T 01873 890611   **F** 01873 890611
E halfmoonllanthony@talk21.com
Licensee: Christine Smith
Directions: From Abergavenny turn left A465

There's no mistaking this as a truly rural pub. The downstairs consists of a traditional public bar plus a smaller lounge area and a dining room. The bar has an original flagstone floor and has the feel of an old country inn where time can stop while you enjoy a relaxing drink. There are splendid mountain views, and being situated amid popular walking country, the pub makes for a welcoming refreshment stop for the more energetic. The quiet imposing ruins of Llanthony Priory are close by. A stalwart supporter of the Cardiff-based microbrewery, Bullmastiff, beer may occasionally be sold from the barrel.

- Four double, two twins, one single, one room with two bunk beds, one family room with one double and two bunk beds
- **£** ££
- **Bullmastiff Gold, Son of a Bitch** and **Addlestones** Cider
- Lunch, evening and snack menus
- Credit cards not accepted

Kagan's Brasserie (Cross Lanes Hotel)

Bangor Road, Marchwiel, Wrexham LL13 0TF
T 01978 780555   **F** 01978 780568
E guestservices@crosslanes.co.uk
www.crosslanes.co.uk
Licensee: Michael Kagan
Directions: On A525, three miles from Wrexham

Proving that even sophisticated hotels can sell real ale if they really want to, the Cross Lane Hotel is home to Kagan's Brasseries, which has a large open plan lounge set around a big central servery. Beer from the Plassey Brewery, Wrexham is served on draught, normally the full bodied and distinctive Bitter. Set in six acres of beautiful grounds and countryside the hotel has Jacobean panelling in the entrance which dates from 1620. It was rescued from Emral Hall at Worthenbury, which was burnt down in 1875, and has been carefully restored. A local history exhibition has been set up, adding pertinent interest to a thoroughly ambient establishment.

🛏 13 double, five twin, three single
£ ££££
🍺 Plassey Bitter
🍴 Lunch, evening and snack menus
💳 Credit cards accepted

MILWR near Holywell

The Glan Yr Afon Inn

Dolphin, Milwr, Holywell, Flintshire CH8 8HE
T 01352 710052   **F** 01352 714329
Licensee: Pepe Pastor
Directions: Off the old A55 – the A5026 follow signs

Hidden away in the Welsh countryside, records show that parts of the inn date back to the 16th century, as do parts of the neighbouring houses. It's a sympathetically extended Welsh long house, which now has seven en suite bedrooms, some with disabled facilities. The inn is also listed in the Guinness Book of Records as being in the same family for over 400 years from 1559 to 1997. The food is excellent and regular mini beer festivals are held. An ideal base for a walking, riding or golfing holiday it is close to Flint, Rhuddan and Conway Castles.

🛏 Five double, two twin
£ £
🍺 At least four, changes weekly
🍴 Lunch, evening and snack menus
💳 Credit cards accepted

NORTHOP

Soughton Hall & Stables Bar

Soughton Hall, Northop, Flintshire CH7 6AB
T 01352 840811   **F** 01352 840382
www.soughtonhall.co.uk
Directions: Off A5119 between Northrop and Sychdyn

The fabulously expensive Soughton Hall was originally built as a Bishop's Palace in 1714 and it is now an elegant country house hotel with its own splendid 150 acres of grounds. The 14 bedrooms are individually decorated and furnished with fine antiques and fabrics. There are several large public rooms furnished in character.

A bar and restaurant offers a contrast to fine dining in the main hotel. The bar has a heavily beamed ceiling, wood panelling and rustic furniture, while upstairs the haylofts have been opened up to provide a characterful restaurant, with bare brick walls and high beamed ceilings. Diners can select their food from a large display in the open kitchen area and watch the meal being prepared if they wish. A blackboard, bistro-style menu here, where the emphasis is on fresh fish and meat, provides an informal alternative to the upmarket restaurant in the hall itself, which is where the luxurious guest rooms are located. The large rooms are decorated and furnished in period style to a high standard; all are en suite and enjoy views over the surrounding parkland. Children are welcome. Soughton Hall is close to the River Dee and within easy reach of Chester.

🛏 14 double rooms
£ £££££
🍺 **Dyffryn Clwyd Four Thumbs**, **Goff's Jouster**, **Hanby Drawwel**, **Greene King Old Speckled Hen, Plassey Bitter**, plus many guest beers
🍴 Lunch, evening and snack menus
💳 Credit cards accepted

PANTYGELLI near Abergavenny

Crown Inn

Old Hereford Road, Pantygelli,
Abergavenny, Monmouthshire NP7 7HR
T 01873 853314
E yeoldecrowne@aol.com
Licensee: Amanda Campbell
Directions: Off A465, four miles north of
Abergavenny

A thriving pub and restaurant in a small hamlet outside Abergavenny. All the guest rooms all have extensive views over open countryside towards the Skirrid Mountain. The Crown was runner-up in the 2002 Gwent Pub of the Year competition and the landlord, who is a CAMRA member, takes a great pride in the quality of his beers, which always include at least one guest from an independent brewery.

Food varies from full à la carte to filling bar snacks, with children catered for. The large, open-plan interior is divided into discrete drinking areas, with the restaurant separate. A large, flower decked patio enjoys wide ranging views and is popular, particularly with walkers, in summer. Situated at the gateway to some of the finest scenery in the Black Mountains, the Crown offers good beer, food and accommodation to visitors enjoying the physical recreation available locally, or equally with those just seeking to relax amidst beautiful scenery.

One double, one twin, one single – they share a private toilet, bathroom and shower
£ £
Draught Bass, **Worthington Bitter**, **Fuller's London Pride** plus guest beers
Lunch evening and snack menus
Credit cards accepted

RUABON

Wynnstay Arms Hotel

High Street, Ruabon, Nr Wrexham LL14 6BL
T 01978 822187
Licensee: Nicholas Marshall
Directions: On junction B5605 and B5097 in town centre

An early 19th century coaching inn on the Holyhead and Ireland route, retaining plenty of character, including the archway to one entrance of the car park. It has two main rooms, a comfortable busy locals lounge – cluttered with prints – and a more frugal bar with TV. There's a proud entrance corridor with an old settle and a quieter overflow side room with arm chairs and a more sedate atmosphere. Very friendly convivial – it is a lovely balance between old and modern. It has seven en suite bedrooms and is an ideal base for touring north east and mid Wales and the Marches.

Three twin, three double, one family
£ £££
Robinson's Best Bitter and **Hartleys XB**

Wynnstay Arms Hotel, Ruabon

🍴 Lunch, evening and snack menu. No food Sunday evening
💳 Credit cards accepted

SOLVA

The Harbour Inn

31 Main Street, Solva, Pembrokeshire SA62 6UT
T 01437 720013
Directions: On A487 road adjoining harbour car park

Harbour Inn is nestled amongst the Welsh Hills in the picturesque village of Solva – recognised as one of the most attractive on the West Coast of Wales. This ancient port and fishing village surrounds a beautiful harbour and river, sheltering yachts and small boats from the Atlantic Ocean. The pub has an idyllic view across the harbour and its situation makes it a superb base from which to explore the whole of Pembrokeshire. With its traditional atmosphere, the inn is popular with locals and visitors.

🛏 One double, one twin, one twin
£ £ single £££
🍺 **Draught Bass**, **Worthington** and guest
🍴 Lunch evening and snack menu
💳 Credit cards accepted

TINTERN

Wye Valley Hotel

Tintern, Monmouthshire NP16 6SQ
T 01291 689441 **F** 01291 689440
E wyevalley.hotel@ukgateway.net
www.wyevalleyhotel.co.uk
Licensees: Barrie and Sue Cook
Directions: Situated on the A466 between Monmouth and Chepstow

The Wye Valley Hotel is situated in an area of breathtaking natural beauty at Tintern in the heart of the Wye Valley, described by the poet Wordsworth as the most romantic valley in Wales. The Wye River runs through the village, less than 100 yards from the hotel. The world famous 12th century Tintern Abbey is only a five-minute walk away. The Wye Valley is a paradise for walkers,

birdwatchers and those simply wishing to escape the rat race.

The hotel is a large, attractive 1930s 'roadhouse style' hotel of red brick at the north end of the village that displays a profusion of floral colour when in season. Formerly an alehouse called the Carpenters Arms, the comfortable bar hosts the landlord's large collection of beer bottles from breweries past and present. The restaurant uses fresh local produce. Sited in a popular but not over-commercialised tourist spot, the general area is good for walking, canoeing, angling, or just relaxing with a pint of good real ale.

🛏 Eight doubles/twins (two could be used as family rooms)
£ ££ and £££
🍺 **Wye Valley Bitter**, **Butty Bach**
🍴 Lunch, evening and snack menus
💳 Credit cards accepted

USK

Kings Head Hotel

18 Old Market Street, Usk, Monmouthshire NP15 1AL
T 01291 672963
Licensee: Steve Musto
Directions: Reached off A449 or Pontypool Road. Main Street running through Usk, take road off Bridge Street, by bridge over river, into old Market Street. The Kings Head is on left at bottom of road

A centrally placed pub in a quiet location ,providing a good base from which to stay and explore the town and surrounding area, which includes Usk Castle, Gwent Rural Life Museum, antique shops, floral displays and a unique town clock. The pub's large lounge has a dark décor and a variety of furniture and various bric-a-brac dotted around to give it a nice cosy feel. The landlord's passion for fishing is reflected in pictures of past triumphs that may have become just a little exaggerated over time! The huge fireplace is used to burn logs and provides a welcoming and warming focal point in winter. Tasty food may be enjoyed in the lounge or the small dining room adjoining it. A former Gwent CAMRA Pub of the Year winner that has maintained its high standards for good beer quality. A popular haunt for locals and visitors alike.

🛏 Eight double/family plus eight rooms in cottages (single/double/family)

🍺 **Brains Rev James, Fuller's London Pride, Timothy Taylor's Landlord**

£ ££ and £££

🍴 Lunch, evening and snack menus

💳 Credit cards accepted

traveline
public transport info
0870 608 2 608

Join CAMRA

If you like good beer and good pubs you could be helping to fight to preserve, protect and promote them. CAMRA was set up in the early Seventies to fight against the mass destruction of a part of Britain's heritage. The giant brewers are still pushing through takeovers, mergers and closures of their smaller regional rivals. They are still trying to impose national brands of beer and lager on their customers whether they like it or not, and they are still closing down town and village pubs or converting them into grotesque 'theme' pubs.

CAMRA wants to see genuine free competition in the brewing industry, fair prices, and, above all, a top quality product brewed by local breweries in accordance with local tastes, and served in pubs that maintain the best features of a tradition that goes back centuries.

As a CAMRA member you will be able to enjoy generous discounts on CAMRA products and receive the highly rated monthly newspaper *What's Brewing*. You will be given the CAMRA members' handbook and be able to join in local social events and brewery trips. To join, complete the form below and, if you wish, arrange for direct debit payments by filling in the form overleaf and returning it to CAMRA. To pay by credit card, contact the membership secretary on (01727) 867201.

Full single UK/EU £16; Joint (two members living at the same address) UK/EU £19;
Single under 26, Student, Disabled, Unemployed, Retired over 60 £9; Joint retired over 60,
Joint under 26 £12; UK/EU Life £192, UK/EU Joint life £228. Single life retired over 60 £90,
Joint life retired over 60 £120. Full overseas membership £20, Joint overseas membership £23.
Single overseas life £240, Joint overseas life £276.

Please delete as appropriate:

I/We wish to become members of CAMRA.

I/We agree to abide by the memorandum and articles of association of the company.

I/We enclose a cheque/p.o. for £   (payable to CAMRA Ltd.)

Name(s)

Address

                                  Postcode

Signature(s)

                CAMRA Ltd., 230 Hatfield Road, St Albans, Herts AL1 4LW

Instruction to your Bank or Building Society to pay by Direct Debit

Please fill in the whole form using a ball point pen and send it to:

Campaign for Real Ale Ltd
230 Hatfield Road
St. Albans
Herts
AL1 4LW

Originator's Identification Number

9	2	6	1	2	9

Reference Number

Name of Account Holder(s)

FOR CAMRA OFFICIAL USE ONLY
This is not part of the instruction to your Bank or Building Society

Membership Number

Name

Postcode

Bank/Building Society account number

Branch Sort Code

Instructions to your Bank or Building Society
Please pay CAMRA Direct Debits from the account detailed on this instruction subject to the safeguards assured by the Direct Debit Guarantee. I understand that this instruction may remain with CAMRA and, if so, will be passed electronically to my Bank/Building Society

Name and full postal address of your Bank or Building Society

To The Manager   Bank/Building Society

Address

Postcode

Signature(s)

Date

Banks and Building Societies may not accept Direct Debit instructions for some types of account

 -

This guarantee should be detached and retained by the Payer.

The Direct Debit Guarantee

- ■ This Guarantee is offered by all Banks and Building Societies that take part in the Direct Debit Scheme. The efficiency and security of the Scheme is monitored and protected by your own Bank or Building Society.

- ■ If the amounts to be paid or the payment dates change CAMRA will notify you 10 working days in advance of your account being debited or as otherwise agreed.

- ■ If an error is made by CAMRA or your Bank or Building Society, you are guaranteed a full and immediate refund from your branch of the amount paid.

- ■ You can cancel a Direct Debit at any time by writing to your Bank or Building Society. Please also send a copy of your letter to us.

CAMRA Books
Buy more books about pubs and real ale directly from CAMRA

All our books are available through bookshops in the UK. If you can't find a book, simply order it from your bookshop using the ISBN number, title and author details given below. CAMRA members should refer to their regular monthly newspaper *What's Brewing* for the latest details and member special offers. CAMRA books are also available by mail-order from: CAMRA Books, 230 Hatfield Road, St Albans, Herts, AL1 4LW. Cheques made payable to CAMRA Ltd. Telephone your credit card order on 01727 867201. Or pay by secure credit card ordering via the website at **www.camra.org.uk**

Carriage of £1.00 per book (UK), £2.00 per book (Europe) and £4.00 per book (US, Australia, New Zealand and other overseas) is charged.

Good Beer Guide
ROGER PROTZ

CAMRA's annual guide to the best 4,000 pubs in the UK. A third of the entries change every year and all the descriptions are brought up to date by CAMRA branches who visit all the pubs in the guide. Real ale quality has to be of the highest order to get into the guide and branches are looking for top quality in all respects if a pub is to be listed.

800 pages approx
Published annually in September.

CAMRA's Good Cider Guide
David Matthews

CAMRA's guide to real cider researched anew for cider's fifth Millennium. Features on cider around the world, and cider-making, plus a comprehensive and detailed guide to UK producers of cider. The brand new listing of outlets includes pubs, restaurants, bars and small cider makers – with full address and contact numbers. Also provided are details of ciders available and, where appropriate, items of interest in the pub or area.

£**9.99** *(400 pages)*   ISBN 1 85249 143 4

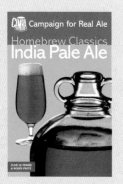

India Pale Ale (Homebrew Classics series)
Clive La Pensée *and* Roger Protz

Roger Protz goes on an historical hunt for the origins of the most famous British beer of all time – IPA. He uncovers the original brewery where IPA was devised as an export for the colonies, an invention that made its brewers extremely wealthy men.

Brewer La Pensée conjures up the smells and sounds of breweries and brewers spanning three centuries, making their version of IPA.

£**8.99** *(196 pages)*   ISBN 1 85249 129 9

Stout and Porter (Homebrew Classics series)
Clive La Pensée *and* Roger Protz

An introduction for the home brewer to the history and historic preparation of Stout and Porter. Roger Protz gives a brief account of the history of Porter brewing and consumption, including sketches of successful Porter/Stout brewing companies while Clive La Pensée investigates the history of this drink in more depth from the brewing perspective.

£**8.99** *(176 pages)*   ISBN 1 85249 129 9

Good Bottled Beer Guide
JEFF EVANS

The definitive guide to real ale in a bottle:

- *Every UK bottle-conditioned beer*
- *tasting notes to help you choose*
- *the background to each beer*
- *where to buy the beers*
- *key dates in beer history*
- *how to buy, store and serve bottled ales*
- *the best foreign beers*

Highly commended by the British Guild of Beer Writers, the Good Bottled Beer Guide is for those who like to try the most creatively brewed beers in the world. More than 300 to choose from, all from the comfort of your armchair!

£8.99   *(224 pages)*   ISBN 1 85249 185 X

Good Beer Guide to Northern France
ARTHUR TAYLOR

Compiled with the help of French organisation Les Amis de la Biere. Breweries, bars, shops, museums. Recipes for cooking with beer, French style.

£7.99 *(224 pages)*   ISBN 1 85249 140 X

Good Beer Guide to Belgium & Holland
TIM WEBB

The gold standard guide to understanding and finding Belgian and Dutch beer. Details of the 170 breweries and 1100 beers in regular production. 640 of the best hand-picked cafes. Every known brewery tour, beer festival and museum of brewing. Useful travel tips for the independent tourist.

£11.99 *(352 pages)*   ISBN 1 85249 174 4

Pubs for Families
ADRIAN TIERNEY-JONES

This is your independent guide to real ale pubs with family-friendly facilities: Visit these pubs in the confident knowledge that there will be suitable food choices, secure play areas and games for the kids. Some of the pubs host seasonal events, bouncy castles and children's entertainment.

The real ale choices will always be tip-top. Many of the pubs offer accommodation. Most have extensive, and inventive, menus for lunch and evening meals.

- *Traditional pubs that cater for children – from toddlers to teenagers.*
- *Articles full of useful consumer advice – from what makes a child-friendly pub to pub food for kids beyond the ubiquitous chicken nugget.*
- *Organised by British Tourist Authority regions.*
- *Mini-guides to leisure activities and tourism close to each pub entry.*

Adrian Tierney-Jones is a food and drink writer whose work has appeared in *What's Brewing*, the *Field* and the *Guardian* amongst other publications and he is also the author of *Westcountry Ales* (Halsgrove). He is tireless in the task of seeking out family-friendly pubs.

£**9.99** (*256 pages*)   ISBN 1 85249 183 3

CAMRA's London Pubs Guide
LYNNE PEARCE

The guide to CAMRA's favourite London pubs, chosen because they sell traditional real ale, often brewed in the capital itself. The guide points you to the features you will want to discover on your trip around London: the architecture, personalities, history, local ambience and nearby attractions.

Practical aids include transportation details and street level maps, information about opening times, food, parking, disabled and children's facilities, plus the range of beers.

Feature articles include a history of brewing in London, a guide to London's best pub food, and London pubs with stories to tell. What could be better?

£**9.99** (*224 pages*)   ISBN 1 85249 164 7

Heritage Pubs of Great Britain
MARK BOLTON *and* JAMES BELSEY

It is still possible to enjoy real ale in sight of great craftsmanship and skill. Feast your eyes and toast the architects and builders from times past. This full-colour 'coffee-table' production is a photographic record of some of the finest pub interiors in Britain. As a collector's item, it is presented on heavy, gloss-art paper in a sleeved hardback format. Photographed by architectural specialist Mark Bolton and described in words by pub expert James Belsey. Available only from CAMRA – call 01727 867201 (overseas +44 1727 867201)

£16.99 *(144 pages, hardback)*

The Landlord's Tale
BARRIE PEPPER

Hugely enjoyable and humorous yarn about a 1950s Yorkshire pub and the characters within. Bernard Ingham states in his foreword: "As the old News of the World advert put it 'All human life is there'. It certainly is in Wilf Lowe's Coach and Four. This is a very human tale, and entirely credible."

£6.99 *(160 pages)*   ISBN 1 85249 171 X

Dictionary of Beer
CAMRA

A unique reference work. Where else would you find the definitions of: parachute, Paradise, paraflow and paralytic? Or skull-dragged, slummage and snob screen? More than 2000 definitions covering brewing techniques and ingredients; international beers and breweries; tasting terms; historical references and organisations; slang phrases and abbreviations; culinary terms and beer cocktails; and much more.

£7.99 *(208 pages)*   ISBN 1 85249 158 2

Home Brewing
GRAHAM WHEELER

Recently redesigned to make it even easier to use. The classic first book for all home-brewers. While being truly comprehensive, Home Brewing is also a practical guide which can be followed step by step as you try your first brews. Plenty of recipes for beginners and hints and tips from the world's most revered home brewer.

£8.99 (*240 pages*)   ISBN 1 85249 137 X

Brew Your Own British Real Ale at Home
GRAHAM WHEELER *and* ROGER PROTZ

This book contains recipes to replicate some famous cask-conditioned beers at home or to customise brews to your own particular taste. Conversion details are given so that the measurements can be used world-wide.

£8.99 (194 pages)   ISBN 1 85249 138 8

Brew Classic European Beers at Home
GRAHAM WHEELER *and* ROGER PROTZ

Keen home brewers can now recreate some of the world's classic beers at home. Brew superb ales, stouts, Pilsners, Alt, Kölsch, Trappist, wheat beers, sour beers, even fruit lambics. Measurements are given in UK, US and European units.

£8.99 (196 pages)   ISBN 1 85249 117 5